IN GREAT WATERS

ALSO BY SPENCER DUNMORE

FICTION
Bomb Run (1971)
Tower of Strength (1973)
Collision (1974)
Final Approach (1976)
Means of Escape (1978)
Ace (1981)
The Sound of Wings (1984)
No Holds Barred (1987)
Squadron (1991)

NON-FICTION
Reap the Whirlwind: The Untold Story of 6 Group, Canada's Bomber Force of World War II (with William Carter) (1991)
Wings for Victory: The Remarkable Story of the British Commonwealth Air Training Plan in Canada (1994)
Above and Beyond: The Canadians' War in the Air, 1939–45 (1996)

IN GREAT WATERS

The Epic Story of
the Battle of the Atlantic

1939 – 45

SPENCER DUNMORE

M&S

Cloth edition published in 1999
Trade paperback edition published in 2000

Canadian Cataloguing in Publication Data

Dunmore, Spencer, 1928-
    In great waters : the epic story of the battle of the Atlantic, 1939-45

Includes bibliographical references and index.
ISBN 0-7710-2929-2 (bound)   ISBN 0-7710-2936-5 (pbk.)

1. World War, 1939-1945 – Campaigns – Atlantic Ocean.   2. World War, 1939-1945 – Naval operations.   I. Title.

D770.D85 1999   940.54'21   C99-931362-2

We acknowledge the financial support of the Government of Canada through the Book Publishing Industry Development Program for our publishing activities.

We further acknowledge the support of the Canada Council for the Arts for our publishing program.

Set in Bembo by M&S, Toronto

Printed and bound in Canada

McClelland & Stewart Ltd.
The Canadian Publishers
481 University Ave.
Toronto, Ontario
M5G 2E9
www.mcclelland.com

2 3 4 5   03 02 01 00

CONTENTS

This book is dedicated to all those "that go down to the sea in ships, that do business in great waters."

Psalms 107:23

PROLOGUE

THE SHIP'S DYING made her famous. In her lifetime, she had been little known, just another passenger vessel, one of thousands plodding around the globe from port to port, an unremarkable part of the maritime scenery. She had never been numbered among the world's glamour liners; not once had her decks echoed to the promenadings of the likes of Noël Coward or Marlene Dietrich. Reporters and photographers seldom covered her arrivals and departures; the Society press had little interest in her passengers, mostly minor government officials and apprehensive immigrants, junior officers and unimportant couples on unimportant missions. For sixteen years, the ship had plied the oceans, earning a reputation for comfort rather than luxury. If the "Queens" could be likened to the greatest, most splendid hotels in the world, she had to be categorized as a well-run boarding house of the sea; she provided the basics and not much more.

Most passengers professed to prefer her informality to the pomp and splendour found aboard the *Queen Marys* and *Mauretanias*. It wasn't simply a matter of economy, they assured one another. Repeatedly. The cosy atmosphere of the ship counted for a lot, they said. Her single funnel, tall and slim, bore the red-white-and-blue insignia of the Donaldson Line. It accorded the ship an engagingly Edwardian appearance; the officers wouldn't have looked out of place had they sported stiff, white, wing collars, mutton-chop whiskers, and short-peaked caps.

She had left Prince's Dock, Glasgow, at noon on Friday, September 1, 1939, bound for Belfast, Liverpool, and Montreal. In command was Captain James Cook, a veteran sailor, now embarking on his fourteenth transatlantic voyage as master. On this day, he had spent longer than usual looking about the ship and the dockside, studying the faces of the boarding passengers, pondering them and their intentions. Was it any wonder? At that very moment, Hitler's forces were smashing through the weak defences on the Polish border – and a new word was about to be added to the lexicon of modern times: *Blitzkrieg*. The war everyone had feared for years seemed about to boil over into a general conflict. But why, millions asked themselves, should we march into battle over *Poland*, of all places? To most of the passengers, Poland was a remote and vaguely exotic place. Few knew any Poles; even fewer had been to the place; and many were unsure precisely where it was.

The news hadn't improved by the time the ship called at Liverpool, the last port before the Atlantic crossing. People had been swarming around the company office for days, trying to obtain passage to North America. First Class or Third, it didn't matter – as long as they could get out of European waters before the balloon went up. The ship sailed with a passenger list swollen by two hundred, for a total number aboard of 1,103. Makeshift dormitories had been set up in the ship's gymnasium and the Third Class smoking room. Most passengers were Canadian or American. In Glasgow they had been startled by jeers from dockyard workers, who apparently believed them to be Britons scurrying away to safety in North America.

While the world waited in fearful anticipation, the ship slipped out of Liverpool and headed through the North Channel to the Atlantic. The sun shimmered on placid waters. Passengers enjoyed a hearty dinner before retiring to the lounge. The tiny orchestra soon began scraping out the popular dance tunes of the day: "South of the Border," "The Lambeth Walk" . . .

The next morning dawned fair and bright. It was Sunday, September 3. No run-of-the-mill morning, this; everyone knew it. A nagging air of tension seemed to weigh every moment. Men kept glancing at their watches. Conversations were clipped and hushed, as if the speakers were anxious not to miss other, more important words. As eleven o'clock neared, passengers and crew members began drifting to the ship's radio room. At the hour, the words of British Prime Minister Neville Chamberlain crackled through from Downing Street. Sounding slightly bewildered, apparently still unable to believe what had happened, the PM announced that no reply had been received to Britain's demand for Germany's withdrawal from Poland. Thus, a state of war now existed between Britain and Germany. While the assembly absorbed this, a messenger took the text of the PM's announcement and pinned it to a noticeboard outside the purser's office. Passengers read it again and again, as if repeated readings would reveal some hitherto hidden truth. People shook their heads and sighed. No one seemed surprised. The news had been expected for weeks. In fact, it was a sort of relief. Now the wondering and worrying had ended once and for all. The passengers kept telling each other that Adolf was going to find out that he had bitten off considerably more than he could possibly chew.

The hours passed quietly enough. Everyone agreed that the Germans must be completely mad to throw themselves into another war with Britain little more than twenty years since the disastrous conclusion of the first. Would they never learn? What did they hope to accomplish? Some seemingly well-informed individuals told their fellow passengers that there was little to worry about. At this very moment, peace negotiations were underway between London, Paris, and Berlin. The whole absurd business would be cleared up at the conference table. A few differences of opinion had to be ironed out; a bit of give here and a spot of take there; it shouldn't be beyond the capabilities of the boys in pin-stripes, should it?

The afternoon brought cloud, although the sea remained calm. Passengers became more relaxed the further they journeyed into the Atlantic. Europe was a good place to get away from at this moment in history.

The ship seemed to be alone in an empty ocean. She wasn't. Some two hundred miles west of the Hebrides, a five-hundred-ton U-boat cruised on the surface, her lookouts diligently scanning every point of the compass. None had to be reminded that his country was now at war. The submarine had been delivered from the builder a matter of months before. Her captain was younger than most U-boat commanders. Fritz-Julius Lemp, twenty-six, was the son of an army officer. He had joined the navy in 1931 when he was eighteen, volunteering for the embryonic U-boat service in 1936. His rise had been meteoric, and in November 1938, he had been promoted to command U30, a rare achievement for one so young.

Lemp was immensely proud of his boat. U30 was a Type VII vessel, just over two hundred feet in length, with a beam of nineteen feet. Her cigar-shaped pressure hull was divided into six compartments. Her four forward torpedo tubes occupied the bow compartment, in company with ten torpedoes and twenty-four of the crew, who lived and worked in cramped and frequently insanitary conditions and were subject to violent pounding in heavy seas. Aft of the main torpedo section came a compartment containing half the ship's batteries, used to propel the boat underwater. Above the batteries were accommodations for the captain, three officers, and half a dozen petty officers and midshipmen. The control room, the nerve centre of the boat, was situated amidships, presenting to the uninitiated a bewildering confusion of dials, gauges, controls, and valves, upon which the ship and her crew depended for survival in the uncertain world beneath the surface.

Aft of the control room were more accommodations, more batteries, and the ship's galley, with its electric range and miniature ovens. Next, the engine room, with two 1,160-horsepower engines. And finally, the electrical room, containing two 375-horsepower engines, actually motor generators. A single torpedo tube was located in U30's stern; it had to be fired by remote control.

Life aboard U30 was acutely uncomfortable, with sanitary facilities that would have precipitated riots in penitentiaries, and a lack of space that would have sent any claustrophobe into hysterics, although the conditions seemed to affect some men much less than others. As Werner Hirschmann, who served as a U-boat engineering officer, points out: "We had three meals a day, slept in dry bunks, and our biggest pain was endless boredom. To prevent mental atrophy, we had contests for the dumbest jokes, chess tournaments, an extensive library, and we developed intense relationships with the occasional fly that emerged from somewhere in the middle of the Atlantic."[1] Whatever their feelings, the men of the U-boat service never complained; they counted themselves fortunate to be part of the elite U-bootwaffe. The force of Type VII U-boats was augmented by the larger, longer-range Type IX. On the outbreak of war, fifty-seven U-boats were available for operations, two-thirds of them Type VIIs, the remainder Type IXs.

The sighting of the British ship set off a flurry of excitement aboard U30. The boat's young skipper could barely contain his glee: a target, a fat one, on the first day of the war! He would be the envy of the entire service! He scrambled up to the conning tower and studied the merchantman through his Zeiss binoculars. A good-sized ship, he noted with satisfaction, probably an auxiliary. Undoubtedly British. A legitimate target, no question about it. Lemp ordered an immediate dive. He was pleased with the crew's quick reaction. He had trained them well. In a matter of moments, the long, grey hull was splashing its way beneath the surface. But already an ache of uncertainty began to nag at the skipper. Could he get into an attacking position before the big merchantman slipped away? Since the U-boat's electrical motors could propel the vessel underwater at only a few knots, the attack had to be well planned. He didn't have the speed underwater to outpace the enemy, so he would have to outmanoeuvre her. The merchantman had shown no sign of having seen U30. To intercept a ship underwater, you had to second-guess her captain, get into his mind and look around until you knew what he was going to do next. As the moment neared, Lemp could feel himself becoming calmer; no nerves, no jumping the gun. Unless he had made a significant miscalculation, the big merchantman would come within range in a matter of minutes . . .

Shortly after seven-thirty, as many of the passengers were sitting down to dinner, a salvo of torpedoes hit the ship. One slammed into its target amidships, sending up a spectacular column of smoke and spray. As if in slow motion, fragments of spinning wreckage rose and fell, hitting the sea with huge splashes. The big ship rocked. For a terrifying instant, she appeared to be turning turtle, but she recovered. Passengers seemed more confused than afraid, as if they couldn't believe this was happening. One moment the ship had been sailing along strongly, purposefully, the next she lay dead in the water, a sickening stink of explosive pervading every nook and cranny. Dozens of passengers found themselves trapped in the dining room. The torpedoes had blown the main stairway into a tangle of wreckage. Now, with a grinding and creaking, an unhappy sighing, the ship assumed a thirty-degree list to port – and at the same time, her stern began to sink. Abandon ship!

But for ten awful minutes, the crew couldn't launch the lifeboats because of the list; passengers had to stand and wait as the liner sank beneath them. Then, miraculously, she righted herself. Hurriedly, more than a thousand passengers and crew scrambled into the boats. Most were saved, but 112 lost their lives, including twenty-eight Americans. Sixteen children went down with the ship – the *Athenia*.

News of the sinking troubled Hitler. The last thing he wanted at this delicate stage of negotiations was unfavourable press in America. Hadn't he been vigorously working to negotiate the British and French out of the war? "Of course we are in a state of war with England and France, but if we on our side avoid all acts of war, the whole business will evaporate," he had instructed his inner circle, convinced that the Western powers had declared war simply to save face.[2] In Berlin, the propaganda ministry lost no time in reporting that no U-boats had been anywhere near *Athenia* when she went down. Propaganda minister Joseph Goebbels' people told the American chargé d'affaires, Alexander Kirk, that the British were to blame; they had sunk the ship for political reasons, hoping to provoke the United States into declaring war on Germany. It all smacked ominously of the *Lusitania* crisis of 1915.

In Berlin on September 16, thirteen days after the sinking, Grand Admiral Erich Raeder, the sixty-three-year-old commander-in-chief of the Kriegsmarine, told the U.S. naval attaché the same story. It was all the result of a nefarious British plot; Germany was blameless. Chances are, Raeder believed the story. He knew nothing of Lemp's attack: U30 was still at sea. Not until September 27 did the boat return to Wilhelmshaven. Commodore of U-boats Karl Dönitz was waiting on the quayside. Lemp came ashore and asked to speak to Dönitz in private. Dönitz noticed that the young man looked uneasy, and later noted that Lemp admitted "at once that he thought he was responsible for the sinking of the *Athenia*."[3] Dönitz sent Lemp off to report to the naval war staff in Berlin. Predictably perhaps, the meeting resulted in further vehement denials of culpability from the Germans and assertions that Winston Churchill himself had ordered the sinking in a futile attempt to involve the Americans in Britain's war. Lemp was ordered to remove the appropriate pages from his log and to substitute doctored accounts. Dönitz talked to the crew and swore every man to secrecy.

I

THRUST AND PARRY

"Power is not revealed by striking hard or often, but by striking true"
— Honoré de Balzac

THE AIRMEN'S INTENTIONS couldn't be faulted. The Anson dived out of a cloudy sky, its two Cheetah engines banging away at full power, rather less than three hundred horsepower each. The aircraft headed purposefully for a submarine lying motionless on the ocean's surface a mile or so distant. A perfect target! Two 100-pound bombs fell from the aircraft's rack.

Both missed. Worse, both bounced like ping-pong balls when they hit the sea. They skipped back into the air, sailing skyward as if propelled by rockets. To the dismay of the Anson's crew, the bombs exploded directly beneath the aircraft, sending it wobbling and skidding, barely under control. The pilot managed to right it, but fuel — gallon after precious gallon of it — streamed from the peppered tanks in a highly inflammable mist. The engines didn't catch fire; they ran dry, coughing and spluttering into silence. In a matter of minutes, the Anson glided down to a wheels-up landing in the sea. A trawler picked the crew up and took them to safety.

Meanwhile, the submarine slipped away, undamaged. It was as well, for the craft belonged to the Royal Navy.

A few days later, two Blackburn Skua dive-bomber/fighters took to the air from the aircraft carrier *Ark Royal*. Their aim was to destroy the German U-boat U30, which had sunk the liner *Athenia* earlier that month. Their bombs exploded in midair, bringing down both aircraft. Two of the airmen survived and were captured. So far, British anti-submarine weapons had brought down three British aircraft and killed two British airmen without inflicting even a scratch on a U-boat.

On September 17, with the war already two weeks old, eight Fairey Swordfish biplanes set out from the veteran British aircraft carrier *Courageous* in response to reports of U-boat activity in the Bay of Biscay. The five-thousand-ton British freighter *Kafiristan* had been torpedoed and sunk. The merchantman's crew had taken to their lifeboats while the radio officer succeeded in transmitting an SOS, with a somewhat vague position report.

The Swordfish began a diverging search. The freighter was thought to be about one hundred miles south of *Courageous*, on the Atlantic side of the Bay of Biscay. But was it? The Swordfish crews, huddled in their open cockpits, saw nothing but sea. At the controls of one of the Swordfish sat twenty-five-year-old Fleet Air Arm Lieutenant Charles Lamb, on his first operational sortie; he saw no sign of U-boats or the freighter's crew. The ocean stretched as far as the eye could see, apparently into eternity. A daunting vista, one to make a man dwell on the reliability of the Bristol Pegasus nine-cylinder radial engine clattering away up front.

At last his fuel gauge told Lamb to head for home. He shook his head; there was nothing more he could do. He turned, hoping that one of the other crews might have spotted the lifeboat. Lamb's navigator, Bob Wall, gave him a course for the carrier. He nodded. It was a disappointing conclusion to their first flight in anger. The only positive prospect was that of a stiff drink in the wardroom after landing. Lamb stared ahead. The carrier should be coming

into view . . . *there*. But the sea remained empty, a vast area of
absolutely nothing but water. He swallowed the desire to ask Bob
for confirmation of the course. It was correct; Bob was always
correct. Wispy fragments of mist clung to the sea like cotton wool.
How long before darkness crept over the pewter-coloured ocean?
Lamb tried to think of other things, particularly of his forthcoming marriage.

The Fleet Air Arm had not yet seen fit to install radio telephony
(R/T) in its aircraft; their Lords of the Admiralty had, however, in
their wisdom and generosity, provided aircrews with Aldis lamps.
With these, aircrew could communicate with ships by Morse, pro-
vided of course that aircraft and ships were in visual contact. Which
Lamb most certainly was not.

The knot of anxiety tightened with every passing moment. A
few days earlier, the squadron had experienced its first loss. The circumstances were ominously similar to today's. A Swordfish was
returning from patrol but couldn't find the carrier because of low
cloud. Although the aircraft had flown right over the carrier, and
although searchlights had played on the clouds and flares had been
fired to attract the pilot's attention, the Swordfish flew on. Nothing
more was ever heard of it or its crew. At the time, Lamb had suggested to his squadron CO, Pat Humphreys, that the Swordfish
might have been shot down by the enemy. Humphreys thought the
notion preposterous; the enemy was nowhere in the vicinity, he
pointed out. Lamb wrote:

> The tragedy had given me the opportunity of saying some-
> thing that had been bothering me for a week. "I know it's a
> very remote possibility, but it isn't impossible; and I think it's
> time we armed the aircraft guns." The Swordfish had a
> Vickers gun in front, which was fired by the pilot by press-
> ing a button on the control column; the gun then fired
> through the propeller. We also had a Lewis gun in the rear
> cockpit, which was fired either by the observer or the air

gunner if one was lucky enough to be carrying such a luxury as a third member of the crew.

"You've been watching too many films about the last war!" said Pat Humphreys scathingly. "What on earth do we want bullets in our guns for?"[1]

The remark seemed to sum up the RN's collective frame of mind in the early days of the Second World War. The extraordinarily complacent, numbingly anachronistic service never entertained a moment's doubt about its innate superiority over every other service anywhere. Indeed, its officers and men were well trained and bursting with enthusiasm, but they were poorly educated in comparison with the officers of other industrialized nations. Change was viewed with deep suspicion, an odd characteristic for a service that had become great through revolutionary tactics and technology. Although the RN had pioneered in the use of aircraft for "spotting" duties, the service went into the Second World War believing that it was the Navy's job to sink any enemy ships that the aircraft might find – and that aircraft posed little danger to a properly crewed man o' war.

With only about forty-five minutes' fuel remaining, Lamb began a standard square search: four minutes west, four minutes north, eight minutes east, eight minutes south, and so on. His uneasiness intensified as the mist thickened and daylight began to fade. Lamb turned again . . . and saw something glinting on the water miles away to port.

A U-boat! No question about it! Lamb could see the conning tower clearly. He passed the word to Wall and Doug Hemingway, the third member of the crew. Prepare to attack! Helmeted heads nodded dutifully. Lamb put the aircraft into a shallow dive, throttling back as he prepared to drop the bombs mounted on racks beneath his lower wing. He didn't allow himself to fret over the fact that his Swordfish carried no bombsight; it took miraculous judgement – or phenomenal luck – to kill a U-boat with the equipment currently in service. So far in this war, no one had done it; how eminently satisfactory it would be to be the first.

Approaching the U-boat, Lamb frowned at his fuel gauge as if willing it to register a more optimistic reading. He had sufficient for this attack – he hoped – but no more. Perhaps the most unpalatable possibility was that of running out of fuel at the moment of dropping the bombs; in that case he might end up in the water with his intended victims. Then again, he thought, the chances were awfully good that he would be shot down and killed before he had time to drop the bombs.

Eyes narrowed, he concentrated utterly on the task at hand. There was no time to be apprehensive. It had to be now or never.

But something didn't make sense. The target seemed to be growing in size but not getting any nearer. With a jolt of surprise, he realized what had happened. What he had taken for a U-boat's conning tower was in fact the huge island of his own ship, *Courageous*; he had been given a helping of the sort of fantastic luck that is usually reserved for those who win the pools or break the bank at a certain municipality in Monaco. Simultaneously relieved and disappointed, Lamb jettisoned his bombs (it was forbidden to land on a carrier with bombs aboard) and turned to approach the carrier which was at that moment swinging into wind to receive its aircraft. Lamb glanced at his fuel gauge for the umpteenth time. It registered empty and had been doing so for several minutes. Ponderously, the great carrier continued its turn. Lamb couldn't wait. If his engine cut out he would end up in the sea, perhaps right in the path of that enormous steamroller of a ship. Cutting his circuit short, he darted at the flight deck with the batsman frantically waving him off. Lamb ignored him. He had no choice. Sideslipping off his excess height, he arrived on the deck with an almighty thump. Fortunately, the Swordfish's muscular landing gear could take the shock. Before the aircraft had come to a halt, the engine coughed into silence, its last ounces of fuel consumed.

With the propeller still turning, the deck crew busied themselves with folding the broad wings, the drumtight fabric emitting irritable little pings that seemed to be echoed by the bracing wires in a higher pitch. Experiencing the slight giddiness familiar to people who have spent a few recent moments cheek by jowl with eternity, Lamb clambered out of the Swordfish and followed Bob Wall to the wardroom. He asked Wall what he would like to drink.

Wall didn't have time to answer.

It sounded as if the world had been ripped asunder. Lamb heard – and felt – two explosions a split-second apart. They were the loudest, most violent bangs he had ever heard. "If the core of the earth exploded, and the universe split from pole to pole, it could sound no worse. Every light went out immediately and the deck reared upwards, throwing me backwards, and the hot blast which followed tore at the skin on my face and plucked at my clothes. There was something Satanic about it, and unreal. In the sudden deathly silence which followed, I knew the ship had died."[2]

Unknowingly, Lamb had flown over a U-boat as he approached the carrier. Had he been looking for it, he might have seen U29, a five-hundred-ton oceangoing Mark VII submarine, virtually identical to U30, which sank *Athenia*. At 1800, the U-boat's skipper, Otto Schuhart, had spotted the veteran carrier, which had been laid down as a battle cruiser in 1916, then converted to a carrier in the early 1920s. Schuhart had observed with interest that the carrier was escorted by only two destroyers. He longed to attack, but too many factors weighed against him. The U-boat could manage only a paltry eight knots underwater. He dared not surface; the carrier's aircraft would be sure to spot him. For some ninety minutes, Schuhart followed the carrier, the distance between them steadily growing and the likelihood of a successful attack diminishing at the same pace.

Then, to Schuhart's astonishment, *Courageous* began to turn in his direction! He saw Lamb's solitary Swordfish approaching to

land. It touched down on the deck and was dragged to a rapid halt
by the arrester wires.

For Schuhart, it was a perfect opportunity! At a range of three
thousand yards, he fired a fan of three torpedoes. Two hit the carrier.
A gigantic white cloud of smoke and spray obscured the scene;
massive explosions seemed to rock the very ocean. Sections of steel
plate spun high into the air like playing cards tossed away by dis-
gruntled players; the carrier rolled slowly to port. Boats and aircraft
went slithering across the crazily angled deck. Water – or was it fuel?
– sloshed over the deck and into the sea. Something fell across the
lanyard connected to the steam siren, which proceeded to blare
without pause, a melancholy dirge underscoring the catastrophe.

Minutes earlier, Doug Hemingway had ordered an ale in the
petty officers' mess. He wasn't able to take a sip before the torpedoes struck. The ship shivered, groaning; the lights went out; men's
voices sounded disbelieving more than alarmed. This couldn't be
happening; it simply wasn't *on*. The very air seemed to tremble in
the appalling din of breaking glass and clattering pots and pans as
every shelf, every cupboard, every table, shed its contents on the
tilting of the ship. With a shock, Hemingway remembered that he
had left his lifejacket in the aircraft. He scrambled up the darkened
companionway and managed to grab the jacket out of Lamb's
Swordfish just as it began its last journey across the sloping deck
and into the sea. As Hemingway joined his shipmates in abandoning ship, he noticed a squad of Royal Marines struggling to stand
at attention as the ship rolled to port. They had been well trained,
refusing to break ranks until they received the appropriate order.

Fifteen minutes after being hit, the 22,500-ton carrier sank; 519
of her 1,260-man crew went with her, including the captain, W. T.
Makeig-Jones.

In minutes, the escort destroyers roared off in hot pursuit of U29,
determined to avenge *Courageous*, the first major Royal Navy ship
to be lost in the war. Angry mushrooms of spray erupted as depth

charges peppered the sea. Surely no U-boat could survive such an assault. It must already be in pieces on the floor of the ocean.

It wasn't. To the fifty-man crew of U29, however, death seemed imminent; some tried to prepare themselves for it, a few even wished for it. Anything was preferable to this torture. The detonations tore at one's very soul. It was as if huge hobnailed boots were kicking the U-boat's metal hull, straining every pipe, every stanchion. Their senses reeling, the crew crouched defenceless in their reeking metal cocoon, every man fighting the battle of his life, summoning every ounce of courage and will to keep himself under control. Charge after charge burst in chilling proximity, sending great waves of energy bursting over the sub and her huddled occupants. Lights failed; streams of icy water found a way in through minuscule cracks opening in the hull. How long before the slim steel body collapsed under the awful stress? Schuhart and his crew could do nothing but cling like limpets to anything substantial. And hope for the best.

It lasted a lifetime: four hours. Then, at last, the awful punishment suddenly ceased. Silence seemed to enfold the U-boat like something physical. Men glanced at one another, hardly daring to hope. The sounds of the destroyers gradually faded. Schuhart guessed that the destroyers had used up their supply of depth charges. He waited, listening intently as he nodded to his crew, according them little grins to tell them that there was absolutely nothing to worry about, that this episode would soon be over and life would return to normal, or at least what they had come to accept as normal. It seemed to help. The men began to relax; their features softened. Cautiously, Schuhart ordered the boat underway. He used the almost soundless electric motors until he was well clear of the area. He couldn't wait to radio his sensational news to Dönitz, heading home in high spirits, knowing what an enthusiastic welcome he would receive in Wilhelmshaven. He was not disappointed; the Third Reich knew how to lionize its heroes. In this instance, however, Hitler would have been happier had *Courageous* not been sunk. Not then. He still entertained hopes of negotiating the British and French out of the war.

Schuhart received the Iron Cross (the Ritterkreuz) First Class; every member of his crew got the Iron Cross Second Class. The men knew the heady experience of being flattered by the nation's luminaries, of being interviewed by reporters, seeing their pictures in the paper, having their hands shaken by total strangers. In a matter of days, these anonymous servicemen became known all over Germany, admired, emulated. But it lasted less than a week. All too soon, they learned how fleeting fame can be.

∽

Thus the German U-boat force captured headlines from the first days of the war, establishing a reputation for daring and efficiency just as they had in the Great War of 1914–1918. In that conflict, there was never any doubt as to who had the most powerful navy. In the years leading up to war, the Germans had made herculean efforts to match the naval strength of the British. (Kaiser Wilhelm's mother, the daughter of Britain's Queen Victoria, gushed indulgently to a relative, "Wilhelm's one idea is to have a Navy which shall be larger and stronger than the Royal Navy" – as if discussing an amusing new hobby.[3]) Soon the two nations were embroiled in a no-holds-barred race to build bigger and more powerful warships, then the ultimate weapon.

Britain won the first round with the revolutionary *Dreadnought*, the first major ship to incorporate steam turbines, resulting in an attractive combination of great power and amazingly smooth operation. *Dreadnought* was fast, capable of ripping through the bounding main at twenty-one knots, and she packed a tremendous punch in her ten 12-inch guns. She was the best battleship in the world.

Germany responded with a number of technically excellent vessels, most of them better armed, and better armoured, than their British counterparts. But when war broke out in 1914, Britain still had the edge in naval strength. The RN ached to engage the German fleet in a pitched battle in the Nelson tradition, a grand and glorious conflict that would change history. Admiral Alfred von Tirpitz had other ideas. With his spectacular forked beard and hairless cranium, he looked as if he belonged in the cast of something by Gilbert and Sullivan. In fact, Tirpitz had a first-class mind. Holger Herwig, the leading historian of the imperial German navy, described him as "ruthless, clever, domineering, patriotic, indefatigable, aggressive yet conciliatory, pressing yet patient, and stronger in character and drive than the three chancellors and seven heads of the Foreign Office who were destined to be his co-actors on the political stage."[4]

Tirpitz had little confidence in the prospects of the German navy in a head-to-head confrontation with the RN. He rapidly came to the conclusion that Germany's best, indeed only, chance of winning a naval war was to employ a recent addition to the arsenal of naval weapons: the submarine. At the time, the world's navies had scant regard for the undersea craft. Dirty, dangerous, lacking any of the *elan* admired by most sailors, the smelly, furtive contraptions posed more of a danger to their crews than to any enemy. Ambitious naval officers avoided the beastly, malodorous things like the plague. Tirpitz himself had originally dismissed the submarine, but now he had second thoughts. He pondered long and hard on the fact that Britain relied on the importing of vast tonnages of food and other supplies. Britain's immense mercantile fleet, the largest in the world, existed to serve that need. Destroy that fleet, Tirpitz reasoned, and Britain could no longer fight.

The Hague Convention had a few things to say about the unrestricted use of the U-boat against merchant ships. The rules required warships of all types, including the U-boat (*Unterseeboot*), to send boarding parties to examine the cargoes of merchantmen suspected of carrying contraband. It was a time-wasting procedure that put such vessels as submarines at considerable risk. Of what importance were such niceties when the future of Germany was at stake? Tirpitz envisioned a new form of warfare in which underwater craft sank merchant ships without warning. Inhumane? Was it any more inhumane than the British blockade, which, if successful, would result in starvation for countless Germans?

He was soon rewarded by a stunning success. At dawn on September 22, 1914, U9, under the command of Lieutenant Otto Weddigen, surfaced near the Dutch coast. To Weddigen's delight, he immediately spotted three large ships: British cruisers, elderly vessels, but splendid targets nevertheless. And particularly attractive because they appeared to have no escorts.

At a range of five hundred yards Weddigen fired a torpedo at the cruiser *Aboukir*. A perfect shot! The ocean trembled; debris tumbled through the air and splashed into the sea. *Aboukir* settled by the stern. Her commander, Captain Drummond, signalled to the other two cruisers for assistance, convinced that his ship had hit a mine. None of the British crewmen apparently saw U9. At 0655, Weddigen fired both bow torpedoes at the second cruiser, *Hogue*, now stationary in the water as she picked up *Aboukir's* survivors. Both missiles found their mark, and the venerable cruiser began to heel over, members of her crew scrambling frantically up the slanted deck.

Weddigen could scarcely believe his eyes. Two cruisers down and still the British hadn't spotted him! He surfaced, to find the third cruiser, *Cressy*, picking up survivors struggling in the chilly water. Weddigen thought rapidly. His batteries were by now almost completely exhausted. But he still had three torpedoes. And the remaining cruiser still floated.

He had to try to get her!

Crewmen on *Cressy* spotted the U-boat as it came near. The cruiser captain ordered full speed ahead. He nearly evaded Weddigen's torpedo, but not quite. One of two torpedoes hit *Cressy*. The crack of the explosion seemed to gather strength as it sped over the water. The ship came to a halt, wallowing helplessly. Weddigen launched his last missile. His aim was unerring. He watched the venerable vessel slipping beneath the surface, a splendid sight, yet infinitely sad. "For long minutes we were lost as if in some kind of trance," Weddigen later wrote.[5] When he pulled away, hundreds of men still struggled in the water. He couldn't stop to pick any up; he had no room for prisoners.

Weddigen's victory stunned Britain. Three magnificent ships gone, 1,400 men dead. Winston Churchill, at the time the First Lord of the Admiralty, came in for particularly bitter criticism. Why did he permit his cruisers to sail in such dangerous waters without escort? Predictably, perhaps, the RN dismissed the incident as another example of Teutonic dirty tricks. A court of enquiry placed the blame squarely on Captain Drummond for not zigzagging his formation (just as a few months later, the captain of Lusitania would be criticized for not zigzagging the famous liner). The court censured the captains of the cruisers for stopping their ships to pick up survivors. All three should have posted extra lookouts in those U-boat-infested waters, declared the court, its members infinitely wise so long after the event. In fact, at that stage of the war, the possibility of U-boat attack seemed remote to most British sailors. They didn't realize that a new and frightening era in maritime warfare had begun.

By the end of 1916, U-boats were sinking an average of 300,000 tons of British shipping every month. Even Britain, with her huge mercantile fleet, could not withstand such losses for long. Something had to be done. That something was to organize convoys. Convoys had their critics, particularly the ships' owners, who complained that their vessels could sail only when suitable convoys were ready – at the speed of the slowest ship. Convoys were ruining them, they said. Escorting convoys was also an unpopular task in the RN. Most naval officers preferred the idea of RN patrols scouting ahead and clearing the sea lanes for merchantmen. Experience soon proved, however, that such patrols were largely a waste of time and effort. The ocean was too vast, the target, the U-boat, was too small.

In the end, the use of convoys proved to be the most successful anti-submarine weapon of the First World War. In 1917, Germany declared unrestricted warfare on the high seas, and thereafter food supplies in Britain dwindled alarmingly; some politicians spoke seriously of the nation going down to defeat in six months if no relief was forthcoming. Then the Americans joined in. President Woodrow Wilson declared that armed neutrality was no longer enough to protect American interests and lives. U-boats tipped the scales in favour of war; "a wanton rampage against mankind," Wilson called them, adding that the "status of belligerency had been thrust upon the United States by the actions of Imperial Germany and her associates."[6] Despised a few years earlier, the submarine was now important enough to change world history.

In the last years of the war, a British and French team, led by Canadian scientist R. W. Boyle, set out to find a means of locating submerged U-boats. The team concentrated their efforts on sound pulses, reasoning that if a sound pulse could be emitted and later picked up after it had rebounded from a submarine's hull, the elapsed time could be measured to calculate the distance. It took years to perfect, but Asdic, named after the Allied Submarine Detection Investigation Committee that invented it, seemed to be the answer to a vexing problem. Confident that they would have little trouble with U-boats in the future, the British neglected the construction of anti-submarine and escort vessels in the years between the wars. They would regret the omission.

~

In the early days of the Second World War, most senior Allied officers would have been amazed had they known how few U-boats the Germans possessed. Britain and France each had more: the RN about fifty, the French navy some seventy. Germany had twenty-seven (plus thirty 250-ton Ducks, small training submarines, each equipped with three torpedo tubes). In those days, it was rare for more than a dozen U-boats to be on patrol at any given time. They sailed individually to areas west of Britain and in the Bay of Biscay, attacking merchant ships as they encountered them – although unrestricted warfare against shipping was still *verboten*. The Führer insisted that the U-boat crews conduct themselves in accordance with international Prize Regulations. Only those ships directly assisting the enemy's war effort could be attacked – and even those had to be stopped, boarded, and examined, and their crews put safely in lifeboats. It is hard to imagine a vessel less suited to such duty than the U-boat. Deadly beneath the surface, it was awkward and unstable on the surface. The U-boats would not have to put up with such restrictive practices for long.

What Germany lacked in numbers of submarines, it more than made up for in superb training and dedicated personnel. At the helm of the U-boat service was a slim, somewhat lugubrious-looking individual of forty-eight, Karl Dönitz. No swashbuckler, Dönitz out of uniform might have been taken for an assistant bank manager or a local politician. Born in Berlin in September 1891, he was the younger of the two sons of Emil Dönitz, an engineer with the Zeiss optical company. Dönitz's mother died before he was four; his father never remarried. Although the family had no maritime tradition, both sons went to sea: the elder boy, Friedrick, joined the merchant marine, and Karl in 1910 joined the imperial navy. He revelled in the life. After service afloat as a cadet, he went to the naval academy at Kiel and won a commission. On the outbreak of the First World War, he was a junior officer on *Breslau*, a cruiser later handed to the Turks by Germany in exchange for their joining the Central Powers. Dönitz subsequently qualified as an air observer. He married Ingebord Weber in May 1916, and in the same year volunteered for service in U-boats. He became watch officer on U39, commanded by Walter Forstmann, Germany's second-ranking U-boat ace of the Great War and holder of the coveted Pour le Merite. Dönitz sailed on four patrols with Forstmann, in the course of which they sank a remarkable total of thirty-two ships. Promoted to command UC25, an elderly minelayer, Dönitz won the Knight's Cross of the House of Holhenzollern – the Ritterkreuz – for laying two minefields and torpedoing five ships. His superiors thought highly of him, describing him as charming and dashing, a first-rate officer. In September 1918, he was promoted again, to command UB68. The following month, with the war almost over, he attacked a convoy and sank one ship, after which his vessel was damaged and went out of control. He had to scuttle the boat and was captured. As a prisoner of war in England, he feigned mental problems in order to be repatriated. British interrogating officers described him as moody and unpleasant even to his fellow countrymen.

The ploy worked. In mid-1919, Dönitz rejoined his wife and daughter in the uncertain world of postwar Germany. He remained in the Reichsmarine, commanding a destroyer before being assigned to the naval staff in Berlin. And it was in Berlin that Dönitz met Rear Admiral Erich Raeder, the man who would command the German navy in the first half of the Second World War. Raeder thought the world of Dönitz, assessing him as "smart and industrious, possessing excellent professional knowledge."[7] Dönitz had found his mentor. In the mid 1930s when Hitler ordered Raeder to create a new U-boat force, the man selected for the job was Karl Dönitz. Raeder couldn't have chosen a more capable man. Although Dönitz may have had some fleeting regrets about not commanding one of the magnificent new capital ships then under construction, he soon thrust himself heart and soul into his new job. In so doing, he became the world's leading submariner, a man who brought totally new thinking to underwater warfare, and who developed a stunningly efficient force from a mere handful of officers and men. He personally selected every one, determined to create a force that, if not the biggest in the world, would be by far the best.

Dönitz's training regimen became infamous in the German navy, a six-month endurance test, an utterly exhausting routine of mock attacks both on the surface and underwater, with rigorous and repeated exercises on every conceivable aspect of submarine operations. Dönitz insisted on his crews learning a veritable encyclopedia of facts about their vessels, so that they were ready to deal with any emergency. In his memoirs, he commented, "I wanted to imbue my crews with enthusiasm and a complete faith in their arm and to instil in them a spirit of selfless readiness to serve in it. Only those possessed of such a spirit could hope to succeed in the grim realities of submarine warfare. Professional skill alone would not suffice. One of the first things I had to do was to rid my crews of the ever-recurring complex that the U-boat, thanks to recent developments in British anti-submarine defence, was a weapon that had been mastered."[8]

He never spared his crews – and they never failed him. To those who didn't know him well, he seemed a rather distant and pedantic figure who looked as if he never cracked a smile. To his crews, particularly those who had just returned from successful patrols, he was unfailingly jovial. He possessed a puckish sense of humour which made itself known at unexpected moments. A famous story tells of his radio message to a U-boat skipper announcing the birth of a daughter. A new boat had been delivered, Dönitz transmitted – minus a periscope.

From the start, Dönitz made sure that he spent every available moment in the company of his crews. He also insisted on his men receiving awards quickly; there would be no red tape and administrative delay. Within a day or so of returning from his latest patrol, the submariner could go off home on leave, proudly displaying his newly won decoration for the admiration of his friends and relatives. Dönitz regarded this practice of immediate awards to those engaged on operations as psychologically important. In the uncertain world of underwater operations, the danger was too great that a man might lose his life before he could wear his decoration. No one ever disagreed with him on that score.

Initially, the Allies had far more respect for Germany's capital ships than for her U-boats. After all, hadn't Asdic put paid to underwater craft? Not completely, as it turned out. Operational experience revealed that the device was far from perfect. It had two glaring limitations that, incredibly, seemed to have escaped everyone's attention during development. First, the device was of little use in detecting U-boats on the surface, a major disadvantage because that was where Dönitz's U-boats spent most of their time. Secondly, even though it could detect subs beneath the surface, it had no way of determining their depth. Although film and fiction have depicted U-boats lurking in the depths, darting at unsuspecting prey like ravenous sharks, the fact is, submarines of that era were really surface craft with the ability to submerge for short periods. If the Admiralty had taken the trouble to purchase a copy of a book published shortly before the war, *Die U-bootwaffe* ("The Submarine Weapon"), their lordships would have found the facts clearly enunciated by the author, one Karl Dönitz. Astonishingly frank considering the international tensions of the times, Dönitz told his readers that the best way to use a submarine force was at night and on the surface, in the largest possible numbers. He considered every aspect of the science, asking, "How far is it possible to exercise command over a number of U-boats? Is it possible during the actual attack or only as far as to ensure coordinated action before the attack? What is the ideal balance between the exercise of overall command and giving the U-boats independence of action? Must command be exercised by a person actually at sea? In a U-boat? Or in a surface vessel? Is it, anyway, possible to exercise command from a U-boat? Can command be exercised wholly or partially from the land? Would it then be necessary to have some sort of subordinate, intermediate command post at sea? If so, where would the division of responsibilities between the two lie?"[9]

Dönitz put his theories to test in large-scale exercises carried out in the fall of 1937. From a command post on a submarine depot ship at Kiel, he directed the movements of U-boats in the Baltic by radio. The experiment was, he states, a "complete and impressive" success – although he feared that he could never keep

these group tactics a secret.[10] Later, during the war, he was astonished to learn that the British had been caught unawares by his
"wolfpack" tactics and by his method of attacking by night on the
surface. Dönitz claimed that this was largely due to the emphasis
on surface ships, the bigger and heavier the better, in RN training.
Undoubtedly he was correct.

Dönitz always maintained that German forces at sea – whether
over, on, or below the surface of the water – should form one
entity under the command of the navy. "In opposition to this
view," Dönitz wrote, "stood General Göring who, from the time
when a start was made in 1933 with the raising of a new German
Air Force, adopted the attitude: 'Everything that flies belongs to
me!' From 1933 right up to 1939, Grand Admiral Raeder did his
utmost in long and stubborn discussions to persuade the
Government of the need for an independent naval air service. All
his efforts were in vain."[11]

Most British naval officers convinced themselves that any U-
boat unwise enough to come nosing around any of His Majesty's
ships would be taken care of by means of "hunter" groups of
destroyers and other speedy warships. The concept of naval forces
dashing around the seas like the cavalry of old must have appealed
to Churchill, who had made his name in the saddle during the
Boer War. It went against the grain to have naval vessels waiting to
be attacked by these damned furtive U-boats. Far better to go out
and find them, then sink them! It was all very spirited and inspir-
ing, but not particularly efficient. There was simply too much
ocean and too few ships. U-boats rarely experienced much
difficulty in steering clear of destroyers. As the number of merchant ships sunk grew at an alarming rate, it became clear that the
time-tested system of running convoys must be employed again.

In addition to its U-boats, the Kriegsmarine had eight formidable warships at its disposal in September 1939: two battle cruisers, *Scharnhorst* and *Gneisenau*; three of the so-called "pocket
battleships" (*Panzerschiffe*), with their powerful armament and light

structure, *Admiral Graf Spee*, *Admiral Scheer*, and *Lützow* (formerly known as *Deutschland*, the name being changed because of Hitler's nagging concern about the blow to the nation's morale should a ship called Deutschland be lost); three large cruisers, *Admiral Hipper*, *Blücher*, and *Prinz Eugen*; and finally, the pride of the German navy, the two "super battleships," the greatest in the world, *Bismarck* and *Tirpitz*, both of which had been launched but not yet completely fitted out. Although small in number, the new German battleships represented the very latest thinking in naval warfare. By any standard, they were exceptional vessels, faster and more heavily armed than their British counterparts, most of which were of First World War vintage (although five new ships were under construction for the RN). The jewel in the British naval crown was *Hood*, and, at twenty-one, she was beginning to show her age. The British intended to employ groups of battleships against the formidable German vessels. In addition, assistance was expected from the French, although that nation tended to be more interested in the Mediterranean than the Atlantic. As in the First War, the RN's principal base in the British Isles was Scapa Flow in the Orkney Islands, north of Scotland, windswept and forbidding, but strategically important. Here the British Home Fleet had five battleships, two battle cruisers, two aircraft carriers, twelve cruisers, seventeen destroyers, and an assortment of other naval hardware. Submarines were based at Dundee, Scotland, and Blyth in northeast England. On the British south coast, two battleships, two aircraft carriers, three cruisers, and nine destroyers constituted the Channel Force. Six shore-based commands controlled various sections of the country. Of these, none could match the strategic importance of Western Approaches Command, which controlled southwest England and the Irish Sea, and hence the sea lanes between Britain and North America.

Long before hostilities broke out, the Germans had decided that in the event of war one battle cruiser would go to the North Atlantic, the other to the South Atlantic, both to be accompanied by supply ships. Sixteen U-boats would occupy waiting positions off the Atlantic coasts of Britain and France, as well as the Strait of Gibraltar. In addition, a small naval force would be available for duty against the diminutive Polish navy. Admiral Raeder was frankly pessimistic about the prospects of his naval forces in combat with the British. In his memoirs, he wrote that they could do little against such overwhelming strength except die gallantly. He underestimated them.

~

The Germans lost their first U-boat of the war on September 14, 1939: a case of defeat at the moment of victory. U39, a long-range Type IX boat, under the command of Gerhard Glattes, came across the British aircraft carrier *Ark Royal* west of Scotland. *Ark* was a new ship, launched in April 1937, commissioned in December 1938. She carried sixty aircraft, Skuas and Swordfish. On September 3, 1939, *Ark Royal* had received the same Admiralty cipher message sent to all Royal Navy ships: "Total Germany." Eleven days later, she was attacked. She had received word that the merchant ship *Fanad Head* had fallen victim to a predatory U-boat. The carrier and its escort of four destroyers hurried to the scene. *Ark Royal* turned into the wind to launch her Skuas, but in so doing, she drew away from her destroyer escort.

When Glattes got the splendid new carrier in the crosshairs of his sight, he could scarcely believe his good fortune. He had been on patrol for more than three weeks with nothing to show for his efforts. Now he had the RN's newest and greatest aircraft carrier at his mercy! At 1507 hours he fired a fan of three torpedoes equipped with magnetic firing mechanisms.

In an agony of suspense, the crew of U39 waited while the torpedoes streaked through the water. A perfect shot! It couldn't miss . . . couldn't, *couldn't*. Men held their breath for long, agonizing moments. Someone talked about seeing flashes and smoke. And hearing an explosion. Or something. But the minutes passed. The carrier steamed on, apparently undamaged. Glattes cursed. Those damned useless tin eels again. Someone should be put up against a wall for sending such weapons out on operational patrols. He would report the incident to Dönitz at the first opportunity.

He didn't get that opportunity.

Like avenging angels, three British destroyers suddenly came speeding for U39. They were *Ark Royal's* escorts, *Foxhound*, *Faulkner*, and *Firedrake*. They had seen the torpedoes slicing through the water, and now their crews bristled with determination to get the U-boat that had tried to sink the *Ark*. They launched depth charges, scores of them, sending them splashing into the ocean to sink to preset levels where they exploded, unleashing great waves of energy. If they exploded within a few feet of a U-boat, the effect was usually lethal.

Asdic conditions were excellent. The destroyers' operators obtained strong signals that fixed the U-boat's position as clearly as a radio voice from below. The hapless submarine crew could only wait, wincing with every shattering detonation. The depth charges kept coming, rocking the very ocean, punishing every square inch of the U-boat's steel skin. Crewmen stared blankly at the hull; you could *see* it absorbing the dreadful punishment, bending, straining. Would the next charge be the last one? Would the hull collapse, crushed like an eggshell? Lights dimmed; sea valves leaked; salt-water got into the batteries, spewing out poisonous chlorine gas, the narrow space becoming a fiendish underwater laboratory. All electric power failed. The boat went out of control, a mad thing goaded beyond endurance, twisting and turning, writhing in its death agonies. Glattes ordered the crew to abandon ship. He blew the main ballast tanks and surfaced, only to find himself surrounded by the three destroyers, their guns blazing. The firing ceased when U39's crew began jumping overboard. The scuttling charge exploded and the sub went down bow-first. The three triumphant destroyers launched boats and picked up all forty-three members of the crew. The episode had a happy ending for the RN, but it had been a frighteningly near thing. Only a fault in a torpedo had saved the Navy's pride and joy.

~

In the first months of the war, Canada's aerial coastal defences were virtually non-existent. Some work had begun on site surveys for airfields on the east coast, but none was ready on the outbreak of war. Only one squadron, No. 5 (General Reconnaissance), was at its war station, at Dartmouth, Nova Scotia. Other units had to make their way east from various locations. No. 3 Squadron flew its obsolete Westland Wapiti biplanes from Calgary, with only half reaching their destination on the east coast, the remainder having got hung up at various locations along the way. Three landed at Millinocket, Maine, due to technical problems, and RCAF officers feared that the U.S. authorities might intern them. In fact, the Americans seemed only too glad to see the venerable biplanes continue on their way.

Eastern Air Command (EAC) had an immense area of responsibility, extending from eastern Quebec to Newfoundland. On the outbreak of war, several squadrons were ordered to the coast. They found few facilities. No. 10 Squadron set up at Halifax's civil aerodrome. No. 8 Squadron set to work to create a seaplane base at the mouth of the Sydney River in Cape Breton. "All property along the shore line is privately owned," noted the unit diarist, "and great difficulty is expected in being able to establish a base from which to operate. To date movement of personnel to and from aircraft has been made in a small row boat hired from Mrs. Georgia Piercey, from her property."[12] By mid-September, the slow and poorly armed Stranraer biplane flying boats of 5 Squadron, and 8 Squadron's Northrop Deltas, were searching for U-boats off Halifax harbour and flying convoy escort patrols. Later, Hurricanes of No. 1 Squadron, based at Dartmouth, Nova Scotia, flew "coastal sweeps" and local patrols. On November 3, 11 Squadron arrived at Dartmouth equipped with Lockheed Hudsons, EAC's first modern maritime-patrol aircraft, capable of a top speed of 230 mph, compared with the Stranraer's maximum speed of 130 mph. By the end of the year, Douglas Digby bombers equipped 11 Squadron.

Eastern Air Command was beginning to take form, although none of its aircraft was equipped with the radar and other equipment that would soon be considered essential in maritime patrol work.

~

During the war's first few weeks, Dönitz began to think seriously about an idea that had fascinated him for years: Penetrating rocky, forbidding Scapa Flow, the Scottish base of the British Home Fleet, by U-boat. At first glance, the notion seemed suicidal. Scapa Flow was a sort of nautical Maginot Line, a heavily defended base nesting secure behind a series of impenetrable barriers. But were they really impenetrable? Dönitz had been studying charts and photographs of Scapa Flow and had come to the conclusion that there might be a way through. Reconnaissance by aircraft and submarines had confirmed the existence of hulks blocking the half dozen channels surrounding the base. Resting on the bottom, the hulks were held in place by cables anchored on land, effectively denying access to all channels. All, that is, except one: Kirk Sound, in the northern part of the base. There appeared to be a gap of about fifty feet through which a U-boat's slender form could slip. Dönitz noted in his war diary, "Here, I think, it would certainly be possible to penetrate by night, on the surface at slack water. The main difficulties will be navigational."[13]

Dönitz needed a brave and resourceful skipper for the job. He knew just the man: Günther Prien, the thirty-one-year-old son of a Lübeck judge. The good-looking Prien was a former merchant marine officer who had qualified just as the Great Depression settled over Europe. Prien, like millions of others, had been tossed out of work. In the grim early 1930s, he took any odd job that came his way, hoping against hope that he would eventually be able to make a living at sea. In 1933, the year Hitler became chancellor of Germany, the Reichsmarine (later to be known as the Kriegsmarine) opened its officer-candidate program to merchant marine officers. Prien immediately volunteered, opting for the submarine service. To his delight, he was accepted. In 1935, he became an officer, and by the outbreak of war in September 1939, he had been promoted to command U47, a Type VII boat. Two days later, he sank a small British freighter, *Bosnia*. It was a significant sinking: the first British merchant ship lost in the war. The following day, he sank another, *Rio Claro*, then yet another, the 1,777-ton *Garvaton*, sending her to the bottom after her crew tried unsuccessfully to ram him. Prien rapidly became one of the brightest stars in Dönitz's firmament.

On October 1, the commodore told Prien about the proposed attack on Scapa Flow. Prien immediately volunteered, but Dönitz said to think it over for forty-eight hours before making up his mind. Like a businessman considering an interesting deal, Prien took the file home for the weekend and studied it. Dönitz had chosen his man well. The young commander was experienced enough to recognize the formidable dangers involved, yet ambitious enough to find them irresistible. Prien was soon back in Dönitz's office. He would be honoured to undertake the mission.

On October 8, Prien's U47 slipped unceremoniously from its berth at Kiel, proceeding along the canal to the sea. Only when he was well clear of land did Prien inform his crew of the nature of the task they had undertaken. Their reaction delighted him. Every man was enthusiastic, eager to reach Scapa Flow, a name denoting defeat to every German sailor, for the high seas fleet had been scuttled there soon after the end of the First World War. If morale counted for anything, the job was as good as done.

The journey to Scotland seemed endless. During daylight hours, Prien hid in the depths of the North Sea, U47 lying on the murky bottom like some predatory crustacean. The crew rested and waited. Only at night did the grey monster stir itself, pumping out its ballast, easing itself out of the silt, beginning the long ascent through hundreds of feet of ocean, cautiously approaching the surface after exhaustive hydrophone searches to detect the sound of any ship in the vicinity. All quiet above. At periscope depth, Prien surveyed the surrounding sea. Still quiet. No sign of life. All clear to surface. The chief engineer ordered all ballast tanks blown. Compressed air hissed into the tanks. The U-boat emerged, almost invisible in the darkness. Now her motion changed. No longer a creature of the dark and tranquil deep, she had to cope with the turbulent surface. She shuddered as the diesel engines' gears took the load. Her long slim nose sliced the swirling water and she moved forward. It was choppy; she wallowed, rolling, dipping, her steel hull slapping the sea as she gained speed, literally bouncing from wave to wave, jarring everyone and everything inside. Spray drenched the lookouts on the conning tower. They huddled in their oilskins, their red-rimmed eyes scanning the almost-invisible horizon, their fancies creating destroyers and aircraft out of wispy flecks of moonlight and shifting shadows. Approaching the British base, a shock awaited Prien; he found the area illuminated by aurora borealis. The streaky, uncertain light accorded the scene an oddly theatrical quality. He considered postponing the operation for twenty-four hours; then he decided to push on. He confirmed his position by the Orkney navigational lights. Shortly after 11:00 P.M., as he neared the entrance to Holm Sound, he was startled by the black, impenetrable form of a merchant ship looming out of the darkness. Heart thumping, he waited until the merchantman had gone on its ponderous way.

Just before midnight, U47's bow slid into the channel Prien believed to be Kirk Sound. It wasn't. He realized his error in the nick of time. Ordering the diesels switched off and replaced by almost silent electric power, he pushed on into Churchill's sanctum sanctorum. Ahead lay the rusting hulks.

Prien felt the tug of the currents elbowing his boat this way and that. The passage became a test of nerves; at one point, his craft scraped the bottom, grinding its way along the stony bed before it pulled free. Relief flowed like was a fresh breeze through the damp, fetid sewer pipe of an interior. Prien's smile broadened. It was twenty-seven minutes past midnight. He was in the heart of the British base — and old Winston would have a heart attack if he knew.

The shielded headlights of a car on the coast road startled the U-boat commander and his lookouts. The car's lights disappeared into the night and darkness enfolded the scene. Prien wondered where the big ships were. He pushed on into the bosom of the enemy camp. Still no sign of capital ships.

Prien became uneasy; the surreal half-light seemed to suggest a trap. Were destroyers and cruisers waiting around that promontory? Were gunners at this moment squinting into their sights, preparing to blast the U-boat out of the water? He stared until his eyes ached. The fifteen-mile-long inlet seemed deserted. Why? This was a major naval base. Even in the early hours of the morning, the place should be bustling. He edged to the north.

Moments later he saw them. Two battleships lying at anchor. Sitting ducks! With the assistance of his first officer, Engelbert Endrass, Prien identified the ships as *Royal Oak* and *Repulse*, two important RN vessels.* Ironically, Scapa Flow was virtually deserted, because the German cruisers *Gneisenau* and *Köln* had struck out into the North Sea on the same day that Prien had sailed from Kiel. Most of the RN ships then in Scapa Flow had gone in pursuit. German aircraft had attacked the RN force but had done no damage. Of all the battleships sent to intercept the Germans, only *Royal Oak* had returned to Scapa Flow; the others had put into

---

*   In fact, Prien and Endrass correctly identified only one ship: *Royal Oak*, an elderly veteran of the Battle of Jutland. The second ship was an old seaplane transport, *Pegasus*. At that hour, *Repulse* was snug in harbour at Loch Ewe in northwest Scotland.

Loch Ewe. Poor communications between the various arms of the German navy had robbed Prien of several attractive targets.

At 0055 Prien fired four torpedoes, two at *Royal Oak* and two at the ship he believed to be *Repulse*. Of the four, only one found its mark. It hit *Royal Oak* near her bow and blew a fifty-foot-wide hole above the waterline adjacent to the paint and anchor chain lockers. Exhibiting remarkable sang-froid, the ship's captain, William Benn, grumpily ordered an inspection, after which he concluded that spontaneous combustion had been responsible, causing a minor explosion in the paint locker. It probably never crossed his mind that a U-boat might have slipped into Scapa and done the deed. The master-at-arms was of the opinion that the noise had come from an exploding carbon dioxide bottle. In any case, it wasn't serious. No one had been hurt. The ship's watertight doors had sealed off the damaged section. Everyone went back to bed.

Meanwhile, Prien, unsure what he had achieved and puzzled by the lack of response, prepared for another attack. He fired his stern torpedo but missed, the missile ending up on shore. Then he fired his three remaining torpedoes at *Royal Oak*. This time all three missiles hit their target, blowing the old ship's starboard flank to pieces. One torpedo struck the engine room, another smashed its way into the magazine, setting off an uncontrollable blaze. Trembling as if in pain, the battleship slowly rolled over to starboard. Another shattering explosion heaved the ship almost clear of the water. Her great bulk crashed back, creating a veritable tidal wave smashing through the harbour. All the ship's lights went out; the intercom failed, so the order to abandon ship could not be heard; burning cordite fouled the vents; men coughed and spluttered as they groped around in the darkness, trying to find a way out. Suddenly, convulsively, the splendid old ship turned turtle and sank, taking with her more than eight hundred of her twelve-hundred-man crew. A survivor recalled the deafening din as the ship rolled: every can of food, every racked shell, every cup and plate and pot and pan went bouncing and crashing about on the pitch-black decks, making more noise than the torpedo. Captain Benn, who had evinced remarkably little interest in the attack, was tossed bodily into the water. He survived.

Prien scurried away, convinced (incorrectly) that he would be pursued by British destroyers. Two and a half hours after entering Scapa Flow, he escaped into the open sea. The next day, the Admiralty released the humiliating news that *Royal Oak* had been sunk with heavy loss of life. Berlin heard the bulletin but withheld comment until Prien had reported. He did so in the early hours of October 16, stating simply: *Royal Oak sunk, Repulse damaged.* The following day, Raeder and Dönitz were waiting on the dockside as U47 purred into Wilhelmshaven. They conferred the Iron Cross First Class on Prien and the Iron Cross Second Class on every member of his crew. Hitler made no attempt to conceal his glee. Prien's incursion into Scapa Flow was just the sort of daring exploit to capture the imagination of the German people and put the fear of God into the British. The Führer sent his personal aircraft to fly Prien and his crew to Berlin. At Templehof airport, thousands of Berliners turned out to greet the heroes. Thousands more lined the road into the city. During the heady days of celebration in the capital, Prien and his crew revelled in the adulation of the people, enjoying the finest food and entertainment, meeting the mighty, shaking thousands of hands, answering countless questions. In London, Winston Churchill stood up in Parliament and, grim-faced, described Prien's attack as a remarkable exploit. He then went to Scapa Flow and ordered the camouflaging of the oil tanks and the building of dummy tanks for the Luftwaffe to waste its bombs on. He also took the opportunity to fire Admiral Sir William French, flag officer in command of Orkney and Shetland.

Hitler promoted Dönitz to Admiral in recognition of the brilliant exploit. But the promotion didn't alleviate Dönitz's frustrations. He had shown what his submarine force could do, yet his appeals for more U-boats had borne no fruit. Hitler had convinced himself that the war would be over in a matter of weeks or months and there would be no need for more U-boats. The American journalist William Shirer reported that the press in Germany was talking openly of peace; Hitler had declared that he had no desire to wage war against Britain and France, adding that if those nations refused to discuss peace, it proved that they were responsible for the war's continuation. In reply, Neville Chamberlain, the weakling who in 1938 had sold Czechoslovakia down the river, surprised Hitler with his firmness. Calling the German leader's proposals "vague and uncertain," and noting that "they contain no suggestions for righting the wrongs done to Czechoslovakia and Poland," he said that no reliance could be placed on the promises of the present German government.[14] The tragedy was that he hadn't employed such strong rhetoric a year earlier.

∾

The successes enjoyed by Dönitz's U-boats alarmed the British, dependent as they were on imports of an immense array of supplies. It was clear that a furious fight was about to commence in the Atlantic. With some reluctance, they reinstituted the convoy system, which had done so much to beat the U-boats in the First World War. Although it was popularly believed that the speed and firepower of the escorts were what had made convoys so successful, in reality it was simply the grouping of ships together. Winston Churchill explained it succinctly: "The sea is so vast that the difference between the size of a convoy and the size of a single ship shrinks in comparison almost to insignificance. There was in fact very nearly as good a chance of a convoy of forty ships in close order slipping unperceived between the patrolling U-boats as there was for a single ship; and each time this happened, forty ships escaped instead of one."[15]

On October 1, Dönitz, recognizing the effectiveness of Allied convoys, had written in his war diary, "In view of the incorporation of enemy shipping into convoys, I do not consider it advisable to distribute the U-boats singly over a very wide area. Our object must be to locate the convoys and destroy them by means of a concentrated attack by the few U-boats available. The finding of a convoy on the high seas is a difficult task. Our operations therefore must be concentrated against those areas in which the enemy sea lines of communication converge and join – namely, off southwest England and in the vicinity of Gibraltar."[16] Because of the acute shortage of U-boats, Dönitz could not initiate his so-called wolf-pack tactics for another year.

Convoys moved under the control of the RN, a fact resented by many merchant skippers who claimed, not without justification, that they had infinitely more experience of the sea than the average naval officer; they bitterly resented being ordered about by pip-squeaks whose "wavy navy" insignia hadn't even acquired a decent salty patina.* Throughout the war, relations between the navy and merchant sailors ranged from grudging respect to outright hostility.

At first, convoys were usually escorted only a certain distance either east or west into the Atlantic, after which they dispersed and sailed independently to their destinations. That was considered good enough at a time of relatively little action. In the early days, only ships capable of travelling at between nine and fifteen knots were put in convoy; the rest sailed independently (to be known as Independently Routed Ships, or IRSs). In general, the larger the convoy, the better the protection against enemy action it provided – and later in the war, some convoys would consist of close to two hundred ships. On the other hand, the larger the convoy, the more unwieldy it was and the greater the risks posed by violent storms and poor visibility. At times, fog or mist could entirely obscure the ship next door, and even if actual collision was avoided, the convoy could quickly become scattered over a vast area of ocean, where-upon escort vessels dashed around like furious sheepdogs, trying

---

*   Members of the Navy's Volunteer Reserve wore "wave-like" cuff rank badges in contrast to the straight badges of the regular officers.

to get the ships in line again. The stress on masters was unrelenting.

Collisions seemed sometimes to haunt certain ships, or groups of ships. A particularly tragic example involved the Canadian destroyer *Margaree* (formerly HMS *Diana*). She had been acquired by the Royal Canadian Navy to replace HMCS *Fraser*, lost in a collision during the last days of the evacuation from France in 1940. Confusion in signals between *Fraser* and the British cruiser *Calcutta* led to the disaster. *Calcutta* sliced through *Fraser*'s foredeck, her entire bridge and its occupants ending up on the cruiser's bow. The destroyer *Restigouche* rushed to the wreck to offer assistance, taking on sixty of *Fraser*'s crew. Meanwhile, the severed bow drifted away in the darkness. Forty-seven Canadian and nineteen British sailors lost their lives.

Fraser's replacement, *Margaree*, sailed from Londonderry on October 20, 1940, escorting a small convoy of five ships. Amongst her crew were many of the survivors from *Fraser*. Two days later, during an inky, stormy night, *Port Fairy*, the leading merchant ship in the port column, smashed into *Margaree*'s flank and cut the destroyer in half, the bow section sinking in moments. The crew of the merchantman threw calcium flares as the captain positioned his ship alongside the after part of *Margaree* to take on survivors. Despite his efforts, *Margaree*'s commanding officer and 141 of her crew were lost.

The most important naval action in the closing months of the war's first year involved the German navy's much-vaunted pocket battleship *Admiral Graf Spee*.[*]

Graf Spee had taken up position in the South Atlantic prior to the outbreak of war. She sank nine ships in the Atlantic and Indian oceans before suffering engine troubles. Uncomfortably aware that

---

[*] Pocket battleships were so called because they were relatively small, to meet the dictates of the First World War peace treaty limiting Germany to ships of less than 10,000 tons. Nevertheless, they carried powerful armament. To the Germans, a pocket battleship was known as a Panzerschiffe.

his cruise had produced paltry results to date, Captain Hans Langsdorff was keen to score more victories before he headed home for repairs. He had been told of a convoy in the River Plate area off the coast of Uruguay and decided to intercept it. What Langsdorff didn't know was that his move had been anticipated by Commodore Henry Harwood RN, whose Force G was one of several formed to hunt the German battleship. When Langsdorff spotted the British force, he mistook it for the convoy he sought. Eagerly, he changed course.

The light cruiser *Ajax*, Force G's flagship, carried a Fairey Seafox seaplane mounted on a catapult. It took off in search of the German battleship. The Seafox looked about as threatening as the Tiger Moth trainer, but it did its job, quickly spotting the German ship. Langsdorff, who had been looking forward to easy pickings on the South Atlantic convoy routes, found himself in a fierce fight. In addition to *Ajax*, Commodore Harwood had under his command the light cruiser *Achilles* and the larger *Exeter*. He attempted to minimize the Germans' superior firepower by attacking from two quarters simultaneously. He was, however, only partially successful, for Langsdorff concentrated his radar-directed fire on *Exeter*. (At this time, RN ships had not been equipped with radar-directed guns.)

Only the fact that several German shells failed to explode saved *Exeter*. She had to withdraw, listing badly and taking in water. It seemed questionable whether she would remain afloat. *Ajax* and *Achilles* saved the day with a gallant gesture, dashing into the battle, guns blazing, drawing the German ship's fire away from the badly damaged *Exeter*.

Ajax and *Achilles* eventually retired under cover of a smoke screen, while Langsdorff, his ship suffering from the effects of several direct hits, put into Montevideo to effect repairs and tend to his wounded. The Uruguayans proved unexpectedly inhospitable. *Graf Spee* could stay in Montevideo up to seventy-two hours, they said, but no longer. Langsdorff kept hearing disquieting reports of a massive British buildup of naval forces – just waiting for him to attempt an escape from Montevideo. He did his best to charter an aircraft to check for himself, but none was available – at least, to him. Langsdorff received intelligence reports of the British laying in large quantities of fuel oil, sufficient to power two capital ships. The situation was becoming nastier by the hour. Langsdorff cabled Berlin for instructions. Admiral Raeder replied, "Attempt by all means to extend time in neutral waters in order to gain freedom of action as long as possible. Fight your way through to Buenos Aires, using remaining ammunition. No internment in Uruguay. Attempt effective destruction if ship is scuttled."[17]

On the evening of December 17, the German battleship sailed out of Montevideo. At sunset, she hove to. With representatives of many of the world's newspapers watching, she blew up, scuttled by her own crew.

Three days later, Langsdorff lay down on his hotel bed in Montevideo, pulled a German naval flag over himself, and ended it all with a bullet in his head. Hitler regarded the episode as a disgrace to German arms. Scarcely able to contain himself, he summoned Admiral Raeder, then exploded in one of his monumental tantrums, savagely criticizing the navy and its officers. Quite apart from the loss of an important ship, Germany had suffered a humiliating defeat in the battle of propaganda. Hadn't the German public been told that *Graf Spee* had achieved a spectacular victory, sending the British cruisers limping away, utterly defeated? Now this. How was it to be explained to the nation? Raeder had no suggestions. And a day or two later, a funereal-voiced radio announcer broke the news that Captain Langsdorff had gone down with his ship, but not before heroically fulfilling the expectations of his Führer, the German people, and the navy.

The sinking of *Graf Spee* was treated as a major victory in Britain. At the Admiralty, they took pleasure in crossing out the name of one of their principal foes, and at that stage of the war, battleships were still seen as the most dangerous threat to shipping. Langsdorff's ship had impressed the British. Although she now lay at the bottom of the sea, their lordships eventually paid the Uruguayan government fourteen thousand pounds for her. She revealed the uncomfortable truth that the RN's warships were no longer the last word in naval hardware.

∿

During this period, Allied defences against submarine attack were feeble. RAF Coastal Command and the RN's Fleet Air Arm so far had little influence on the battle now brewing – although the so-called Scarecrow patrols by light training aircraft probably deterred some U-boats from making attacks. Hundreds, even thousands of long-range, heavily armed aircraft were needed to patrol the sea lanes.

Maritime aircrews had to rely on the anti-submarine bomb, an uncertain weapon that usually posed more danger for the aircraft and its crew than for the enemy. The only way to sink a sub was with a direct hit – a difficult task, since the aircraft carried no bombsights. In the spring of 1940, Coastal Command tested the RN's Mark VII depth charge. It proved satisfactory and was soon put into service. For the aircrews, the introduction of depth charges added significantly to the dangers they faced, for attacks now had to be carried out at low level, usually at about fifty feet, dropping "sticks" of depth charges about one hundred feet apart. The aim was to straddle the target; even near-misses could be fatal, the concussion sufficient to fracture a U-boat's hull. The first Coastal Command victory over a U-boat came in January 1940, when a Sunderland of 228 Squadron, the destroyer *Whitshed*, and the sloop *Fowey* combined forces to sink U55 near the Isles of Scilly.

∿

The weather was an implacable enemy in the early months of 1940. Record-breaking cold gripped Europe. People almost forgot about the war in their ceaseless struggle to keep warm. But if the people thought little about the war, it occupied Hitler's thoughts totally. And the focus of his thoughts was Norway. That country was the bridge to Sweden, with its high-grade iron ore. Before the war, the Third Reich annually imported some ten million tons of Swedish ore. Now, Germany's need was even greater. During the warm weather months, the ore could be transported from northern Sweden down the Gulf of Bothnia, across the Baltic to Germany. In winter, that route became icebound. So the ore travelled by rail to the Norwegian port of Narvik, thence by ship down the Norwegian coast to Germany, safe, thanks to Norway's neutrality, from interference by Allied ships or aircraft.

On November 30, 1939, the balance of power had shifted in northern Europe. Russia attacked Finland. Initially, the smaller nation's armed forces did well against the Soviets, but soon, however, superior strength began to tell. In January, Britain and France concocted a plan to send forces to Norway and Sweden to protect both countries against a German attack, a plan that evoked a singular lack of enthusiasm among the countries involved. Then the Finns sued for peace. The situation might have settled down, at least temporarily, but for the *Altmark* incident.

Altmark had been a supply vessel for Captain Langsdorff's *Graf Spee*. When the German pocket battleship was destroyed, *Altmark* set off for Germany carrying some three hundred captured Allied merchant seamen. A British destroyer flotilla, commanded by Captain (later Rear Admiral) Philip Vian, attempted to intercept her in neutral waters but was prevented by Norwegian naval units. *Altmark* escaped into Joessenfjord. Determined not to let her get away, Churchill, the First Lord of the Admiralty, ordered Vian to storm the Norwegian fjord and take the ship. The dashing Vian was the right man for the mission. Blithely ignoring the fact that he was committing an act of war, he went careering into the fjord, boarded the German ship, and freed the prisoners.

The legality of the action was of no concern in Britain, where newspapers revelled in the boarding party's cry "The Navy's here!"

Churchill declared of the action: "In a cold winter, it warmed the cockles of the British heart."[18] The Norwegians complained bitterly, although most other nations shrugged it off, reasoning that the Germans never let legal niceties stay their hand, so why should the British? The *Altmark* incident probably decided Hitler. The flow of Swedish iron ore into Germany was far too important to leave to chance. On March 1, he issued formal directives for the invasion of Norway and Denmark. Churchill wanted to lay mines in Norwegian territorial waters. Chamberlain and Lord Halifax, the foreign secretary, wouldn't hear of it. Chamberlain seemed convinced that the German buildup of naval forces in Baltic ports was merely a warning to the British not to mine Norwegian waters. But the deteriorating situation soon persuaded the War Cabinet to take more cogent action. It was too late. The Germans were already on their way to invade Norway. An expeditionary force of British, French, and Free Polish troops, some twelve thousand troops in all, was hastily assembled and sent off to Trondheim. Irresolutely led, they did poorly against the efficient German forces.

Dönitz's U-boats became involved in the campaign in Norway. It was the first time in history that submarines had taken part in a major military campaign, cooperating with air, sea, and ground forces. Initially, the U-boats' main job was to prevent the Allies from invading Norway. It proved costly. On March 11, at Wilhelmshaven, an RAF Blenheim bombed U31. The Type VII oceangoing submarine commanded by Johannes Habekost was undergoing sea trials after repairs. Hit by the Blenheim's bombs, it blew up and sank in 102 feet of water, killing Captain Habekost and his crew, as well as ten shipyard workers. U31 was the first U-boat in history sunk by an aircraft.* Then a Type IX U-boat, U44, struck a mine in the Helgoland Bight and went down with all hands. In addition, two

---

*   Subsequently U31 was raised and repaired. The pilot of the Blenheim, Squadron Leader Miles V. Delap of 85 Squadron, RAF Bomber Command, was shot down little more than two months later during an attack on Gembloux, Belgium. Delap survived to be taken prisoner.

of the small training subs, known as Ducks, U21 and U22, were lost. U21, which ran aground off Norway, was later salvaged; U22 disappeared off the northeastern coast of Scotland, probably the victim of a mine.

So far, the Norwegian episode had turned out to be disappointing for both sides. The only positive note as far as the Allies were concerned was the destruction of the four U-boats; for the Germans, the episode had resulted in the sinking of a handful of small merchant ships. But before long, the Germans and the Allies were engaged in more meaningful combat.

It began on April 9, with simultaneous German assaults on several coastal cities, from Narvik in the north to Oslo in the south, and within a matter of hours, the Germans had captured more important centres. Within two months, the Germans had occupied the entire country, securing their access to Swedish iron ore and other important raw materials. The Allies enjoyed limited success in the campaign, most notably the sinking of the cruiser *Blücher* in Oslofjord. And five small British destroyers under Captain B. A. W. Warburton-Lee attacked ten larger German destroyers at Narvik, sinking two, damaging three others, and sinking five German freighters.* But such successes were few and far between. The Allies' military performance had been desultory. In the last days of the unhappy campaign, the aircraft carrier *Glorious*, sister ship of *Courageous*, assisted in the evacuation from the Narvik area. When attacked by the German battle cruisers *Scharnhorst* and *Gneisenau*, the carrier's captain kept his aircraft secure in their hangars instead of launching them against the enemy, an extraordinary failure that can have few parallels in naval history. One has to wonder what Nelson would have had to say about it. The only morsel of an excuse was that the carrier's captain was an ex-submariner and had little knowledge of naval aviation. It would not be the last time that such ill-chosen officers found themselves commanding British carriers.

---

*   Warburton-Lee won a posthumous VC.

The Norwegian debacle was over in less than two months. It had won Hitler iron ore and other important raw materials, and, of critical importance to the Battle of the Atlantic, a number of strategically located bases for U-boats. The campaign cost the Germans about 5,500 men and more than two hundred aircraft, and several of their most modern warships. The British lost some 4,500 men, including 1,500 on the carrier *Glorious* and two destroyer escorts. One of the few bright spots in the story was that the huge Norwegian merchant fleet sailed to England to avoid impressment into German service, thus helping to compensate to some extent for the massive losses suffered by the merchant marine since the outbreak of war.

~

The BdU (Befehlshaber der Unterseeboote), the high command of the U-boat force, made an alarming discovery during the Norwegian campaign. Most of its torpedoes were faulty. Dönitz's leading "ace," Günther Prien, patrolling in the vicinity of Bygden Fjord, came upon a magnificent target: half a dozen transport ships escorted by two cruisers. Hundreds of troops were transferring to fishing boats. Prien and his first watch officer, Engelbert Endrass (soon to become an ace in his own right), planned the attack carefully. They would make their approach submerged, fire four bow torpedoes (three with impact pistols, one with a magnetic pistol, as Dönitz recommended) at four ships, reload the forward tubes, then surface to escape at top speed, firing the bow tubes again at the four other ships. It would be the greatest, most successful submarine attack in the history of warfare. But it didn't happen. None of U47's torpedoes worked. One swerved hopelessly off course immediately after launching, slamming into a cliff far from its intended target. The rest simply vanished. In his fury and frustration, Prien ran on to an uncharted sandbar. It took hours to get the sub free, after which the starboard diesel failed under the strain. Prien aborted the patrol and returned to base, complaining bitterly to Dönitz as soon as he was on shore.

Only after many months of investigation was the problem solved. It lay with the detonators. U-boats carried two types: magnetic and contact. The former was intended for use against heavily armoured targets, such as battleships, using the victim's own magnetic field to set off the warhead. In Norwegian waters, the highly sensitive detonators were thought to have been affected by the proximity of the North Pole and iron-ore lodes beneath the seabed. The contact detonator was essentially a percussion cap. It was intended for "soft-skinned" targets, including merchant ships. Its design was flawed. The twin-bladed screw on the nose would work only if it struck the target at precisely ninety degrees. The Germans solved the problem by capturing a British torpedo and copying its detonator mechanism. But the investigations revealed other difficulties. Wartime service meant that torpedoes were forever on the move, subject to great changes in temperature and pressure, which had unexpected effects on the missiles' delicate systems. In addition, the chamber for the hydrostatic valve, which controlled the torpedo's horizontal steering fins, was not airtight. Frequent changes in air pressure brought about by repeated dives and other operational manoeuvres affected the missiles' accuracy. Many "point-blank" shots that went astray may have been the result of such difficulties.

Technical problems were to be expected, Dönitz declared, but not bureaucratic incompetence, and that was the principal culprit in this case. He was right. Complaints about torpedoes went back to prewar days. The files bulged with long-winded reports of technical problems, with equally verbose excuses – but no explanations. A full-scale enquiry led to six months' imprisonment for the senior officer of the torpedo experimental institute, Rear Admiral Oskar Wehr. Thereafter, torpedo quality began to improve, but it took time.

Despite the modest number of U-boats in service and their chronic technical problems, Dönitz's force had succeeded in sinking more than two hundred ships since the outbreak of war, amounting to over 800,000 tons. Dönitz had every reason to be proud. Its period of greatest triumph was about to begin.

2

THE HAPPY TIME

"Happy as kings"
– Robert Louis Stevenson

THE WEHRMACHT'S STUNNING defeat of France and the Low Countries had an enormously significant impact on the Battle of the Atlantic. It gave the Germans control of the European coastline from Norway to the Atlantic coast of France. Never in its long history had Britain faced such a critical situation. Historian John Keegan states: "At a stroke, the distance which U-boats were obliged to travel to their patrol stations was halved and the dangers of the passage eliminated. Instead of having to negotiate the minefields of the Dover Straits, use of which the Germans had abandoned after three U-boats had been sunk, or make the long traverse round the north of Scotland, U-boat captains could launch themselves from Lorient, later also from Saint Nazaire, Brest, La Pallice, and La Rochelle, direct into the convoy tracks."[1]

The Germans quickly discovered that in addition to the advantageous positions of the French bases, they had acquired repair facilities at Lorient superior even to those in Germany. Dönitz was pleased to note that such facilities soon had a decided impact on the operational performance of his U-boats: "Whereas during the period September 1939–July 1940, 2.35 operational boats were required to keep one boat permanently at sea, in the period July 1940–July 1941 the figure fell to 1.84, which represented an improvement of 22 per cent. A higher proportion of the total of U-boats available were now at sea than ever before. Nor was that all; of the increased number of days at sea thus obtained, fewer were now being expended in proceeding to and from the area of operations. Before July 1940, the U-boats had to make a voyage of 450 miles through the North Sea and round the north of Great Britain to reach the Atlantic. Now they were saving something like a week on each patrol and were thus able to stay considerably longer in the actual area of operations. This fact, in its turn, added to the total number of U-boats actively engaged against the enemy."[2]

The tempo of U-boat operations increased. Excellent work by B-Dienst, the German navy's decoding department, provided Dönitz with consistently accurate information on Allied convoy movements. Within a few weeks of the outbreak of war, the Germans were regularly reading British naval signals. In addition, Dönitz obtained valuable data on Allied convoy movements from an unlikely source: American insurance firms, which continued to share their risks with European insurers even after the outbreak of war. Cables went to and fro across the Atlantic detailing names of ships, cargoes, sailing dates, and other important data. A large underwriter in Zürich made a practice of sharing its shipping information with a firm in Munich – making a mockery of the thousands of posters all over Britain cautioning citizens not to reveal any secret information such as ships' sailing dates. One has to wonder how many seamen lost their lives because of this extra-ordinary state of affairs. Incredibly, the outflow wasn't stemmed until early 1943.

Between July and October, Dönitz's U-boats sank a total of 217 ships, well over a million tons. No wonder the Germans called it the Happy Time. Remarkably, during this period, there were rarely more than half a dozen U-boats in the Atlantic on any given day, although nervous sailors on freighters and tankers were convinced that the ocean seethed with hundreds of the vile, furtive things. You *might* see a luminescent streak in the dark water if you happened to be looking in that direction. But chances were, you wouldn't know anything until the torpedo hit. It might be a shattering, end-of-the-world bang or a mere thud. It all depended on where you found yourself at that moment. The ship would recoil like a frightened animal, the air instantly sour with the stink of explosive. Fire might sweep the deck. The hull might fracture. You saw shipmates trapped. You saw them burnt alive. Your world, so normal, so *dull*, was transformed in a minute or two, even less in the worst cases. Now life consisted solely of survival. If you were lucky, the lifeboats were undamaged. You could get away without even getting your feet wet. Most didn't. Most found themselves struggling in the water, bone-numbingly cold no matter what the time of year. Some merchant seamen went through the frightful process several times during the war. Nearly thirty thousand of them lost their lives.

For the Allies, the only positive event to be recorded at that dark time was the occupation of Iceland. The country was then a neutral state under Denmark, which had fallen to Germany in the spring of 1940. It was said of Iceland that whoever controlled her controlled the North Atlantic. Hardly surprisingly, both the British and Germans looked to the country as a key element in the Battle of the Atlantic. For once, the British beat the Germans to the punch, in one of the most important yet poorly publicized actions of the war. When the British landed in the spring of 1940, they declared that the action was intended to pre-empt the Germans and that there would be no interference with Iceland's internal affairs. They kept their promise, though British and Canadian forces, and the Americans who followed, received a generally cool reception from the locals.*

~

Churchill made a practice of keeping President Roosevelt informed of every development in the war. He did all he could to foster the idea that Britain and the still-neutral United States were inextricably linked in the war against fascism. He revelled in the idea of the two countries being "mixed up together in some of their affairs for mutual and general advantage" – although it would have been hard to find comparable enthusiasm on the other side of the Atlantic. Churchill became positively prolix on the subject: "No one can stop it. Like the Mississippi, it just keeps rolling along. Let it roll. Let it roll on full flood, inexorable, irresistible, benignant, to broader lands and better days."[3]

When British Foreign Office officials were told that the Germans were using French Atlantic ports as U-boat bases, they dismissed the notion as absurd; the French would not permit it, they claimed. (The Foreign Office personnel who made such statements seemed to be of the same breed as the experts who kept insisting that the German economy would soon collapse under the intolerable burden of war.)

Most of the world, including a majority of Americans, believed that a German victory over Britain was just a matter of time. Although he was all too aware of Britain's appalling situation, both military and economic, Churchill, by now prime minister, kept making defiant speeches; in July he declared in a BBC broadcast: "We await undismayed the impending assault. Perhaps it will come

---

* In 1944, Iceland became an independent republic. Churchill instructed British staff officers to refer to the country in their reports as "Iceland(c)," the reason being that early in the war, a ship had been sent to Ireland instead of Iceland because of someone's poor handwriting.

tonight. Perhaps it will come next week. Perhaps it will never come. We must show ourselves equally capable of meeting a sudden, violent or, which is perhaps a harder test, a prolonged vigil. But be the ordeal sharp or long, or both, we shall seek no terms, we shall tolerate no parley; we may show mercy; we shall ask for none."

Shipping losses had averaged some eighty thousand tons per month for the first few months of the war; a serious matter, but by no means catastrophic. Now, the slaughter of merchant ships – and their crews – was on the rise. From the beginning of June to the end of December 1940, Dönitz's U-boats accounted for a dreadful average of 240,000 tons of merchant shipping a month, 343 ships in all, most of them sunk by U-boats.

Although convoys were effective against U-boats, the RN found itself critically short of escort vessels, since so many destroyers and frigates had been lost in Norway and at Dunkirk. Fortunately, before the war, orders had been placed for a whaling ship design that, it was thought, might be useful for coastal convoy duties. The ship was known as the corvette. The RN ordered its first corvettes a few weeks before war broke out, awarding the work to the Yorkshire firm of Smith's Dock Company. In September, the Canadian government undertook to build twenty-eight corvettes in a dozen Canadian yards. Despite being dubbed the "cheap and nasties" by Churchill, the corvettes, cheeky little vessels that looked like overgrown tugboats, proved to be invaluable in the convoy war. Although originally earmarked for coastal escort work only, they soon found themselves slogging across the Atlantic, helping to protect convoys all the way. With their rounded bottoms, they bobbed like inebriated corks when the weather turned rough. In full-scale Atlantic storms, they became things possessed, rolling with a devilish vigour, apparently enjoying themselves. Frank Curry was a seaman on *Kamsack*, and recalls the corvette's behaviour in rough weather: "The sea roared over the length of the ship, filling the port and starboard passageways waist-deep, sending sheets of glistening spray over the bridge. Seawater shot into mess decks and into the galley. One moment we were buried and water-logged; then the trawler design came through and our bows rose to the skies."[4] Crewmen spent days prostrate in their hammocks, *hors de combat*. Keeping a bucket by your side usually made matters worse, for in the vicious conditions of the Atlantic, it could be counted on to distribute its contents in every direction.

Few members of corvette crews were prepared for the grim realities of convoy escort work in the North Atlantic. Their vessels were too short to straddle the waves, resulting in violent up and down movements, not unlike those of an aircraft in heavy turbulence — except that the vertical motions, unpleasant enough on their own, were augmented by sudden rolls and yaws. Atlantic storms had a particularly nasty quality, and sailors had to find their sea legs in a hurry. Some never could. One Canadian corvette ran into a storm that blew incessantly and with enormous strength for four days; one of the crew became irrational because of the strain and was put in the wheelhouse, where the motion was slightly less violent. On his return to shore, the man was hospitalized and never sailed again.

Crew comfort was of no more concern in corvettes than in U-boats. Cooking was often impossible in heavy weather, for seawater kept slopping down ventilator shafts, making unpleasant living conditions unspeakable. Water dominated a corvette sailor's life. His clothes were always soaked, so was his food. In the early days, such conditions were particularly unpleasant because of the shortage of so many essentials of shipboard life: weatherproof outfits, duffle coats, and the like. By any definition, the corvettes were an acutely uncomfortable mode of transportation, yet most seamen acquired a perverse affection for them. The noise was deafening; the very structure of the ship cried out in pain at the frightful treatment she had to endure, day after hideous day, as she plodded her weary way across the world's most violent ocean. Designed to accommodate twenty-nine in none-too-salubrious surroundings, the corvettes soon had crews of about fifty, then close to a hundred, as more and more specialists were required to fight the increasingly technological battle.

The 205-foot-long corvette had a four-cylinder, triple-expansion engine producing 2,750 horsepower. Early corvettes had large boilers of the simplest type. The big boilers provided a good deal of steam in reserve for quick acceleration: perfect for chasing whales or U-boats. Corvettes were agile ships; their basic armament was a four-inch gun on the foredeck, plus one or more machine guns and some sixty depth charges. The first corvettes to enter service lacked many items of equipment, including the standard four-inch guns mounted on the foredeck. In an effort to conceal this fact from any predatory U-boats or other enemy vessels, fake guns were often mounted. The fakes soon looked bedraggled after a spell of Atlantic weather; in a number of cases, their wooden barrels drooped, inevitably generating rude signals from accompanying ships.

The corvettes were tucked around convoys, shepherding the merchant ships like fussy, irritable corgis around a herd of sheep. Most corvette crews consisted of one or two professional sailors, or "regulars," the rest being hastily – often inadequately – trained volunteers. Shakedown cruises could reveal startling shortcomings in both vessels and men. One corvette hit the open sea off Vancouver Island, British Columbia, whereupon the heavy stove in the galley began to stir like some primeval monster awakening from a long sleep. One of the ship's cooks, Charlie Appleby of San Diego, recalls, "The stove started moving back and forth. My assistant, Jock Glasgow, and I leapt up and held the crossbars on the skylight, feet on the sink. Pots, pans, dishes, everything came loose and rolled back and forth, smoke belching. There were no crossbars on the shelves to hold anything in place."[5] During construction, the stove had simply been placed in position, and there it sat, waiting for someone to weld it to the deck. That someone never arrived – just another glitch on an overheated wartime production line.

The ships were full of devices, electrical and mechanical (and soon, electronic), all of which had their idiosyncrasies. *Cobourg*, an RCN corvette, went to war with a fatal flaw in her four-inch gun that no one discovered until it was too late. Her gunnery officer, Tom Blakely, recalls that the problem was a simple cotter pin in the steering mechanism in the tiller flats just above the rudder. At slow speeds, if quick turns were made by the helmsman, the cotter pin would become dislodged. The gun would no longer traverse; but a moment later, the impish pin would drop back into position and the gun would function perfectly, leaving no clue as to what had taken place. This little quirk sparked many a battle of words between members of the crew. Nor were the qualities of the gun ever likely to inspire much confidence. When the gun fired, you could spot the shell as it went on its way. On one occasion, Gordon Johnson, the six-foot-six skipper of *Cobourg*, exclaimed, "I saw the damned thing!" The first lieutenant, Kenneth Christmas, went one better: "Hell, I could read its licence plate!"

~

RAF Coastal Command's job was to guard Britain's trade lifelines from above. Curiously, in spite of the obvious importance of the job, Coastal had to make do with miserably inadequate equipment. On the outbreak of war, the command had twenty operational squadrons, eleven of which flew the mediocre Avro Anson – which soon made its most valuable contribution to the war effort in Canada, as a trainer with the British Commonwealth Air Training Plan. Initially, relations between Coastal Command and the RN were somewhat strained, but sailors and airmen alike soon came to realize how much they depended upon one other. Thereafter, Coastal Command and the RN enjoyed a mutually advantageous relationship, one that came to be envied by the services of other nations.

As far back as December 1911, the potential for aircraft to spot submarines was recognized by the Committee of Imperial Defence. Meetings were held to delineate the duties of the various services in the event of a European war. The idea of floating aerodromes was singularly appealing. A British naval officer, Commander C. R. Samson, demonstrated the feasibility of the idea by flying a Short pusher biplane off a modified deck on HMS *Africa*. The aircraft was equipped with floats as well as wheels. Although the Short landed in the water of Sheerness harbour without damage, it was unable to take off again, because the designers had not realized the necessity of "stepping" the floats to break the suction created during the takeoff run. In 1912, the same Commander Samson made history by dropping the first bombs from a seaplane.

In the First World War, Britain's Royal Flying Corps (RFC) and the Royal Naval Air Service (RNAS) operated almost totally independently of one another. The RFC procured most of its aircraft from the Royal Aircraft Factory, the RNAS purchased its equipment from a handful of aircraft manufacturers in Britain and elsewhere. There appears to have been remarkably little operational coordination between the two forces, and in fact naval aviators began bombing German targets before the RFC.

Between the wars, Coastal Command flew a not-very-impressive collection of aircraft, the majority being large biplane or triplane flying boats. In fact, considering the paucity of funds available for new aircraft development, it is amazing how many flying boats came into being and flew at least in prototype stage during those lean years: the Nile, the Iris, the Felixstowe Fury (a behemoth of a triplane), the Kittiwake, the Puffin, the Pintail, the Titania, the Cromarty, the Pellet, the Vulture, the Seagull, the Swan, the Ayr, to name just a few, all of them massive aircraft with gigantic fabric-covered wings braced by wires as taut as bow strings. The first aircraft incorporating such modern features as an enclosed cabin for the crew and a retractable undercarriage was the Anson, designated as a general reconnaissance type. Developed from a civil design, the Avro 652, the Anson was powered by two Cheetah engines of about three hundred horsepower. In its original service form it carried a crew of three with a grossly inadequate bomb load of two 100-pound and four 20-pound bombs. Underpowered, with a poor range, the Anson won little glory as an operational aircraft. A far more successful development of a civil aircraft was the Hudson, which evolved from the American Lockheed 14 airliner. Although its appearance in Coastal Command angered the British aircraft industry, the Hudson met an urgent need at a critical time. It was a modern, high-performance aircraft, by no means perfect for the role it was given, but vastly superior to the outdated flying boats and open-cockpit biplanes that then equipped most Coastal Command units. Pilots accustomed to the gentlemanly flying characteristics of these elderly warbirds were initially alarmed by the Hudson with its high-wing loading and powerful flaps. The Hudson was considered quite a handful. The first production aircraft reached British shores in 1939 equipped with such unfamiliar luxuries as the Sperry Gyropilot, de-icers, and a fuel-jettisoning system. Despite their initial caution, Coastal Command crews soon came to respect the converted airliner; in fact, it was a Hudson of 224 Squadron that shot down the first German aircraft to fall to the RAF in the war.

Much was expected of the British-made Bristol Beaufort, the first examples of which went to 22 Squadron at Thorney Island, near Portsmouth, in 1939. The Beaufort proved, however, to be a demanding aircraft to fly and its Taurus engines were notoriously unreliable, seldom delivering their promised power. Most of the new aircraft were soon wrecked in accidents, many of them the result of engine failures. The Beaufort went on to operate in the Middle East and Far East and became a successful operational type powered by Pratt and Whitney Twin Wasp engines. High hopes were also held out for a new product from Blackburn, the Botha. A handsome, high-wing torpedo bomber, it emerged from the factory in the spring of 1939, immediately acquiring a dubious reputation. It was soon relegated to training duties. Another disappointing dud.

The Botha had an unfortunate habit of shedding ailerons in flight. Test pilot H. A. Taylor described it as "operationally useless."[6]

The one Coastal Command aircraft capable of undertaking moderately long-range maritime patrols was the hefty Short Sunderland four-engined flying boat. A development of the prewar Empire flying boat flown by Imperial Airways, the Sunderland equipped only three Coastal Command squadrons on the outbreak of war, and production had already ceased. In their wisdom, the Air Staff had discontinued the Sunderland in favour of the Stirling heavy bomber, a product of the same company. At the time, the Stirling was seen as a key instrument to realize what many considered the air force's *real* function: blowing Germany's strategic targets to bits. To replace the Sunderland, the Air Staff selected a twin-engined flying boat, the Saunders Roe (Saro) Lerwick. It was hopeless, as viciously unstable in the air as it was on the water. Most of the Lerwicks were wrecked in accidents; the rest were scrapped, to the intense relief of their crews. Most Lerwick units found themselves flying Stranraers, Londons, or Singapores, venerable biplane flying boats with admirable handling qualities ("like overgrown Tiger Moths," according to some who remember them) but hardly suited to the conditions prevalent in the Battle of the Atlantic's first months.

Coastal Command went to war possessing no effective anti-submarine weapons. Its bombs were, in the main, general-purpose type 250- and 500-pounders, with a dismal reputation for reliability. New weapons were urgently needed. Early in 1940, Coastal Command undertook a series of tests using the Navy's Mark VII depth charge, essentially an oil can bulging with Torpex and equipped with a hydrostatic pistol that could be set to detonate at various depths. Aircrews found that the "D/Cs" worked satisfactorily if dropped at low altitude and at just the right speed; too high or too fast meant that the missile would explode when it hit the sea.

It was no easy job attacking a U-boat from the air. U-boat crews maintained a diligent watch when surfaced, and so in most cases the sub had time to dive before an approaching aircraft was over-head. Only a swirl would be left when the aircraft arrived on the scene. Other than killing vast numbers of unfortunate fish, Coastal Command's depth charges seldom accomplished much.

In the war's early days, twenty-five feet was considered an effective setting for D/Cs. Later, with the benefit of countless hours of operational experience, charges were set to detonate at much greater depths, with the British Mark VII Heavy having the great-est depth-setting of all: 259 metres (850 feet).

It had long seemed obvious to countless sailors and airmen that if every ship had its own aircraft constantly circling overhead, the U-boats would be virtually eliminated, at least during daylight hours. The trouble was, there simply weren't sufficient numbers of aircraft available. The supply of VLR (very long range) aircraft would be one of the most contentious issues of the war.

In the early days, convoys headed out into the dangerous Atlantic shipping lanes from two principal starting points: the Thames Estuary and Liverpool. The naval escort would shepherd the mer-chantmen only part of the way across the Atlantic. Thereafter the escorting vessels met incoming convoys, escorting them into British waters. The first eastbound convoy of the war left Halifax, Nova Scotia, in mid September 1939. It arrived safely. From then until the end of 1939, 5,756 ships sailed across the Atlantic in convoy. Only four were sunk. The U-boats kept away, preferring individual victims, of which there was seldom a shortage. Indepen-dently routed ships were much easier to attack and sink, and some U-boat skippers were already running up impressive scores, despite the persistent problems with torpedoes. At this time, Britain's annual shipbuilding capacity represented only about one-third the average monthly loss rate; in other words, Britain was losing ships far more rapidly than she was building new ones.

The successful U-boat commanders were national heroes in Germany. Names like Günther Prien, Otto Kretschmer, and

Joachim Schepke resounded the length and breadth of the land, the men's features as well known as those of movie stars. Dönitz personally made sure that successful crews returning from patrol found their docks crowded with military bands and plenty of attractive nurses and servicewomen. The returning heroes came home to the best that wartime Germany could provide. Dönitz provided official rest and recuperation centres, with a tempting array of sports and entertainment facilities, but the majority of U-boat men seemed to prefer finding their own fun – and there was plenty available. If you wore a U-boat uniform and had just returned from patrol, you had little trouble finding female companionship. Everyone knew your pockets were stuffed with back pay and you had spent weeks or even months at sea, jammed into a U-boat with at least fifty other men as grubby and smelly as you. Plainly, female companionship was high on most men's agenda. Some preferred professionals and in the French Atlantic ports in particular, the names of notably desirable or innovative *filles de joie* quickly circulated among the U-boat crews, although later in the war, the submariners were warned not to talk freely with prostitutes, because so many of them were said to be in the Resistance.

Hardly surprisingly, Dönitz's men later looked back at that period of 1940 as the best they ever knew. The war was going splendidly; U-boat crewmen were the nation's heroes, lionized by relatives and friends, and often by total strangers. Life on the home front had hardly changed since the days of peace. The shops bulged with goods; food was plentiful and of the best quality. Life was good.

The U-boat crews thought highly of Dönitz. He was a former submariner, respected for his innovative thinking, and he never relaxed his efforts to do everything in his power for his men. There was nothing flamboyant about Dönitz's leadership, but it set precisely the right tone for the men of the Ubootwaffe. They trusted Dönitz implicitly. And they admired him. After all, he had been an "ace" in the Great War and was an internationally renowned expert on underwater operations.

Dönitz did an excellent job of achieving and maintaining superb morale among his crews even into the later years of the war, when the casualty lists made devastating reading and a U-boat crewman had less than a one-in-three chance of surviving his next patrol. Like most servicemen in highly dangerous occupations, a U-boat man tended to fall back on the totally unfounded belief that *it* would always happen to the other guy, that the luck that had brought him this far would continue to hold. There can be little doubt that the force's high morale was also influenced by belief that they belonged to an elite unit – in fact, *the* elite unit.

~

For the RN, the few months following the fall of France in mid-1940 were exceptionally difficult. Called upon to provide vessels and crews for the evacuation of Allied forces from Norway and France, the RN also had to prepare for operations against the French navy in North Africa (controlled by the pro-Nazi Vichy regime), the Italians in the Mediterranean, as well as the probable attempted invasion of the British Isles in the not-too-distant future. Recent operations had cost the RN fifteen destroyers sunk and more than twenty seriously damaged. Many convoys had to sail with a single corvette or destroyer as escort. In August 1940, with the RAF and the Luftwaffe embroiled in the Battle of Britain, Dönitz decided to shake the British with a forceful attack on her ocean lifelines. It was the beginning of the "wolfpack" operations.

Initially, things did not go smoothly. Thirteen boats left their bases. U25, commanded by Heinz Beduhn, struck a mine and went down with all hands. Then the RAF spotted U37 and U51 and bombed them, inflicting serious damage; in fact, the 210 Squadron Sunderland crew attacking U51 believed they had sunk the U-boat. They had seen it turn turtle and disappear, leaving quantities of oil on the surface. But the boat had survived – only to be sunk by a British submarine, HMS *Cachalot*, four days later. Another of

Dönitz's force, U65, had two secret agents on board. The plan was to land the two men in Ireland, one of whom was Sean Russell, a veteran of the IRA, the man responsible for most of the prewar bombings in England. But some hundred miles west of Galway, Russell collapsed, suffering agonies from a perforated ulcer. He died soon afterward and was buried at sea, his body wrapped in a Nazi flag.

A depleted force of nine U-boats now made its way to the Western Approaches, England's southwestern waters, and the Irish Sea. Dönitz was gravely concerned; his entire force seemed to be in jeopardy with few successes against the enemy. But the picture soon changed. Heinrich Liebe, commanding U38, and Hans Roesing, commanding U48, both sank two ships for a total of some twenty thousand tons; Joachim Schepke in U100 and Fritz Frauenheim in U101 sank British freighters for a total of about fifteen thousand tons. In all, though, the results were disappointing: eight ships sunk and two damaged.

Then the Germans came upon an unexpected hitch: the British changed all their encoding systems. It was a shock to the U-boat command, but in fact their list of victories grew longer, as if the crews were making special efforts to compensate for the decryption problems. Viktor Oehrn, commanding U37, sank a remarkable total of seven ships in four days for 24,400 tons. Joachim Schepke in U100 increased his score by five ships, totalling 21,000 tons. U46, under the command of Engelbert Endrass, sank four ships with a combined tonnage of close to 30,000 tons. Ten more Allied or neutral ships went to the bottom – victims of U48, U32, U101, and U28 – during the latter days of August.

The renowned Günther Prien was a late arrival on the scene, having left Kiel on August 27. The previous month, his Olympian reputation had suffered when he attacked an armed liner, the 15,500-ton *Arandora Star*. Prien had been heading back to his base with just one torpedo left, which he believed to be faulty, an every-day problem at that time. Prien had already attempted to fire it at a target in the Western Approaches. It had failed. Now the damned thing was still snug in its tube, a potential danger to every man on board. God only knew what might happen if he tried to fire the thing again. Possibly nothing. But just as possibly, it could blow up in its tube and send U47 and her crew to the bottom. Prien would have been fully justified in heading straight home, but that wasn't his style. There was a perfect target dead ahead! He could no more ignore it than fly.

His target was zigzagging toward him. Prien held his breath and, at a range of one mile, fired the suspect torpedo.

It worked! A hiss and a clatter marked its departure through a forward tube. The boat shifted, its balance jogged by the torpedo's exit.

The eel functioned perfectly, carving a steady path through the choppy water. A cheer went up in the stale air in the U-boat. A wonderful shot! It hit the liner fair and square. The ship seemed to come to a shuddering halt in the ocean, smoke and flame bursting from her flank. She staggered as an explosion ripped through her. Massive pieces of steel plate went spinning into the sea, a mast collapsed. No doubt about it, the ship was settling; soon she would go down. Prien decided it would be unwise to wait and watch her final plunge; it was daylight, and in a minute or two the sea would be boiling with escort vessels bent on revenge. Having used up all his torpedoes, he slipped away, heading for base. He was in good spirits; the patrol had been the most successful of his career, in fact the most successful of the war to that time, with ten ships to his credit for a remarkable total of 68,587 tons (although this would later be amended to eight ships for 51,483 tons). On his return to Wilhelmshaven, Prien was welcomed by a smiling Dönitz, and soon the entire propaganda machine sang his praise. Here was the ideal Nazi warrior, a hero beyond compare, handsome enough to be an actor, the darling of the German nation. What neither he nor Dönitz nor indeed the German nation knew was that the ship Prien had sunk, *Arandora Star,* had been transporting 1,299

Germans and Italians to prisoner-of-war camps in Canada. Some two hundred British troops guarded them, and the ship's crew numbered 174. A Sunderland flying boat dropped emergency supplies to the boats and rafts striking out from the sinking liner. The Canadian destroyer *St. Laurent* answered the ship's SOS, arriving on the scene in the early afternoon and rescuing more than half of those who had been on board. In all, 826 drowned, 713 of them Germans and Italians. The German public was never told of this unhappy blot on Prien's record.

Now, in early September, BdU instructed Prien to intercept a slow inbound convoy. Two other U-boats would join him: U65 and U101. By September 4, they had formed a north–south scouting line across the convoy's expected track. The weather deteriorated abruptly. Gale-force winds lashed the sea into a frenzy. The U-boats bounced and lurched, great green rollers looming, smashing down on them, straining every component, every rivet, every weld, every square inch of the sub's steel body. Crewmen quickly learned to adapt to their boat's violent movements, walking with a kind of rolling gait in time with the seethings of the storm. It was soon instinctive; and back on shore, returning U-boat men would find it difficult to walk on solid, unmoving earth. It became the practice to look for the arm of a helpful nurse for assistance.

On September 5, U65 made contact with the convoy, but visibility was so poor it could not attack. The same day, the violent weather swept a crewman from U47; he was never seen again. Fritz Frauenheim, skipper of U101, reported engine trouble. He aborted, heading for Lorient. Now only two U-boats remained to take on the convoy.

The weather improved a little, although the seas were still heavy. During the night of September 6, Prien surfaced and sank three ships: two British freighters, *Jose de Larrinaga* and *Neptunian*, plus a Norwegian freighter, *Gro*, for a combined total of over 14,000 tons. He kept tracking the convoy as it neared the British Isles and, on the morning of September 9, he sank the 3,800-ton Greek freighter *Poseidon*. It had been another brilliant performance by Dönitz's favourite ace.

In all, the August/September sorties by Dönitz's U-boats had resulted in the sinking of forty-four ships, representing an impressive 230,000 tons. As was frequently the case, the aces accounted for the bulk of the sinkings; this time Oehrn, Prien, Schepke, Endrass, and Roesing had sunk a total of twenty-nine ships. The victories had come at the cost of two U-boats, U25 and U51. On August 31, U60, commanded by a future ace, Adalbert Schnee, torpedoed a Dutch liner, *Volendam*, carrying more than three hundred children to Canada. Fortunately, the damaged liner could be towed to port and none of the children was hurt.

3

HOSTILE WINGS

"You cannot fly like an eagle with the wings of a wren"
– William Henry Hudson

IN MANY WAYS, the Luftwaffe was just as unprepared for the Battle of the Atlantic as was the RAF. The Germans had for some time recognized the need for long-range aircraft for maritime duties, and in June 1937, the Heinkel company began work on a revolutionary design that promised to answer all the Luftwaffe's maritime patrol needs. Named the He 177 Greif (Griffon), the new aircraft embodied innumerable new ideas. Few worked. Appearing at first glance to be a twin-engined aircraft, the 177 was in fact powered by four engines, two pairs of coupled Daimler-Benz DB 601s occupying a pair of nacelles to minimize drag and increase performance. Mounted side by side and inclined, the coupled engines occupied almost every cubic inch of available space; the inner banks of cylinders were positioned almost vertically, resulting in persistent and dangerous problems with oil leaks and overheating. Another headache was the cooling system. Heinkel wanted to use surface evaporation to supplement conventional radiators, but it proved unsatisfactory. The result: larger radiators had to be installed, adding substantially to airframe drag and, inevitably, reducing speed and range. Heinkel's promised performance – a range of 4,160 miles, with a maximum speed 335 mph and a bomb load of at least 2,000 pounds – began to dwindle day by day. The planned use of remotely controlled "barbettes" had also to be abandoned. Conceptual thinking had overtaken current technology. Wearily, Heinkel accepted the inevitable: conventional manned turrets would have to be installed on the 177, at an appalling penalty in weight and drag. That wasn't all. The Luftwaffe high command now decided that the new bomber had to be capable of diving attacks at as much as sixty degrees, rather than the medium-angle dives specified originally. More beefing-up of the structure, more performance penalties.

The prototype 177s flew, but inspired little confidence among their crews when engines burst into flames, control surfaces developed lethal flutter, and a host of problems afflicted even such conventional features as propeller pitch controls. When war broke out, it was clear that the 177 would be unavailable for many months, if not years. A replacement aircraft had to found without delay. The only remotely suitable type was a former airliner, the Focke-Wulf 200 Condor. First flown in 1937, the Condor was a four-engined aircraft with a span of 107 feet. The type made a name for itself in the immediate prewar period with several well-publicized long-distance flights: among them, Berlin to Cairo, Berlin to New York, and Berlin to Tokyo. Although never designed for military use, the Condor became the interim replacement for the 177. It was quite unsuitable, its structure being too flimsy for military duties. Their maintenance was a headache; it was rare to have more than one in four available for operations at any given time. In addition, the fuel lines ran along the underside of the wings and fuselage, dangerously vulnerable to anti-aircraft fire, particularly in low-level operations.*

---

* A similar problem beset the RAF's Hudson, another converted airliner.

The first batch of six, modified for maritime use, were delivered to the Luftwaffe in the spring of 1940 and met with some success in anti-shipping operations around the British Isles. In June, the improved 200C models arrived at Bordeaux–Merignac. They incorporated minor improvements in the strength of the fuselage, and hand-operated 7.9 mm machine guns had been added on the fuselage amidships and in a small gondola in the ventral position. Now the aircraft's excellent range proved its value. Cooperating closely with the naval command at Lorient, the Condors initiated long-range patrols out across the Bay of Biscay, sweeping over the west coast of Ireland. They had more than a little success attacking targets of opportunity, but their greatest value lay in their ability to find convoys. On spotting a convoy, they immediately transmitted the information to Dönitz's command headquarters. The aircraft usually landed in Norway and refuelled before setting out on another offensive patrol in the opposite direction. These fragile converted airliners (several of which broke their backs in heavy landings) proved to be highly successful. In the six months following the fall of France, they sank some 363,000 tons of Allied shipping. Churchill himself dubbed the Condors "the scourge of the Atlantic," more a tribute to their crews than praise for the airplane itself.

The first Condors engaged in maritime bombing work had no bombsights, so their crews had to take the vulnerable aircraft into low-level attacks, usually at about 150 feet. The Condors, carrying four 500-pound bombs on external wing racks, usually attacked from the beam, so that the victim presented as large a target as possible.

The aircraft's normal operating range was about 1,000 miles; with auxiliary fuel tanks, it could fly round trips approaching 1,400 miles. Fourteen- to sixteen-hour patrols were commonplace. Dönitz thought highly of the converted airliner. He told a staff meeting, "Just let me have a minimum of twenty Fw 200s solely for reconnaissance purposes, and the U-boat success will shoot up!"

But chronic inter-service squabbles plagued the Third Reich throughout its history. All aircraft – in fact, anything that flew – came under the control of the Luftwaffe, and so Göring claimed the Condors as his. The Kriegsmarine disagreed, since the big aircraft would be working on naval missions. The argument went to Hitler. He decided in favour of the navy, something of a blow to Göring. In fact, however, the decision did little to solve the problem, for the Condor unit was not nearly as powerful as Dönitz had thought. Although its complement was nominally some twenty-five aircraft, it was a rare day when more than half a dozen were serviceable. On one occasion, a Condor crew spotted a convoy west of Ireland. They reported the fact to Dönitz's HQ, then attacked, succeeding in sinking two ships. Following this success, the aircraft circled the convoy, awaiting the reinforcements that HQ had promised. None arrived. Every aircraft at Bordeaux–Merignac was grounded with technical problems. Eventually, the Condor's fuel ran low. It had to return to base. The convoy got away.

Dönitz was keenly aware of the value of air power: "Imagine our situation as a land problem, with the enemy convoy at Hamburg, and my nearest U-boats at Oslo, Paris, Vienna and Prague, each with a maximum circle of vision of twenty miles. How on earth can they expect to find the convoy unless directed by air reconnaissance?"[1]

The Condor crews were among the best and most experienced in the Luftwaffe, many being ex-airline pilots. The astonishing thing is the impact they had on the shipping war, considering their modest numbers. The Germans estimated that for every one of them lost in action, the Allies lost thirty thousand tons of shipping.

The Condors' greatest success came in the early fall of 1940, when Oberleutnant Bernard Jope, on his first operational sortie, encountered the magnificent 42,000-ton Canadian Pacific liner *Empress of Britain*, some sixty miles off the northwest coast of Ireland. There was no mistaking her, in peacetime one of the most luxurious ships in service, a favourite of the wealthy and influential.

It was about 0900 on October 26 when Jope's crew spotted the liner, her familiar white colour scheme now replaced by drab wartime grey to suit her role as a troopship.

Jope attacked at once, bringing his Condor around to approach from the stern. He dropped bombs from about two hundred feet – with devastating accuracy. Two bombs smashed through the deck immediately aft of the central funnel, exploding in the Mayfair Lounge, the largest public room on the ship. The eighty-three-by-seventy-foot area erupted in smoke and flames. Despite the energetic efforts of firefighting parties, the fire spread with bewildering speed until the entire midships area was ablaze. Another superbly accurate bombing run by Jope destroyed the stern anti-aircraft gun and set ammunition on fire.

Jope came in for a final pass as his machine gunners sprayed the decks. Then he made off, having sustained damage to the vulnerable under-wing oil lines. Jope succeeded in bringing the Condor safely back to base.

Aboard the liner, fire had taken hold with bewildering rapidity. When the Polish destroyer *Burza* arrived on the scene, one crewman noted that

huge flames began to shoot up from the *Britain*. . . . Bodies [were] in the water, scattered over a wide area, some hanging on to debris, to the sides of an overturned lifeboat. . . . Some of the people clambered up rope ladders but those who could not were hauled over the *Burza*'s side by ropes tied around their bodies. Sailors on deck were waiting to assist the survivors. We had alcohol with which to rub down those who were frozen, and rum to give them to drink. Temptation proved too strong for some sailors, who began to sample the rum, but this did not stop the rubbing process. In fact it gave the process more vigour! We picked up 250 people, and as we were fully loaded, we left for a Scottish port. I remember one man, an Australian. I gave him my extra suit of overalls. Several months later, I received a parcel. Astonished, I opened it and found my suit of overalls, cleaned, pressed, and returned to me by the Australian crewman. Later, when I got around to wearing the suit, I discovered that each of the six pockets had a one-pound note in it![2]

The next day, a Sunday, a boarding party managed to attach hawsers to the still-smouldering hull of the *Empress*, and the oceangoing tugs *Marauder* and *Thames* took her in tow. The liner was an immense burden. The two tugs could barely make four knots, and now the *Empress* was listing to starboard. Nevertheless, the operation appeared to be proceeding well. Soon, it seemed, the liner could be towed back to England and repaired. But Dönitz was fully aware of the situation from radio reports; he ordered three patrolling U-boats, U28, U31, and U32, to intercept the big liner and sink her. What a prize for the successful U-boat! Forty-two thousand tons in a single attack! It was the stuff of a man's dreams! All three U-boat skippers ordered their vessels to proceed at top speed to the designated area. Ritterkreuz-holder Hans Jenisch got there first in the early hours of October 28. Steering a cautious path between the damaged liner and the zigzagging escorts, he had his target lined up. He fired a fan of three torpedoes, one of which exploded prematurely and nearly put paid to the U-boat and its crew. The shattering roar shook the very ocean, sending up an immense blossoming of foam. The U-boat trembled; lights dimmed; steel plates groaned. Tiny leaks sprang open in pipes and fittings. While engineering specialists rushed to repair the damage, crewmen waited for the next explosion, their anxious eyes fixed on the hull, imaginations painting scenes of the steel bending, collapsing, the sub imploding like an old tin can from the awesome pressure of the ocean. They heard a distant bang. They waited. Silence. Could it be . . . ? Yes! Cheers echoed in the metal hull. They had hit the *Empress*!

Jenisch's torpedo struck the ship in line with the third funnel, sending up the familiar tower of water and debris. The strike sent the escorting destroyers into a frenzy of activity. Scurrying about, they fired star shells to light up the area, bent on destroying the U-boat that had done this awful deed. As if in response, another torpedo hit the liner. She staggered, mortally wounded. Water pounded into her, thousands of gallons pouring through the corridors and cabins, the Lounge Deck, the Manicure Room, the Cathay Lounge, the Knickerbocker Bar, the engine rooms, the radio rooms. Crewmen and passengers sloshed about in the corridors, desperate to reach the exits, calling for help, sobbing.

Jenisch dived to safety, out of reach of the destroyers. He headed back to his patrol area, more than satisfied with his night's work.

The drama soon reached its climax. Fire had taken an unbreakable hold on the liner. Thick billows of black smoke rose high over the stricken ship. The tugs could do no more. They released the hawsers. At once, the battered, burning liner listed heavily to port. Ten minutes later, she capsized. Just after two in the morning of Monday, October 28, *Empress of Britain* slipped beneath the surface of the North Atlantic. She was the largest merchant ship to be sunk in the Second World War.

Two days later, Jenisch attacked a solitary British freighter. He had time to fire only one torpedo (which turned out to be faulty) before two destroyers, HMS *Harvester* and HMS *Highlander*, sped to the scene. They quickly picked up a strong Asdic signal. A sub all right! No question about it! Depth charges peppered the ocean, sending up mountains of spray. They inflicted serious damage on the enemy, smashing electric motors, rupturing the stern ballast tank, and fracturing high-pressure air lines. Jenisch dared not dive; he was all too aware that he might not be able to surface again. He could do little but await his fate. The two British destroyers opened up at point-blank range with 4.7-inch guns and machine guns. Jenisch ordered his crew to abandon ship and scuttle. The destroyers rescued thirty-three of the U-boat's crew, including Jenisch; nine died.

The capture of Jenisch led to a brisk little battle between the British and German propaganda machines. Naval historian Clay Blair writes, "The British were glad to have captured Jenisch and most of his crew, the first U-boat POWs to be recovered after those of U26, four months earlier. British propagandists hastened to boast of capturing a U-boat ace, a Ritterkreuz holder, the man who had sunk *Empress of Britain*. In a vain attempt to undercut the British and reassure the German public, Berlin propagandists promptly and vehemently denied the claim. To buttress their denial, the Germans resorted to the bizarre step of broadcasting a fictional account of Jenisch's victorious homecoming, including a detailed first-hand report from Jenisch, describing the sinking of the *Empress*."[3]

U31, the second of the three U-boats to go in pursuit of the doomed liner, encountered the British destroyer *Antelope* on the morning of November 2. The U-boat captain, twenty-seven-year-old Wilfred Prellberg, wanted to attack the destroyer, but he found the sea too rough. Instead, *Antelope* attacked U31, launching six depth charges. They did no damage. Undeterred, the destroyer continued to attack, battling the angry seas as she tried again and again to destroy the U-boat with depth charges. The battle went on for hours, until one of *Antelope*'s depth charges ruptured U31's aft ballast tanks. The U-boat began to sink by the stern. Prellberg ordered every man into the bow compartment. It didn't help; U31 continued to descend. The chief engineer claimed that he could rectify the problem. Prellberg didn't agree, and ordered the boat to the surface for scuttling. What followed had elements of a Keystone Cops comedy. The crew abandoned U31 as the destroyer lowered a whaleboat, its crew intending to board the U-boat and capture any useful documents or equipment. But the now-empty U31 was making adequate speed on her electric motor. The whaleboat couldn't keep up with her. The distance between the two vessels increased, with the whaleboat's crew frantically trying to get another knot or two out of their sluggish craft. The unmanned submarine appeared to be sailing away over the horizon. Then, quite unexpectedly, she swung around, as if in anger. She rammed *Antelope*, puncturing two fuel tanks and a boiler. After this, apparently satisfied that she had done her duty, she went down like a stone. The destroyer picked up most of the U-boat's crew, including Prellberg himself. The British sailors were later intrigued to learn that this was the second time U31 had been sunk. The first time was near Borkum on March 11, 1940, when the sub was commanded by Johannes Habekost. A Blenheim of 82 Squadron sank her, the first U-boat sunk in the war. Remarkably, she was raised yet again after her run-in with *Antelope* and saw more action before being scuttled at the end of the war.

The tempo of operations in the Atlantic continued to increase as Dönitz brought in factory-fresh U-boats and newly trained crews.

Werner Heidel was on his first patrol as skipper of a brand-new Type VII U-boat, U55. He had received instructions to intercept a convoy in the Western Approaches. Heidel found the convoy, and lost no time in sinking a tanker and a Greek freighter, both of about five thousand tons. Pleased with his efforts, he headed away into thickening weather. He had no way of knowing that a British sloop, *Fowey*, was following him. Suddenly the seas erupted in a shattering series of detonations. *Fowey* had fixed U55 with Asdic and had launched depth charges. U55, now down to more than three hundred feet, suffered some damage; a dozen leaks admitted streams of water which the crew worked like beavers to stem.

Fowey wasn't the only ship in pursuit of U55. Two British destroyers, *Whitshed* and *Ardent*, had joined in the hunt, closely followed by a French destroyer, *Valmy*. A four-engined Sunderland flying boat of 228 Squadron also appeared on the scene. Heidel was in a quandary. Remain submerged and attempt to ride out the attacks? Or surface and hope to escape in the thickening weather? Heidel decided on the latter course, in spite of the worsening flooding and visible signs of panic among the inexperienced crew members. At this critical moment, the Sunderland dropped bombs and attacked the sub with machine-gun fire. While returning fire, the breechblock of Heidel's deck gun jammed. The youthful skipper couldn't return the enemy's fire, yet he couldn't dive to safety because of the damage to U55. He had no choice: he ordered the watch officer and the chief engineer to open the vents. The boat sank in a few moments. The British ships picked up most of the crew, but Heidel was not among them.

~

After several months of experience, it was estimated that a convoy needed an absolute minimum of three escorts – plus one more for every ten ships to be escorted. It became an established rule of thumb that doubling the escort quadrupled the U-boat losses for every ship sunk. The dilemma was how to protect convoys from one side of the Atlantic to the other. Air cover provided the best answer, as the lowliest deck hand could testify. But when would enough aircraft with the right qualities be available? No one knew. Moreover, the Canadians, although a central component in the chain of defenders, were dependent on Britain and later the United States for aircraft, always falling at the end of the line for the latest equipment. For many months, the RCAF continued to fly outdated Stranraers and mediocre Digbys, the latter based, not very successfully, on the Douglas DC3. The maritime units had to grapple with what most airmen consider the worst, most unpredictable flying weather in the world. You might take off in good conditions and complete your patrol, then returning to base, you might discover that the winds had changed direction and increased their velocity, vastly increasing your chances of running out of fuel before reaching home. Besides outdated equipment and vile weather, the Canadian airmen had to contend with the senior officers of the Canadian Eastern Air Command, who

were overly parochial in outlook and too often failed to get their priorities right, while Air Force Headquarters in

Ottawa permitted them too much leeway. Eastern Air Command was slow to adapt new refinements of (RAF) Coastal Command's battle-tested methods and, as a result, squandered scarce resources on much less effective methods. Poor tactics sometimes resulted in missed sightings, and certainly prevented the destruction of several U-boats, notably during the German offensive of 1942 in the Gulf of St. Lawrence. There was also a problem with inter-service rivalry. The RCAF was most reluctant to accept the fundamental principle of British anti-submarine practice – that maritime air forces should operate under the appropriate naval direction. Even when the Royal Canadian Navy came under the authority of an American admiral base at Argentia, Newfoundland, in the fall of 1941, the RCAF fiercely maintained its independent stance.[4]

Despite the intractable and short-sighted Canadian high command, the obsolete aircraft, and the miserably inadequate anti-submarine weaponry, the air patrols did a useful job. Their presence was usually enough to force U-boats to dive, after which they had to run on their electric motors that gave them a "flat-out" maximum speed of only a few knots and rendered them fairly innocuous. Although Canadian airmen couldn't point to a huge toll of U-boat sinkings (at this time, they couldn't point to *any* sinkings), their patrols undoubtedly resulted in fewer losses among the hard-pressed merchantmen.

In Britain, a highly efficient organization had been set up before the war to coordinate naval and air forces. Group headquarters maintained control of specific sections of coastline, and perhaps the system's greatest asset was its flexibility: "Squadrons or detachments could be freely moved from group to group according to operational requirements. Group boundaries closely followed those of the Royal Navy's home commands but, more importantly, the group headquarters were located with the corresponding naval

headquarters to form three, later four, Area Combined Headquarters (ACHQ), where the staffs of the two services shared a
common operations room. Air and naval commanders worked
side by side with a common body of information, so that each
service was able to respond rapidly to the requests of the other."[5]
Unfortunately, in the early days of the war, the anti-submarine
organization was limited severely by its lack of aircraft and crews.
To add to the problem, substantial forces were required to maintain Britain's defences against the German invasion, expected ever
since the fall of France.

Dönitz now, in the fall of 1940, began to put some of his "wolfpack" ("*Rudel*" in German) theories into practice. He had more U-
boats, although far from the quantity he felt necessary to do the
job properly. Under his direction, groups of U-boats took up
positions across convoy routes. The U-boats invariably attacked at
night, since Asdic couldn't locate them on the surface and Coastal
Command could do little to help, most of its aircraft having no
radar. Radar (still often referred to as radio location) was as yet
severely limited. The original versions of ASV (air to surface vessel)
radar provided little more than a bewildering array of trembling
dots on operators' screens, when the sets were functioning, which
they frequently weren't. Operators required the skill of scientists at
laboratory microscopes to interpret them accurately.

As Dönitz had anticipated, the wolfpacks dealt a serious, almost
fatal blow to the convoy system. The weak escort forces found
themselves unable to cope with sudden attacks by a number of U-
boats simultaneously. The bolder U-boat skippers penetrated the
convoys on the surface at night, then sailed along the lines of merchantmen, sinking them one after the other.

Deeply concerned about the catastrophic loss of merchantmen,
Churchill demanded an immediate expansion and improvement
of anti-submarine forces. Coastal Command bases were opened in
Northern Ireland and Iceland; it took time for them to become

effective, but it was a beginning. Now Coastal could patrol effectively about 350 miles from Northern Ireland and a similar distance from the new bases in Iceland. Gradually, therefore, Dönitz began to lose some of the enormous areas of the Atlantic in which his subs could operate with impunity. As the U-boats were forced away from the critical shipping areas near the British Isles, "the Admiralty gained sea room in which to route convoys around the packs, whose positions could often be accurately plotted by intelligence."[6] But if a modicum of progress for the Allies seemed to be gained in one area, bad news from another would inevitably follow. The Italians invaded Greece in October 1940. The British countered by sending forces from Egypt to occupy the islands of Crete and Lemnos. A large part of the RN's strength was committed to the Mediterranean when the possibility of an invasion of the British Isles, though not as likely as during the anxious weeks after the fall of France, was still seen as a distinct possibility. Particularly worrisome was the shortage of destroyers; the Norwegian campaign and the evacuation from Dunkirk had cost far too many of these ships, and the shortage was keenly felt in the North Atlantic.

High hopes were held out for the new Hunt-class destroyers just entering service. They turned out to be a bitter disappointment. Top-heavy, unstable in rough weather, they lacked range and could carry only fifty depth charges each. Glumly, the admirals acknowledged the fact that they would have to look elsewhere for ships to escort convoys.

Churchill cabled Franklin Delano Roosevelt, asking for "fifty or sixty of your oldest destroyers." He went on: "Mr. President, with great respect I must tell you that in the long history of the world this is a thing to do now. Large construction is coming to me in 1941, but this crisis will be reached long before 1941. I know you will do all in your power, but I feel entitled and bound to put the gravity and urgency of the position before you. I am sure that with your comprehension of the sea affair, you will not let the crux of the battle go wrong for want of these destroyers."[7] Roosevelt faced a dilemma. He had little doubt that the United States would eventually find itself at war with the Axis powers. He also knew that it would be political suicide to say so publicly. Most Americans seemed to recognize the menace of the Nazis but didn't want their government to do anything about it. Isolationism was a cogent political force in the America of those days, and Roosevelt, hoping to win an unprecedented third term against the popular Republican Wendell L. Willkie, had been assuring Americans that he was the man who would keep them out of the war. In line with this thinking, Congress passed an act forbidding United States citizens to travel on vessels belonging to belligerent nations. Roosevelt knew, however, that despite Churchill's brave words the odds of Britain's survival were no better than even. No one could have blamed the president if he had turned Churchill's request down; a lesser president would undoubtedly have done so. But Roosevelt and Churchill saw things in much the same terms: this was a pivotal moment in world history, and what the Allied leaders did now would affect generations as yet unborn.

In responding to Churchill, Roosevelt pointed out that he had to have public and congressional approval; he would attempt to obtain the necessary approval if Churchill would guarantee that no part of the Royal Navy would ever be turned over to Germany or scuttled. Churchill readily agreed, although he could not guarantee such things. As a result of the agreement, the United States acquired ninety-nine-year leases on bases in the British West Indies, Bermuda, and Newfoundland.

Roosevelt came up with fifty ships, part of a batch of "flush deck" four-stacker destroyers built in the latter days of the First World War. Each was 315 feet long, with a displacement of 1,200 tons and a maximum speed of twenty-nine knots. Forty-three went to the RN, and were named after towns common to Britain and the United States; seven went to the RCN, and were named after Canadian rivers. Their delivery generated an inordinate amount of publicity. Many newspaper readers were under the impression that the American "gift" had saved democracy. The truth was that, as delivered, the so-called Town-class destroyers were of little value; months of work were required to make them suitable for escort work in the Atlantic, and even then they had serious shortcomings. Canadian Bob Timbrell served on one of them, *Annapolis* (formerly the USS *Mackenzie*), and recalls: "The ships were well built, but were low in the water and were continually wet. There were times when we were convinced we were better off below the water than we were above it; the four-stackers rolled but, nevertheless, they worked."[8] The shortage of absolutely everything in the Canadian Navy at that time resulted in some strange sights. Timbrell remembers seeing corvettes sailing with wooden guns. "In *Annapolis*, sometimes fifty per cent of our depth charges were wood – they would float around when it was wet. They were painted grey and gave the correct appearance when we sailed; if there were any Fifth Columnists in Halifax, they saw what looked like a full rail of depth charges."[9] Harry Beck also served on one of these ex-USN destroyers, *St. Croix*. Its roll was horrific: "We had an inclinometer on the back end of the bridge, and everyone up there kept looking at it, each roll we made, to see how far we'd gone. I think the biggest one was fifty-seven and a half degrees. At forty-five, you have a choice of whether you stand on the wall or the deck."[10] Another Canadian, Ross Campbell, served on *Churchill*. He has few fond memories of the ships: "They were terribly tall and narrow, with awnings on their afterdeck. They had come from the Caribbean and were not really seaworthy in the North Atlantic; it was a crime to use them in that role . . . it was just bloody awful on those things."[11]

By the time these costly vessels had become operational, the need for them had eased, and they soon passed from the operational scene. The destroyers-for-bases deal was good for the United States, the president told Americans, because the bases obtained in exchange for the destroyers substantially enhanced the country's security. He liked to call the destroyers-for-bases agreement

America's greatest foreign deal since the Louisiana Purchase. But far more significant, though little publicized, was Roosevelt's agreement to establish new shipyards on the Gulf Coast and U.S. West Coast to build hundreds of new merchant ships. The admirable American thinking behind the new yards seemed to be that if the U-boats couldn't be sunk fast enough, then the Allies would build merchant ships faster than the U-boats could sink them. Churchill sent blueprints for a simple, 440-foot-long, welded coal-burning cargo ship of ten thousand gross tons, capable of cruising at eleven knots. It was the first step in a remarkable program of merchant ship construction, the greatest ever undertaken. For Britain it was a lifesaver. Washington agreed to build sixty such ships for Britain; Ottawa agreed to build twenty-six more. The Americans also planned to build two hundred for their own use, replacing the coal-fired propulsion system of the original design with oil, and using welding rather than riveting during construction. Officially known as EC2 ships, they soon became famous as Liberty ships.

~

In the latter half of 1941, there occurred an exchange of technical and scientific developments between Britain and the United States that had no parallel in history. Churchill was taking a risk of gargantuan proportions, for the United States was still a long way from entering the war. What would happen if Roosevelt lost the fall election and an isolationist such as Charles Lindbergh won? Heaven only knew what would become of Britain's precious technical secrets – and who might see them – if that scenario were to come to pass. But Churchill had little choice but to play this dangerous game; his back was firmly against the wall. He had to involve the Americans in any way he could. The Germans helped. In September, another "criminal act" by Dönitz's U-boats had the newspapers quivering with righteous indignation. U48, under the command of Heinrich Bleichrodt, intercepted an inbound

Atlantic convoy and sank three ships in rapid succession. Three days later, Bleichrodt came across another convoy, this one westbound and proceeding unescorted. Following normal practice, he tracked the ships during the day, remaining at a range of a few miles, far enough away to keep an eye on the convoy without being seen. He waited until nightfall to make his attack, aiming at a large passenger ship. He fired two torpedoes. He could see his target clearly in the bright moonlight, but the sea was heavy. His torpedoes missed, running away out to sea, apparently without being spotted. Irked by his failure, Bleichrodt attacked again, selecting a five-thousand-ton freighter and the passenger ship that had so narrowly escaped disaster. This time he was successful. He hit the passenger ship, the eleven-thousand-ton *City of Benares*. She carried four hundred passengers, including ninety English children on their way to Canada to escape the Blitz. In the darkness, the inexperienced crew made a mess of letting go the lifeboats. A ghastly scene ensued as boats crashed down upon others, and passengers, including children, went tumbling into the icy sea. Several lifeboats drifted for many days before rescue came. In all, three hundred of the four hundred passengers lost their lives, including seventy-seven of the unfortunate children. Predictably, the Allied press made the most of the incident; in truth, however, Bleichrodt could hardly be blamed for selecting the ship, since it was darkened and unmarked. The Admiralty had not requested safe passage for her. A few days later, Bleichrodt was involved in another highly successful attack on an Atlantic convoy. First spotted by the daring Günther Prien, the convoy comprised some forty ships. Dönitz sent five U-boats to deal with it, and they were devastatingly successful. In a matter of some twenty-six hours, the U-boats sank eleven ships: 72,700 tons in all. Star of the attack was undoubtedly Joachim Schepke in U100, who courageously slipped into the middle of the convoy and sank seven ships, totalling over 50,000 tons.

Convoy SC7, carrying a variety of supplies, including oil, sailed from Sydney, Nova Scotia, on Saturday, October 5, 1940. The convoy consisted of thirty-five slow ships, three of them lakers designed to operate on the Great Lakes, most of the rest ancient merchantmen that would have gone to the scrapyard had it not been for the war. The motley assembly of aging vessels sailed into the most dangerous waters on earth with just one escort, a thousand-ton sloop, HMS *Scarborough*, armed with two four-inch guns and depth charges. A Sunderland flying boat would patrol from land for the first two days of the voyage only, a measure of the critical shortage of suitable patrol aircraft.

On the very first day, one of the merchantmen vanished from the convoy, probably due to impatience on the part of the skipper rather than any action by the enemy. More ships slipped away over the next few days. South of Iceland, shortly after noon on the eleventh day, in heavy weather, the Canadian Lake steamer *Trevisa* took a torpedo fired by U124, a long-range Type IX U-boat commanded by Georg-Wilhelm Schulz. The ship sank quickly, taking six of her crew with her.

On October 17, as the convoy still plodded in its glacial way across the ocean near Iceland, it became the subject of much interest to the skipper of U48, Heinrich Bleichrodt. He immediately notified BdU in Lorient by short-wave radio. Dönitz alerted five U-boats patrolling only a few hours away. He ordered them to attack en masse. The convoy, and its inadequate escort, appeared to be in imminent danger of being wiped out.

The five attacking U-boats made contact during the evening of October 18, in ideal conditions of calm seas and a full moon. One, U99, was commanded by a highly successful skipper, Otto Kretschmer. In the calm, moonlit conditions, he found a treasure trove of heavily laden ships. The vessels could be picked out without difficulty, overlapping one another to create huge targets. Torpedoes streaked across the tranquil sea, tracing luminescent trails. Never had the U-boat men seen better targets or conditions. Even the scores of torpedoes that failed to hit their intended targets were seen to strike others nearby. Kretschmer fired a torpedo at a big freighter which turned in the nick of time; the torpedo ran into another ship, still larger than the first. Inside the U-boat, the crew could hear an almost constant roar of explosions. To the U-boat crews and the tense and apprehensive merchant seamen on the ships still unscathed, it seemed that the convoy was suffering the worst slaughter in the history of the merchant marine. The first reports compiled by Dönitz and his staff indicated that thirty ships of the convoy's thirty-five had been sunk; later calculations revealed that the total was actually twenty. Still, it was a catastrophe of the first order, with more than 50 per cent of the convoy sunk without a single loss to the attackers. The following day, the submariners rested and prepared for the next assault, keeping the convoy in sight from a safe distance. In fact, it was seldom necessary to see the ships themselves; the submariners usually kept a lookout for smoke drifting above the horizon. It told them enough.

The second assault took place that night. Dönitz originally claimed another seventeen ships from the sorely tried convoy, although this figure was later reduced to twelve. It was a shocking defeat for the convoy system. What had gone wrong? One answer can be found in the shortage of escorts – and the lack of training of their crews. At one point, *Scarborough's* captain, Dickinson, picked up a radio report from a Sunderland that had sighted U48. He promptly sailed off in pursuit of the U-boat. He hunted it for twenty-four hours, without success, displaying fine aggressive spirit but paying a regrettable lack of attention to the badly battered convoy, or what was left of it. Dönitz calculated that his U-boats must have sunk forty-seven ships. He described it as a "colossal" success. Prien received a cluster of Oak Leaves to add to his Ritterkreuz. His men had in fact sunk all but three of the convoy's thirty-five ships, for a little over 194,000 tons.

Confusion about victories and losses was as inevitable in a night battle between U-boats and convoys as it was in a big dogfight between fighter planes. Too many things were happening at once for accurate accounting. Countless overoptimistic claims resulted from two or more U-boat skippers launching torpedoes at the same target at the same time. When the intended victim erupted in flames, wasn't it only natural that more than one skipper thought he had scored the victory?

On October 21, 1940, a milestone of sorts was recorded: the day saw the sinking of the five-hundredth British ship lost since war began. The tonnage amounted to a dreadful two million tons, most of which had fallen victim to Dönitz's U-boats. From the beginning of September to December 2, 1940, U-boats sank 157 British and Allied ships, totalling over 800,000 tons, including tankers representing some 140,000 tons. During the same period, Dönitz lost only three U-boats, an exchange ratio of about fifty to one. Many factors had contributed to the slaughter: expert deployment of the few U-boats available; boldness, skill, and confidence on the part of two dozen skippers; and mediocre performance by the ill-equipped and poorly trained escorts.

In early November, the battleship *Admiral Scheer* attacked a thirty-eight-ship convoy, sinking the solitary escort, the 14,000-ton merchant cruiser *Jervis Bay*, and five of the convoy's vessels.

The German battleship slipped away with the Home Fleet in hot pursuit. Haunted by the thought of how much destruction *Admiral Scheer* might inflict on merchant shipping, the Admiralty aborted three inbound convoys, costing Britain far more in desperately needed imports than those carried by the ships sunk. For an unprecedented twelve days, no convoys traversed the Atlantic – an indication of how seriously the Admiralty still took the threat of action by Germany's battleships.

At about this time, the Admiralty demanded that RAF Coastal Command be severed from the RAF entirely and handed over to the RN. "The idea originated," writes Marshal of the Royal Air Force Sir John Slessor, "in an egregious alliance between Lord Beaverbrook, Sir Roger Keyes, and the new First Lord, Mr. A. V. Alexander. These gentlemen were not qualified by temperament or experience to evolve an impartial or professionally sound solution of any problem connected with the employment of air forces. . . . The Sea Lords were far from enthusiastic about the proposal, and it was turned down by the War Cabinet. . . . After a lot of time-wasting argument, a compromise was arrived at by which Coastal Command nominally came under the Admiralty's operational control, which was to be exercised through the Air Officer Commanding-in-Chief."[12] Slessor asserts that "the actual outcome of this was precisely nothing, except a legacy of ill feeling in the Command of which the last traces had hardly disappeared when I took over two years later. The so-called operational control by the Admiralty in effect left the real position just as it had been before all this fuss. . . . Inter-Service relations can only work on the basis of friendly cooperation and that is how the relations of the Admiralty and Coastal Command did in fact work, because the responsible personalities were for the most part reasonable and disinterested people determined to get on with the war."[13]

As 1940 drew to a close, London suffered a series of heavy air attacks. Churchill wanted to cable Roosevelt, telling him that "the scenes of widespread destruction here and in our provincial centres are shocking; but when I visited the still-burning ruins today the spirit of the Londoners was as high as in the first days of the indiscriminate bombing in September, four months ago."[14]

The message was never sent. The British embassy staff in Washington worried that "it might revive the defeatist impression of some months ago."[15] Problems continued to mount for Churchill and his colleagues. Intelligence reports indicated that a German invasion of Greece was imminent, after the humiliating failure of the Italians to defeat the small Greek army. Churchill knew that such an invasion would have a seismic impact on the Balkans, the Aegean, and the eastern Mediterranean. All the gains won by Field Marshal Sir Archibald Wavell would be in jeopardy. Moreover, the American president's attitude to Churchill's pleas for assistance seemed to be hardening. Britain could no longer pay for the arms she so desperately needed. Her gold reserves and dollar balance had dwindled precipitately. The only bright spot on the horizon was the arrival in England of Roosevelt's emissary, Harry Hopkins. His sympathetic presence and his understanding of Britain's situation did much to pave the way for the introduction of the historic Lend-Lease scheme. Under the scheme, the United States manufactured the supplies Britain (and other Allies) needed, leasing them to her on a rental basis with full payment deferred until after the war. It was a lifesaver, but the United States demanded payment of existing debts, in gold, or by the sale of British commercial assets in America. So, on the one hand, America committed herself to giving extraordinarily generous help to Britain; on the other, to what seemed to be a deliberate undermining of British commercial and political power. Did the Americans want to reduce Britain – the most powerful nation on Earth half a century earlier – to a mere protectorate of the United States?

4

SEARCH AND KILL

---

*"The only way you can guarantee that there are no
U-boats in an area . . . is to keep every square mile of it
under surveillance"*
– Rear Admiral Daniel V. Gallery, USN

THE YEAR BEGAN WITH encouraging news. In America, the proposed Lend-Lease legislation appeared likely to be passed, despite bitter opposition from isolationists. Britain had come close to running out of dollars. Roosevelt, ever eager to keep the British fighting, declared his intention to lease the supplies instead of demanding cash payment. It was a way to get the necessary weapons to the British (and others) in sufficient volume and quickly enough so that Americans might be spared the horrors of war – while they enjoyed a bustling economy thanks to the vastly increased production of war materiel. It was a recurring message of Roosevelt's: Wouldn't you much rather make the weapons – and enjoy the revenue derived from them – than have to fight with them?

Events in the Middle East had been moving positively; Churchill fantasized about the Italian colony of Cyrenaica in Libya, now in British hands, becoming the beginning of a "Free Italy." He saw four or five divisions of Italian troops based there, being trained by the British, ready for action. But the day after the PM set this item down on the agenda for discussions with the chiefs of staff, a German major-general arrived in Tripoli. He had made something of a reputation for himself in France in 1940. Now he would upset all Churchill's plans for North Africa. His name was Erwin Rommel. A bold, aggressive commander, he immediately launched a blistering attack that almost drove the British out of Cyrenaica.

The new year rapidly deteriorated. In the Atlantic, the U-boat successes had become catastrophic, threatening to cut off Britain's principal lifelines. One of Churchill's staff incurred the great man's displeasure by reporting yet another convoy disaster, describing it as "distressing." Churchill barked, "Distressing? It is terrifying. If it goes on, it will be the end of us."[1] Although some historians tend to downplay Churchill's frequent wailings on the subject of the U-boats and the losses they caused, it must be remembered that at the time the Americans had yet to agree to build the enormous numbers of merchant ships that would begin to make up for most of the appalling losses in the Atlantic and elsewhere. If left to her own resources, Britain might well have fallen, her merchant marine decimated by the U-boats. The British shipbuilding industry was notoriously inefficient and incapable of raising productivity to any significant extent, despite the looming crisis. The American ship-building program saved the day, as did the integration into the British Merchant Navy (its wartime name) of many ships from European countries conquered by the Nazis – the Norwegian, Dutch, and Greek fleets being particularly useful at a dangerous time. In early 1941, importing capacity shrank to 28.5 million tons, from a prewar level of 42 million tons, resulting in drastic "belt tightening" in Britain. The first nine months of the war had seen about 150 British and Allied ships sunk, a loss made good largely by new building and the capture of Axis ships. The need for more ships had become urgent after the fall of France and the entry of Italy into the war. Now the Channel was closed to deep-sea ships and the

In the uneasy weeks prior to the outbreak of war, several U-boats await action at Kiel. U33 (centre) was a Type VII boat, lost in action in February, 1940. The smaller U-boats are training types. (Imperial War Museum HU-3280)

Karl Dönitz, *Grossadmiral* of Germany's U-boat force, and from January 1943 commander-in-chief of the entire navy. He is seen inspecting coastal defences, spring 1944. (Imperial War Museum A-26643)

A Swordfish interrupts a game of deck hockey on the carrier *Indomitable,* dropping a sleeve target after target practice by air gunners. Note elevator shaft which transported aircraft to the hangars and servicing facilities below. (Imperial War Museum A-10346)

Beaufighters of RAF Coastal Command attack German shipping in Risnes fjord, Norway, a demanding target because of the steep cliffs on either side. Cannon and rocket fire were notably effective in such circumstances. (Imperial War Museum C-5272)

Albacores of the Fleet Air Arm take off from *Victorious* to attack the German battleship *Tirpitz*, March 1942. Intended as a replacement for the venerable Swordfish, the Albacore was not notably successful and had a brief operational career. (Imperial War Museum A-7898)

Guided by signals from the "batsman" on deck, a Wildcat fighter approaches to land on an escort carrier. The Wildcat, originally known as the Martlet in Fleet Air Arm service, was built by Grumman in the United States. (Imperial War Museum A-11642)

The German ship *Altmark*, formerly a supply ship for *Admiral Graf Spee*. When intercepted by the RN in Norwegian waters, she was found to be carrying some three hundred Allied prisoners. (Imperial War Museum HU-27803)

The powerful pocket battleship *Admiral Graf Spee*. Heavily armed and speedy, she ranked as one of Germany's most serious threats to British shipping in the days before the U-boats' rise to dominance. (Imperial War Museum HU-3285)

Two German pocket battleships, *Deutschland* (foreground) and *Admiral Graf Spee*, speed through the Straits of Dover shortly before the outbreak of war. Within weeks, *Graf Spee* had been sunk in the Battle of the River Plate. (Imperial War Museum HU-1032)

The German battle-cruiser *Gneisenau*. Launched in 1936 with her sister-ship *Scharnhorst*, she represented the latest in battle-cruiser design. In 1942, she participated in the famous "Channel Dash" and suffered damage from a mine. (Imperial War Museum HU-3278)

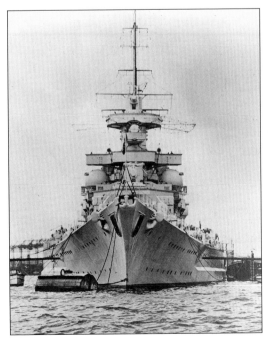

An all too familiar sight during the Battle of the Atlantic: a tanker erupts in flames after being hit by a torpedo. U-boats usually attacked shipping at night. (Imperial War Museum HU-74998)

The Italian submarine *Cobolto* suffered serious damage when shelled by the British destroyer *Ithuriel* in the summer of 1942. *Cobolto* sank soon after, but most of her crew survived. (Imperial War Museum HU-41861)

Two of the RN officers instrumental in the defeat of *Bismarck,* May 1941.
Captain Charles Larcom (left) of the cruiser *Sheffield*, and Vice-Admiral
Sir James Somerville, one of the few admirals with personal experience of
flying in Fleet Air Arm aircraft. (Imperial War Museum A-4120)

A Martin Maryland photo-reconnaissance aircraft of the type that carried
out a notably hazardous sortie over Norway to verify the whereabouts of
the German battleship *Bismarck* prior to the famous battle in which she was
destroyed. (Imperial War Museum A-8223)

This Fleet Air Arm Barracuda overshot during an attempted carrier landing, one of countless such accidents. Surprisingly, the crew escaped without serious injury. (Imperial War Museum A-26688)

The hazards of maintaining non-stop air patrols on Canada's east coast are illustrated by the Canso pictured here and above, destroyed during a take-off crash. The crew lost their lives. (Bill Doherty collection)

Suez Canal closed to ships heading east. Merchant ships had to travel via the north of Scotland to reach the east coast ports, adding at least ten days to the voyage and vastly increasing the dangers of interception by U-boat or surface ships. Voyages to the Middle East now had to go via the Cape of Good Hope, a distance of 21,000 kilometres rather than the previous 4,800 kilometres; it all added up to huge delays, compounded by the inevitable time-wasting of the convoy system itself. Indeed, Britain had her importing capacity reduced by about a quarter.

∿

Early in the new year, the Germans brought an outstanding new warship into service, the battle cruiser *Bismarck*. With her jaunty flared bow, her eight 15-inch guns and her immensely tough armour-plating, she was the pride of the Kriegsmarine and one of the finest warships afloat. In May, she joined forces with the heavy cruiser *Prinz Eugen*. The Germans' plan called for the two ships to break through to the Atlantic and join forces with the battle cruiser *Gneisenau*. And by mid year, it was expected that *Bismarck*'s sister ship, *Tirpitz*, would be completed. With these splendid ships and Dönitz's U-boats, there seemed to be every likelihood that the all-important British transatlantic trade could be destroyed once and for all. Raeder saw his navy winning the war.

Commanding *Bismarck* was forty-five-year-old Captain Ernst Lindemann. An excessively slim individual, he had a pallid complexion that made him look frail, which he wasn't. Although his prominent ears and stern demeanour gave rise to a few wisecracks below decks, Lindemann was a popular commander who did his best to make himself known to every member of his 2,200-man crew. Early in May, the Führer himself came out to Gotenhafen to inspect the new battleship. Never comfortable away from dry land, he seemed ill at ease; the short tender ride out to the *Bismarck* may have upset his stomach, although it's also possible that he was pre-occupied with the assault on the Soviet Union, due to take place in a matter of weeks.

After Hitler and his entourage had departed amid a forest of arms upraised in Nazi salutes, Lindemann and the fleet commander, Admiral Lütjens, got down to the final details of their mission. A study in opposites, the two senior officers maintained correct if not warm relations during their brief time together. They decided that on this mission, *Bismarck* would attack British convoy escorts, while *Prinz Eugen* set about the merchant ships. The Germans were confident that their task force would throw the British Home Fleet into confusion, scattering ships all over the ocean.

On May 17, 1941, *Bismarck* pulled away from Gotenhafen with a full crew, the admiral and his staff, a Luftwaffe contingent to operate and service the ship's Arado 196 reconnaissance floatplane, merchant marine officers to take over captured ships, a platoon of war correspondents to record every detail of the voyage, and an eager assembly of midshipmen from *Tirpitz* to gain combat experience.

Two destroyers and a flotilla of minesweepers formed an escort for the journey northward through the Kattegat, linking Sweden and Denmark. The next morning dawned bright and clear – pleasant conditions, but far from ideal in Captain Lindemann's opinion; he would have preferred cloud or even fog to conceal the ship as long as possible. Who knew how many of those eyes on shore were studying the ships and mentally composing their messages to London? Near Bergen, Norway, the ships slipped into a quiet fjord. *Prinz Eugen* refuelled; inexplicably, *Bismarck* did not. Soon after that, an RAF Spitfire spotted them and took photographs.

At about seven-thirty that evening, the two German battleships and their escorts slipped anchor and headed north.

Aboard his new flagship, *King George V*, fifty-six-year-old Admiral Sir John Tovey, commander-in-chief of the British Home Fleet, waited for the Germans' next move. He had little choice, despite

Churchill's exhortations to action. Really, the PM could be a trial at times. How could the fleet go into action when no one knew where the Germans were heading? Norway? Iceland? The Atlantic? Tovey ordered air reconnaissance of the main escape routes into the Atlantic. The cruiser *Norfolk* had already taken up station in the Denmark Strait; *Suffolk* would soon join her. More cruisers, *Birmingham* and *Manchester*, were patrolling the Iceland–Faroes gap. He ordered the battle cruiser *Hood*, commanded by Vice-Admiral Lancelot Holland, to leave Scapa Flow immediately and head for Iceland with *Prince of Wales*, the rest of the fleet remaining at Scapa, ready to sail at short notice. Tovey planned to lay a trap for the German battleships, once he knew where the enemy lay. Were they still at their refuelling stop near Bergen? Or had they already sailed and were approaching the Atlantic at this very moment? Every instinct nagged at him to set sail and investigate. But hard as it was to accept, he had to stay and await developments. If the Germans decided to slip out between Greenland and the Faroes, aircraft and ships, including *Hood* and *Prince of Wales*, would spot them. Similarly, if they attempted a run through the gap between the Faroes and the Orkneys, the forces at Scapa Flow could deal with them. Provided they could *see* them. The damned weather was closing in again. Because of it, RAF Coastal Command cancelled patrols over the Norwegian coast. Tovey winced at the news. In these conditions, there was every possibility of the Germans eluding him, slipping away in the mist and rain and striking out into the Atlantic to ravage the convoys upon which Britain's survival depended.

It was an unexceptional day at Hatston, in the Orkneys. It rained on and off; it usually did. Target-towing aircraft buzzed around the field, hauling windsock-like drogues about the sky, while fledgling air gunners of the Fleet Air Arm blazed away with their Lewis guns, trying to riddle them with bullets. The station's wireless operator spent most of his days giving permission for the aircraft to land and take off. It was less than thrilling work. But today there occurred something quite out of the ordinary. A voice came over the radio, an unfamiliar voice, a voice tight and urgent. A message for the Coastal Command HQ: *No sign of enemy warships in fjords in the Bergen area.* The simple message was the end result of an extraordinary flight carried out by a scratch aircrew consisting of a highly experienced pilot, Noel Goddard, CO of the target-towing unit, an exceptionally capable navigator, Geoffrey Rotherham, and a veteran wireless operator/air gunner, Petty Officer Armstrong.

The crew received their briefing at 1600 in the Hatston control tower. They took off in an unarmed Martin Maryland target-tower, a mediocre American aircraft originally built as a light bomber. At first the weather was superb: clear skies and lots of sunshine. It didn't last. At briefing, the crew had been told that a front lay over the North Sea and a mass of dense cloud hugged the Norwegian coast. The Maryland droned over a mosaic of islands and forbidding fjords – no place for a forced landing in poor visibility. The horizon began to blur. Minutes later, the airmen saw the cloud, dark and ominous, rising from the water like a blue-black wall of granite.

Goddard took the Maryland down, through the endless strata of clinging murk. Now he was skimming above the ocean. Then he went lower, until he was flying in a strange sort of tunnel, its roof the dark, seething mass of cloud and mist, its floor the speeding water, hurtling just a few feet beneath the aircraft. A gut-wrenching trip, suicidally low. Ease back a fraction on the controls and you would be in the cloud, blinded; relax concentration for an instant and you would find your self in pieces in the sea. He trimmed the nose up a fraction.

Rotherham had to study the sea from time to time to check on winds. He was of the generation of observer/navigators who could tell a great deal about conditions by merely glancing at the sea, "reading" the movements of the water as a doctor interprets the symptoms of a patient. Remarkably, the crew managed not to kill themselves. But it was a nerve-grindingly near-thing.

Marsten Island lies about a dozen miles south of Bergen.

Rotherham had picked it as a checkpoint when plotting his course. He hit it on the nose, neatly skirting the island because it housed a number of flak batteries. In a minute or two, the mainland appeared. So did the flak. Thousands of tiny lights soared skyward, wobbling, curving away, disappearing. The Maryland sped over the rugged terrain broken up by innumerable fjords. The crew saw Norwegians on the ground, gazing up at the unfamiliar aircraft, no doubt wondering if it was lost or experiencing mechanical problems. One thing was sure: no pilot in his right mind would willingly fly this low over enemy territory in such abysmal conditions. Kars Fjord materialized out of the mist, a passageway of dark, forbidding water, but, thank God, free of mist. And flak. No sign of *Bismarck* or *Prinz Eugen*. It appeared that the German battleships had indeed flown their nautical coop.

Or had they merely put into Bergen to wait out the weather? It was vital to find out. Goddard overflew the port – to be met by storms of flak. It peppered the fuselage, wrecking the intercom but miraculously missing the crew. Rotherham studied the ships in the harbour, wincing as the flak came soaring at him at a seemingly leisurely pace, then whizzing past him with unbelievable velocity. Again, no sight of the German vessels. It wasn't easy, concentrating on identifying ships while expecting a bullet or chunk of flak to strike home at any instant. The fact that the Maryland's fuel tanks had no self-sealing material became uppermost in Goddard's mind. One bullet could turn the aircraft into a flaming torch. Blast rocked it, kicked at it. Wobbling, the aircraft continued its perilous journey. The Maryland bounced and swayed like a double-decker bus on a bumpy road. Holes appeared in the cabin windows, admitting screaming blasts of chilly air.

The loss of the intercom complicated matters even further. Rotherham couldn't speak to Armstrong; the wireless operator was snug behind a bulkhead. Rotherham took a piece of paper and wrote: "Signal c-in-c that the battleship and cruiser have left."

He folded the paper and passed it to Goddard, who in turn passed it on to Armstrong. The wireless operator did his best to raise Coastal Command, but he got no response. What to do now? Armstrong had an inspiration: To hell with Coastal Command HQ, contact Scapa Flow, where the day's gunnery practice was in progress. At 1900, then, the radio operator at Scapa picked up the message, blinking in amazement, for all they usually had to deal with were mundane messages concerning training flights. The message went immediately to Sir John Tovey, Commander-in-Chief, Home Fleet.

When the Maryland touched down safely after its remarkable sortie, Rotherham was summoned to the telephone. The Admiral wanted to talk to him. The pilot gave him every detail of the trip. Based on the information provided by Rotherham and the other members of the crew, Tovey ordered the Home Fleet to weigh anchor. One of the most famous and dramatic sea chases in British history was about to take place, made possible by an epic aerial journey in vile weather. None of the crew was ever to win an award for it – and to rub salt in their wounds, the Fleet Air Arm crew later read in the papers that an amazing fact-finding sortie flown by *Coastal Command* had been one of the key elements in the epic battle with the great German vessel.

Aboard *Prince of Wales* was a young Canadian officer, Stu Paddon. He was a rarity: a radar officer. On the outbreak of war, he had been completing his final year at the University of Western Ontario. The head of the physics department approached him and several other students about changing the syllabus to emphasize electronics. It transpired that the request originated with the RN, who had been unable to find enough electronics talent in England, all the likely students having already been snapped up by the RAF.

Paddon was posted to *Prince of Wales*, which had just been completed and was currently fitting out. "*Prince of Wales* was the first ship to get a multiple suit of radar," Paddon explains.[2]

Up until this time, ships carried one radar, now I was to get ten, as follows: one Type 281 radar, air warning principally with a capability for surface detection as well, and nine gunnery radars. . . . During the ensuing period, I received thirty personnel, only one of whom had been to sea before. I was the only "technician"; there were no technicians trained at that time in the Royal Navy for radar duties. Needless to say, I found myself with my head inside a radar set almost continuously, with maybe 40 per cent of the sets not functioning at any one moment. . . . I didn't receive much direction because in those days nobody really knew much about radar . . . and you found two things happening: one, you had to convince somebody it was worth carrying, and when that was achieved, you had to convince them that it couldn't tell you what kind of cigarette a pilot was smoking when he was flying an aircraft.

Prince of Wales still carried some fifty dockyard workers when she set off, in company with the battle cruiser *Hood*. On May 24, the battle began at a range of thirteen nautical miles. The angle of interception proved unfortunate for the two British warships, preventing their full armament being brought to bear. The Germans concentrated their fire on *Hood*. The first salvo fell long by about a hundred yards. The second straddled *Hood*. The third started fires. The next blew it up. In an electrifying, horrifying instant, a cataclysmic explosion ripped the 42,000-ton battleship in two. *Prinz Eugen*'s gunnery officer watched, amazed: "The aft magazine blew up, shooting into the air a molten mass the colour of red lead, which then fell back lazily into the sea – it was one of the rear gun turrets. . . . And in the midst of this raging inferno, a yellow tongue of flame shot out just once more: the forward turrets of *Hood* had fired just one last salvo."[3] Naval experts had regarded *Hood* and *Bismarck* as about evenly matched: both sported eight 15-inch guns; both had similar speed, secondary armament, and armour.

Len Deighton writes: "In the 1930s, *Hood* had been the pride of the Royal Navy, the fastest, most powerful and arguably, most beautiful ship afloat. She had spent so much time showing the flag that there never seemed to be an opportunity for the total overhaul and refurbishing that was so badly needed. Nineteen years older than *Bismarck*, the *Hood*'s 15-inch guns were unchanged in design since those of 1914, while the big guns of the *Bismarck* provided excellent examples of the way in which gun technology had improved."[4] Only three men, a midshipman and two ratings, survived from the crew of 1,419.

Bismarck now concentrated her fire on *Prince of Wales*, which closed to 14,600 yards and scored several hits on the German ship, causing damage to the forecastle, rupturing a fuel tank, and wrecking the fuel transfer system. After this, both ships pulled back to review the situation and consider their next move, angering Churchill in London and Hitler in Berlin, both of whom thought the fight should have continued uninterrupted.

Some 350 miles to the southeast, Admiral Tovey led a force comprising *King George V, Repulse*, the aircraft carrier *Victorious*, and five cruisers. The guessing game had begun. Would *Bismarck* continue on her present course? Or would she turn about when darkness fell? Did she plan to escape to the north or south of Iceland?

The visibility deteriorated. *Bismarck* became a misty form speeding through a forest of gauze. Admiral Frederick Wake-Walker could no longer see her, yet, inexplicably, he became convinced that the German battleship had altered course. He ordered a 360-degree turn to port. In little more than half an hour, the mist cleared. *Bismarck* was dead ahead, less than ten miles distant, steaming at full speed. The hunch had paid off.

One of the oddities of the famous battle with *Bismarck* was the lack of coordination between London and the ships at sea. To Tovey, it seemed certain that *Bismarck* would try to shake off her pursuers during the approaching night. In London, Churchill was of the same opinion – and he could no more leave the decisions to his admirals on the spot than could the senior officer of the Senior Service, Admiral of the Fleet Sir Dudley Pound, the First Sea Lord. Dudley Pound was a desperately sick man, carrying out his demanding duties in spite of a lethal brain tumour and an excruciatingly painful disease of the hip. He should have been in hospital, but he refused to give up. One has to admire the man for his undoubted courage and strength of character; in this case, however, it would surely have served the British cause better had he resigned and let a fit man take over. Never for a moment doubting that he knew far better than the men in action, Pound seemed constitutionally incapable of leaving his admirals alone to get on with their jobs.*

Churchill demanded to know why the British ships were content to trail along in *Bismarck*'s wake; apparently he was unaware that the aircraft carrier *Victorious* was on her way to deliver an attack with its torpedo bombers.

None of the aircrews on *Victorious* were optimistic about their chances, either of sinking the huge ship or surviving the day. They masked their feelings with the usual display of couldn't-care-less. It was expected. Apart from the section leaders (regular officers of the Fleet Air Arm), all the pilots, observer/navigators, and telegraphist/air gunners (TAGs) were fresh from training school; this was to be their first operation.

Les Sayer, a TAG in the crew of Percy Glick, a Dartmouth-trained officer, recalls that *Victorious* had a hangar full of Spitfires in packing cases, destined for Malta.

I wondered what it was all about, and only began to get a vague idea when special authority was given to all TAGs to

---

* He was later blamed for two notable naval disasters: the German operation *Cerberus*, in which the battle cruisers *Scharnhorst* and *Gneisenau*, and the heavy cruiser *Prinz Eugen*, escaped from the French port of Brest to Norway via the English Channel; and the scattering of the Arctic convoy PQ17, with heavy losses, because he believed (wrongly) that it was about to be attacked by the powerful new German battleship *Tirpitz*.

buy one pound of chocolate from the NAAFI. In those days
there were no such things as survival kits, and it seemed to
me that there was a distinct possibility of finishing up in
Greenland, with a comforting pound of chocolate to keep
out the cold. That we were obliged to buy it ourselves out
of our very meagre pay seems incredible today, but it was
something we took quite for granted at the time. . . . Then
came the long period of waiting for something to happen.
Halfway up to the bridge of the carrier, reached by narrow
ladders, there was a small "caboose" and there the TAGs
waited. Six of them, in flying kit, wedged themselves into
this uncomfortable space, which rapidly filled with smoke
and an aroma your best friends wouldn't tell you about.
Apprehensive eyes, not quite knowing where to look,
focused on good luck charms tied to their Mae Wests. . . .
There were periods of uneasy silence broken only by the
steady drone of the ventilation system and the occasional
clang of the sliding door, when someone went out to
nowhere in particular and came back from the same place.[5]

The weather had worsened. The carrier pitched like a seesaw;
stinging hail pounded the flight deck, beating a tattoo on the
fabric-covered wings of the Swordfish. The aircraft had been
"ranged" in preparation for takeoff. Each carried an 18-inch
torpedo slung between its undercarriage legs, most of the missiles
bearing rude messages for Hitler and Göring, scribbled on in chalk
by maintenance personnel – although the slashing spray had already
obliterated many of them.

Sayer clambered aboard his Swordfish, making himself as comfortable as possible in the narrow rear cockpit with its wireless
equipment and Lewis gun. Normally, he wouldn't have been
officially informed what their target was or how it was to be
attacked; in the Navy of the early 1940s, it was not considered necessary for non-commissioned officers to attend crew briefings prior

to sorties. But this attack was different. Everyone knew its purpose: to sink the mightiest battleship in the world. Everyone fought his own private battles with fear and uncertainty. Everyone pretended to be unconcerned about the chances of coming through; they convinced no one, certainly not themselves.

Haunted by thoughts of being shot down and having to paddle about in a frigid ocean, Sayer secreted a tot of rum in his cockpit. He hoped he'd have time to grab it if the aircraft was hit. He checked the rear gun and the radio. Through a tiny peephole in the floor of the cockpit, he could see the bright red fin of the torpedo. Sayer took a deep breath. The moment of truth had arrived; he was about to fly in anger against the enemy, something he had thought about a thousand times. He took another deep breath.

Takeoff was quick in the powerful gale. After a run of only a few yards, the deck dropped away. The Swordfish bounced and skidded in the turbulent conditions. The air was heavy with mist and rain – an aerial obstacle course. Sayer kept looking left and right, but there was nothing to see, just endless grey. The fragile-looking biplanes, nine of them, flew on, every man occupied by his own ruminations. In command of the formation was a short, dapper man "with a strangely wide forehead and the perky look of a bird. A sea bird. He had keen, bright, prominent eyes that, like a bird's, were never still."[6] He was Eugene Esmonde, a veteran pilot of exceptional skill, who joined the RAF in 1928, later transferring to the Fleet Air Arm, with a spell as an Imperial Airways pilot in between. Esmonde was one of those individuals with an in-born ability to lead. It would stand him in good stead.

Several of the Swordfish were equipped with an early form of ASV radar. They picked up a blip. It had to be *Bismarck*. But it wasn't. It was the U.S. Coast Guard cutter *Modoc*, sailing with two other Coast Guard ships on what was known as a "neutrality patrol." Fortunately, none of the Swordfish pilots attacked.

Then, as if materialized by some magician, the German battleship took form through the curtains of mist. At once, sparkles of gunfire punctuated the massive grey shape as every one of the ship's guns opened up. Darts of light criss-crossed the air like a plague of fireflies.

"Going in," announced Percy Glick, Sayer's pilot. He never wasted words. His flight of three Swordfish attacked on the port bow. Les Sayer, in the rear cockpit, kept expecting the upward surge of the aircraft when the torpedo fell away. It didn't come. Percy Glick declared himself dissatisfied with his approach.

"Going around again."

Words to chill a man's soul. Sayer glanced down; sure enough, the bright red tail of the torpedo was still there, mocking him. *Bismarck* looked like a great floating castle, spitting fire from countless guns. Sayer wondered numbly if she was the last thing he would ever see. Shrapnel ripped ugly tears in the wing. Sayer instinctively huddled behind the side wall of his cockpit; an utterly pointless action, since the fabric wouldn't slow a .22 bullet, let alone the hefty ammunition of *Bismarck*'s guns.

The ocean tilted as Glick banked almost vertically, swinging around for another run. The other Swordfish were already heading back to *Victorious*. Sayer saw them disappearing into the shifting walls of mist.

"This time," Sayer recalls, "we had the dubious honour of having *Bismarck*'s undivided attention. With her whole massive armament free to concentrate on one frail, canvas-covered, obsolete biplane, how could they fail to destroy us utterly? One torpedo, two light machine guns, and three men against the might of the German Navy – what a hope. Standing up, I looked over the pilot's shoulder; everything was uncannily quiet – we had not been spotted, or perhaps they could not believe what they had spotted. Closer and closer, the battleship got bigger and bigger, and now my thoughts changed to wondering, 'How can we miss?' The target was huge and the run-in perfect."[7]

Sayer felt the Stringbag surge upward. Thank God, the torpedo had gone at long last! Now the aim in life was to get away from that behemoth and its flashing guns. Great eruptions of water sprang up around the little biplane as flak shells smacked into the sea. Sayer felt the impact when a shell hit the water directly beneath him, tearing the fabric from beneath his seat. A chilly, noisy gale assaulted him. He told Glick, "It's bloody draughty back here!"

Incredibly, all the Swordfish returned safely to *Victorious*, the crews simultaneously elated and badly shaken. They landed with little fuel remaining in their tanks. For his part in the action, Les Sayer won the Distinguished Service Medal.

They had not sunk the great German battleship, but they had hit her with a torpedo; that much was certain. But how seriously had they damaged her? It later transpired that *Bismarck*'s high-speed manoeuvring in heavy seas had done more damage than the torpedo, aggravating a leak in the boiler room incurred during the earlier action. Slowed by her damage, *Bismarck* still managed to elude the British in the thickening weather.

The next day, with no improvement in the conditions, 825 Squadron's aircraft took off from *Victorious* to look for the German battleship. One of the Swordfish, with Lieutenant Pat Jackson at the controls, searched its designated sector but saw nothing. Jackson turned and set course for *Victorious*. He couldn't find her. With his fuel dwindling to the last few pints, Jackson prepared for the inevitable: ditching in the inhospitable Atlantic. It was not a pleasant prospect; although the Swordfish was a good aircraft to ditch, it wouldn't float for long – and the chances of being picked up were about a million to one.

Jackson's observer, Lieutenant D. A. "Dapper" Berrill, suddenly yelled and pointed. By fantastic good fortune, he had spotted an empty lifeboat bobbing in the sea below. "Having dropped a smoke-float to ascertain the wind direction, we made a deck-landing approach into the wind, passing a few feet above the lifeboat and entering the water twenty yards beyond it. By the time we had struggled, drenched and chilly, into our life raft, the aircraft was almost submerged, with just the tail showing above the surface.

The only other thing visible was the lifeboat, its shape outlined by white, breaking water. We drifted downwind towards it."[8]

After using their flying boots to bail out the water from the lifeboat, the three airmen eventually settled down. It was pleasant to have some measure of protection against the frigid wind, but the motion of the boat in the rough seas made them desperately sick.

The lifeboat had come from a Dutch ship, *Ellusa*. It contained a grim-looking bundle amidships; when the airmen opened it, cautiously, they found not a body but a sail-bag containing a rusty axe and a knife, Very light pistols and cartridges, a lug-sail and a foresail, an incongruous suit of clothes, biscuits, water, and a bottle of 1890 Napoleon brandy. Modestly provisioned, the airmen sailed east, then, because of gales, west. They sighted another lifeboat. It was from a Norwegian coal-burner sunk in convoy two weeks before. The two boats nudged each other. The Norwegians suggested the airmen join forces with them. Jackson declined the offer: "We passed over cigarettes and biscuits and went our different ways, ours westward and theirs into oblivion . . ."[9]

After nine days' sailing, the lifeboat encountered the Icelandic ship *Lagerfoss*. "The sight of her crew as they leapt into our boat to help us aboard was one to remember."

Admiral Tovey was a worried man, with the leaden weight of failure growing heavier in his gut as hour followed hour. For thirty-six nail-biting hours, *Bismarck* seemed to have vanished – a disappearing act aided by inexcusable errors on the part of the British navigators, which at one point led to the Home Fleet sailing *away* from the enemy.

Bismarck was in fact speeding toward the French port of Brest, where there were facilities to repair her. Aboard the German ship, engineer officers worried over the fuel leaking from a holed tank. *Prinz Eugen* had slipped away to the west.

For the British, the thought of the German ship escaping was just too awful to contemplate. She had slaughtered Britain's pride, the mighty *Hood*. The British ship had to be avenged.

At 0200 on May 26, airmen clambered aboard aircraft "Z" of 209 Squadron RAF Coastal Command. The crew was unusual: one of their number wore a U.S. Navy uniform. He was Ensign Leonard "Tuck" Smith, from Higginsville, Missouri, recently "lend-leased" to Britain along with the first batch of Consolidated PBY flying boats, renamed Catalina by the British. Smith had been flying the planes for several years; his unit commander said the RAF needed experienced PBY crewmen to help their crews to learn the idiosyncrasies of the new aircraft. Smith volunteered at once. He was sent to Washington with sixteen other pilots, where the Chief of Naval Operations told them he expected the United States to be at war with Germany sooner or later, probably sooner. It was their duty to learn as much as possible before it happened.

The Catalina flew into a pale, wispy dawn, encountering nothing more interesting than sea and sky. One of the crew made a tasty breakfast of bacon and eggs on the midget stove amidships. Then it was back to the eternal searching, scanning the grey, wind-tossed ocean until tired eyes started to play tricks, turning splashing waves into surfacing U-boats and low clouds into exploding bombs.

Smith was the first to see it. He pointed.

"What's that?"

Briggs, the RAF pilot, stared. It looked like a big ship, but you couldn't trust your own eyes in these conditions. Perhaps it was a whale. He indicated to Smith to go closer. Excitement grew as the ship's outline hardened. Yes, no bloody doubt about it! And if there had been any doubt, *Bismarck* herself would have dispelled it with the hail of flak she sent streaming up in the Catalina's direction. It pattered on the aircraft's hull, punching jagged holes through the thin metal. Smith took violent evasive action, tossing one man out of his bunk and smashing half the aircraft's complement of dishes. *Bismarck* was nearly seven hundred miles from Brest. Neither *King*

George V, sailing 135 miles to the north, nor *Rodney*, 125 miles northeast, had a hope of catching up with her before she reached the haven of Brest.

Luckily, there was an RN force between *Bismarck* and Brest. Commanded by a capable, good-natured admiral named James Somerville, the naval group included Britain's best-known aircraft carrier, *Ark Royal*. Therein lay the last hope of stopping *Bismarck* before she reached France. Somerville was one of the very few RN admirals who had personal experience of flying in Fleet Air Arm aircraft – and the aircrews regarded him highly for that reason.

The gale intensified. It howled over *Ark Royal*'s flight deck at more than fifty miles per hour. The big ship's stern rose and fell some sixty feet. Impossible conditions. But the operation had to take place no matter what.

The first Swordfish took off successfully – a heart-stopping business of lumbering forward at a snail's pace into the teeth of the wind, then bounding into the air as the wind whipped over the Stringbag's ample flying surfaces. For the pilots, it quickly became an aerial balancing act, an exercise in juggling with the controls, now pulling up a drooping wing, now correcting a skid, forcing aileron and rudder to fight the effects of the storm.

Bouncing, bucking, the biplanes made their perilous way across the ocean in search of the German battleship. When the Swordfish navigators saw grainy, trembling green signals on their ASV screens, they concluded, not unnaturally, that they had got a fix on *Bismarck*. After all, hadn't they been told at briefing that there were no other ships in the area? The echoes had to be from the German battleship.

They weren't.

The crew of the British cruiser *Sheffield* watched, aghast, as the Swordfish force dived out of the clouds, all of them approaching from different directions. *Sheffield*'s skipper, Captain Charles Larcom, realized at once what had happened. The Swordfish crews had mistaken *Sheffield* for *Bismarck*, although it said little for their ship identification, since the British cruiser possessed two funnels, the German battleship only one. Larcom coolly ordered the gun crews not to open fire on the approaching aircraft. Several Swordfish dropped torpedoes. About half of them exploded prematurely, an astonishing stroke of luck. The others missed *Sheffield*, thanks to Larcom's splendid handling of his ship.

Chastened, the Swordfish crews headed back to *Ark Royal*. On the way, they received a belated signal: "Look out for *Sheffield*."

Despite the screaming winds and the lurching flight deck, all the Swordfish landed back on *Ark Royal*, bouncing, thumping, slithering to safety. Only one aircraft received serious damage during the hair-raising landing. Its remains went over the side. The flight deck had to be kept open. The crews were safe – safe but shaken. No recriminations awaited them, but they were ordered to prepare for another attack in an hour. This time the torpedoes would be equipped with contact pistols instead of the miserably unreliable magnetic firing pistols.

For the second time that day, the Swordfish crews clambered aboard their aircraft, strapped themselves into their open cockpits, and prepared for the ordeal ahead. None had any illusions about their life expectancy. They had already used up far more than their allotment of blind good luck. They couldn't reasonably expect more.

Crouched against the ferocious wind, trouser legs flapping and snapping, the flight deck crews ranged the Swordfish in preparation for takeoff. Rain and snow showers swept the deck, reducing already poor visibility to virtually nil. Below, deep in the carrier's bowels, worried officers stood over the engine like doctors at the bedside of a desperately sick patient. The lubricating oil had caught fire. Now hoses poured saltwater on the engine casing; cans of oil streamed over the glowing components. *Ark* faced a desperate situation. If the engine problems worsened, it might mean the loss of one engine, thereby eliminating any chance of intercepting the German battleship. In the meantime, the engines had to run at top speed. If they blew themselves up, so be it. The only thing that mattered was to keep chasing *Bismarck*.

Tim Coode regarded the ocean without enthusiasm. Cloud, heavy and grey with rain, hung low, little more than five hundred feet from the turbulent water. Lieutenant-Commander Coode, leader of the Swordfish force, had his instructions. First, locate the cruiser *Sheffield*, which was shadowing *Bismarck*, and obtain the latest information on the German ship's whereabouts. Then attack.

The shadowy form of the cruiser appeared through the mist. The enemy was a dozen miles dead ahead, *Sheffield* reported. So far so good. But the cloud thickened as the Swordfish approached *Bismarck*, layer after layer extending upward for thousands of feet. Coode's original plan had been to lead the formation through the clouds, after which the aircraft would attack from every point of the compass to confuse the ship's gunners. But in these conditions, such an attack was impossible. Each sub-flight would have to attack individually.

Coode approached on *Bismarck*'s port beam, watching numbly as the balls of flak floated up, lazily, unhurriedly – then hurtled by. It was like flying into a storm of multi-coloured hailstones. He heard bullets hitting the wing above him. How long before one hit the fuel tank? Or the engine? Or one of the crew? Coode knew that several Swordfish had taken hits, but so far they still seemed to be flying, heading straight for the gigantic, fire-spitting ship.

The rule of thumb for torpedo drops by Swordfish was: speed, 90 knots; height, 90 feet; distance from target, 900 yards. At training school, it had been difficult enough; it was impossible in this bewildering world of flak and fog, cloud and rain, and encroaching darkness. The only thing to do was grit your teeth, press home your attack, and hope for the best.

The extraordinary luck of the Swordfish held; in spite of the concentrated anti-aircraft fire, not one plane was shot down. But no one reported any hits on the German battleship. It was a bitter disappointment; now it seemed there was nothing to prevent *Bismarck* from reaching safety. The Swordfish returned to *Ark Royal*, and again, incredibly, all aircraft and crews landed, although there were some wounds among the men and a multitude of rips and tears among the aircraft. The hangar crews got to work immediately to repair the damage in case another strike was ordered.

The aircrews were dispirited. Twice they had tried; twice they had failed. A miserable, inexcusable flop. And although several of the airmen thought they *might* have seen eruptions of water near *Bismarck*, no one took them too seriously. In such situations, people saw what they wanted to see.

Or did they? *Sheffield* had reported *Bismarck* was now steering 340 degrees. Heading north. Soon there was confirmation from other vessels. Inexplicably, *Bismarck* had changed course again. Wondering, hardly daring to hope, Tovey ordered *George V* south to intercept her.

The weather continued to deteriorate. As the hours passed, it seemed more and more likely that the German battleship had, in fact, been damaged in her steering mechanism. It was a miraculous bit of news; a tonic for the weary officers and men. Now there might be yet another opportunity to put paid to her. There could be no thought of failure. This time the job had to be done.

A veritable armada of ships was gathering: battleships, cruisers, destroyers, all their crews intent on sinking *Bismarck* and avenging *Hood*. As darkness fell, several destroyers engaged the German battleship. Torpedoes streaked through the black water, leaving bubbling trails of fluorescence. Captain Philip Vian, commander of the destroyer force, claimed a hit, so did Commander Stokes in *Sikh*, whose engine room crew reported hearing an underwater explosion. In fact, none of the torpedoes hit its target.

On *Bismarck*, the confidence of the first few days of the voyage had given way to uneasiness. The work on repairing the ship's steering mechanism wasn't going well. The enemy was gathering in increasing strength. An announcement from the captain, Lindemann, did little to raise the crew's spirits; he told them that the Führer had awarded Commander Schneider, the gunnery commander, the Ritterkreuz for sinking *Hood*. It was less than welcome news; the sailors were all too aware that the number of awards handed out tended to be directly proportional to the hopelessness of the situation. Better news was that U-boats were on the way, plus more than eighty aircraft. Seven Swordfish had been shot down, it was claimed, and one destroyer had been sunk and two others were badly damaged and burning. But the crew members could sense the "smell of death in the air and some began to talk openly about what few dared to think; that with every hour that passed, the gap between themselves and *Rodney* and other enemy battleships was slowly but inevitably closing."[10] Like some viciously contagious disease, the conviction spread through the ship that their odds of coming through this were fast dwindling.

At 0500, the loudspeakers throughout *Bismarck* announced that one of the ship's Arado 196 floatplanes would shortly be flown off, carrying the ship's log and some movie film of the sinking of *Hood*. The pilot and observer clambered aboard, hardly daring to believe their good luck. They were going to escape from this hellish situation.

But they didn't escape. The catapult wouldn't work. The Arado remained obstinately stationary. An inspection of the mechanism revealed the reason: a compressed air pipe had been damaged, presumably during the recent action. It couldn't be repaired. The crew turned the Arado's engine off and climbed out; ratings pushed on the wings, and the aircraft ran along the catapult track and tumbled into the sea.

The first glimmers of the new day, writes Ludovic Kennedy, revealed *Bismarck* "wallowing in the unrelenting seas, like a great, wounded, sullen bull. The *picadors* had done their work, thrust their darts deep into flank and shoulders, taken half her power from her. Now she waited for the arrival of the *torero*, for the last trial of strength, whose result was a foregone conclusion. But if she had to die, as bulls did, then she would die bravely and with dignity, that too was determined."[11]

Shortly after 8:00 A.M., the British cruiser *Norfolk* appeared on the port bow, followed a little later by two battleships, *King George V* and *Rodney*. The executioners were assembling.

At precisely 0843 it began, with a salvo from *Rodney*. Then *King George V* opened up. *Bismarck* replied. The salvo fell short, ripping the sea into angry blossomings of water. *Norfolk*'s 8-inch guns joined in, followed quickly by those of the cruiser *Dorsetshire*. The British were now scoring repeated hits on the German vessel. Fires raged on her deck. More shells hit her, and clearly she was doomed. The fact sparked little joy among the British sailors. The scene possessed an infinitely sad quality. The brave ship staggered as more shells thudded into her. The carnage among the crew was ghastly. Men were cut in half by the explosions; shrapnel removed limbs with surgical precision; flames consumed wounded men, whose arms and legs twitched as they were immolated. Many men aboard *Bismarck* simply sat waiting for the end, eyes dulled, resigned to the inevitable.

At about ten, *Bismarck*'s senior surviving officer, Commander Oels, ordered that scuttling charges be placed in position. The end was near. By now, crewmen were jumping into the chilly water, desperate to escape the merciless shelling. A Swordfish from *Ark Royal* droned overhead. The pilot, Kenneth Pattisson, seeing "hundreds of heads bobbing in the water, like turnips in a field of sheep, regretted that he had no dinghy to drop to them, waved in a friendly useless gesture; as he turned away he observed smoke pouring out of *Bismarck*'s decks, smelt her burning, described her main gunnery control as a torch of fire."[12]

The cruiser *Dorsetshire* stopped nearby, and by the score the men in the water splashed their frantic way through the oil and debris to get to her. Numbed fingers clawed at the cruiser's lifelines. Unable to hold on, many fell back into the sea. Others, luckier than their comrades, felt the sturdy arms of British sailors grasping them, dragging them bodily on to the ship.

Then, aghast, the Germans became aware that the cruiser was moving, picking up speed with every yard. Survivors clinging to lifelines, who a few seconds earlier had been thanking their lucky stars for being plucked from the sea, now suddenly found themselves tumbling back into the bone-numbing water. They bellowed with fear and with anger.

Dorsetshire's officers had little choice but to abandon the desperate men. A U-boat had been sighted – at least that's what had been reported. The Admiralty had just sent a signal warning of U-boats, which may have helped foster the thought, but in this place at this time, it was infinitely better to be safe than sorry.

Bismarck slowly rolled over, as if too weary to remain upright. Men crawled over the massive hull like insects, looking in vain for a means of escape. They slithered, scrambling, then fell into the sea.

When *Bismarck* sank, many in the water went down too, dragged to the bottom by the immensely powerful suction. The rest were left struggling in the water.

The battle was over. *Hood* had been avenged. The British publicized it as a great victory – but it wasn't. Churchill declared that the navy had exhibited a dismal lack of offensive spirit. He wanted to court-martial two of the senior officers involved, though cooler heads prevailed, pointing out how damaging to British morale such a trial would be.

The action sparked more controversy among the advocates of big battleships and aircraft carriers. The battleship supporters made much of the fact that only other battleships had been able to sink the mightiest example of them all. Although effectively destroyed *Bismarck* had not in fact been sunk by battleships. They had poured fire into her, hit her with everything they had – even, according to some reports, threatened aircraft in the vicinity in case they dared come near and try to take the prize from the big guns – but still, stubbornly, she remained afloat. In the end, her crew had scuttled her.

The real lesson of the campaign against the *Bismarck* was that aircraft had become a vital element in naval warfare, and that admirals who refused to accept the truth were doomed. Spitfires had spotted the enemy; a Maryland had confirmed that the battleship was on its way into the Atlantic. A Catalina had located her. Carrier-based Swordfish had crippled her steering mechanism. How would the battle have gone had the Germans possessed their own aircraft carrier?

5

NEW APPROACHES

"Greater than the tread of mighty armies is an idea whose time has come"
— Victor Hugo

ON THE DAY *Bismarck* was sunk, a freighter named *Michael E.* sailed into the Atlantic. At first glance it appeared to be just another freighter — but it wasn't. An unusual track had been built on the ship's forecastle. Seventy feet in length, it carried a Hurricane fighter, perched up high like a lonely eagle. *Michael E.* was in fact the first example of the CAM (Catapult Aircraft Merchant) ship, a novel though alarming idea introduced to combat the German Condors, Churchill's "scourge of the sea." The Hurricane fighters destined for use on CAM-ships were old, worn-out aircraft, many of them veterans of the Battle of Britain. Some claim Winston Churchill thought up the idea. Others say that it was Captain M. S. Slattery, the Naval Director of Air Materiel. The only suitable weapon to counter a Condor, he claimed, was a fighter aircraft. Given that there weren't enough aircraft carriers to provide fighters for every convoy, why not have the merchant ships carry the fighters? The idea, while interesting, had one serious disadvantage:

the fighter couldn't land back on its parent ship after its mission. If it was close enough to land on shore (a rare situation), it did so, otherwise, it ditched. What happened to the pilot? He had two choices: bail out or take his chances with his aircraft.

The notion was swiftly taken up, a measure of the desperation of the time. Designers at Hawker said they could modify the Hurricane for use on catapults. A prototype would be ready in five weeks. Fifty catapult kits were procured. Minor modifications to the Hurricane included a "cradle" to position the aircraft on the catapult, as well as an extra-thick pilot's headrest. The vessels selected to become CAM-ships ranged in tonnage from 2,500 to 12,000 tons. Conversion work began immediately at Liverpool, Bristol, Cardiff, and Clydeside. The ships would carry their normal cargoes and would be sailed by Merchant Navy crews and fly the Red Ensign. The pilots would come from the Fleet Air Arm and RAF Fighter Command. *Michael E.*'s pilot was a Fleet Air Arm man, Sub-Lieutenant M. A. Birrell. He never got a chance to fly his Hurricane (more properly, his Sea-Hurricane 1A). On the fourth day of the voyage, a U-boat attacked *Michael E.* and sank her. The survivors, including Birrell, spent twenty hours in the ship's lifeboats before being rescued.

Some merchant skippers resented the presence of the casual young aviators and their maintenance crews. Quite apart from the disruption they caused in the normal smooth running of the ship, they could be viewed as yet another danger in an increasingly unsafe profession. Any U-boat commander, sizing up a convoy and spotting a CAM-ship in the ranks, would have little trouble selecting his target.

On some ships, relations between the Merchant Navy and the MSFUs (Merchant Ship Fighter Units) were excellent; on others, deplorable. It depended upon the individuals involved. In general, the merchant crews thought the RAF/Fleet Air Arm personnel snobbish and possessed of ludicrously weak stomachs; most became violently seasick in the boisterous Atlantic. In some cases, the accommodation provided for the MSFU personnel was substandard – purposely poor, in their opinion, so that they would be encouraged to move on as rapidly as possible and leave the ships to their own business. More serious was the effect of spray and salt upon the Sea-Hurricanes, poised high on the catapults. The conditions necessitated far more work on the aircraft than was normal on airfields, but routine inspections could be dangerous for maintenance crews. The catapult mechanism itself was usually slippery with grease and oil, and the violent pitching of the ship in bad weather could demand the dexterity of squirrels from airframe and engine mechanics accustomed to solid, stationary ladders and metal scaffolding. A salty scum would begin to form on the Sea-Hurricanes within an hour or two of leaving on a voyage. If rough weather was encountered, the scum formed even more rapidly. Gun barrels began to rust inside, although leather covers, specially designed for the job, were soon procured to protect them. The recoiling parts had to be stripped and greased daily. "Dampness caused earths in the firing circuits. Corrosion from salt spray could put trolley wheels out of action, gun wells, breech blocks and barrels, IFF switches, sparking plugs, contact breakers and any part of the electrical system. Dope peeled off everywhere, throttles jammed. 'Very rough sea,' one report ran, 'and 65 mph gale resulted in A/C [aircraft] getting soaked in sea water continuously for four days. Covers were ripped off, airframe corroded, engine mags and all electrical gear setting up currents.' Rough weather could snap aircraft lashings, make bracing wires too slack or too taut, fill the fuselage with water, distort the airframe."[1]

The wonder is that the "catafighters," as they became known, were seldom unserviceable, a tribute to their tireless maintenance crews. Launching the aircraft involved an unvarying routine. First, the raising of the "Aeroplane Flag" (the "F" flag in International Code, a red diamond on a white background). Then, when the pilot was strapped in, the R/T link between him and the FDO (Fighter Direction Officer, usually Fleet Air Arm) was tested, as

were the rockets that propelled the Sea-Hurricane along the catapult track and off into the blue. When the front locking bolt pins
were removed, they were taken to the CDO (Catapult Direction
Officer) with the report, "Catapult ready for firing." By this time,
the Hurricat's Merlin engine was creating a deafening cacophony.
The CDO raised his blue Flying Flag, visible to the master on the
bridge, the pilot in his cockpit, and the rest of the team. The master
raised his own blue flag, which meant, "Launch as soon as ready."

The pilot opened his throttle wide and locked it, pressed
himself firmly against the seat back and headrest, and raised his
hand, the signal that he too was ready. The CDO now had to choose
the moment of launch, a tricky business in rough conditions when
the ship's bow might be rising and falling twenty feet or more. At
what he judged to be the right moment, the CDO pressed the
button igniting the rockets. The bang could be heard even over the
racket of the fighter's Merlin engine. A *whoosh* of flame darted
back from the rocket battery. The fighter tore away down the track
and in a matter of two or three seconds was airborne on its last
flight. There was about two hours' fuel in the tanks.

As far as the official records were concerned, the pilots were
third mates on their respective ships – though their pay and
benefits continued to be on naval or RAF terms. One of the main
problems for the pilots was to keep occupied and keen. At sea, they
had very little to do except wait for something to happen; all were
aware of the fact that they might have to go weeks without flying,
then, in a matter of minutes, be airborne in pursuit of a heavily
armed Condor, engaged in a fight that required every ounce of
skill they possessed. Some volunteered for watches and other duties
on their ships. Others learned to play the saxophone or read the
classics they had been promising to get to for years.

The first action involving a CAM-ship took place on August 3,
1941. On her way to meet a convoy from Sierra Leone, the eight-
thousand-ton merchantman *Maplin* carried two Sea-Hurricanes
(one on the catapult, one stored forward) and three pilots. In the

early afternoon, a big, four-engined aircraft appeared. As it drew nearer, the sailors and airmen recognized it as a Condor. It kept its distance. Obviously a shadower, the sailors told themselves, probably sending reports to U-boats at that very minute. When the Condor eventually headed back in the direction of Bordeaux, a second appeared to take its place. Now was the time to launch. At the Hurricane's controls sat the Australian Bob Everett, a well-known steeplechase rider in prewar days. For the benefit of crew and accompanying ships, the Flying Flag now fluttered. The launch was imminent. The Sea-Hurricane's Merlin engine, already warmed up, started at the first punch of the button. The captain edged the ship around until she faced into wind. In his cockpit, Everett pressed his head firmly against the well padded rest. He ran the engine up and tightened the throttle nut. The aircraft vibrated, tugging like a frustrated animal at the catapult cradle. Now all it needed was the firing of the rockets to break free. The CDO began his count: One . . . two . . . three!

Everett braced himself. Dimly over the engine's din, he heard the bang of the rockets detonating. A giant hand seemed to grab him and thrust him further into his seat. Hard. An instinctive moment of alarm . . . then it was done. He was flying! The ship dropped away beneath him. The sea, choppy and grey, tilted to one side as he turned. It stretched away to infinity. Winding up his flaps, he banked to port and approached the big German aircraft, excitement pulsing through every vein. This was it! Oddly enough, despite the smoke and flashes of the catapult launch, the Condor's crew had apparently failed to notice the Hurricane climbing to attack. Everett smiled to himself. He was going to get this one; he had a feeling.

He was able to fly to within a mile and a half of the Condor before the German aircrew became aware of his presence. Then they acted quickly, swinging to port and opening fire. Everett saw the sparkling shots sliding innocuously below. As he drew level with the big aircraft, he saw the dorsal gunner open fire. Again, the shots went wide, darting away over the misty sea. Everett decided on a beam attack, aiming at the Germans' cockpit. The Hurricane had very little speed advantage over the Condor, and it was no easy matter for Everett to get into the right position to attack. Now on the enemy's starboard bow, he took fire from two more gunners, but nothing hit him. He banked away, turning again, swinging around to the rear of the German aircraft, firing short bursts. A hit! He saw bits of the Condor break away and the flicker of flame within the fuselage. At the same moment, the rattle of the Brownings ended in an impotent hiss of compressed air. Everett had run out of ammunition. A moment later, oil splashed over his windscreen. He called *Maplin*, reporting that his target was alight. The fire appeared to be spreading. With any luck, the Condor would soon be in the drink.

For Everett, the world had shrunk to minuscule proportions; it consisted of him and the Condor. Nothing else. The big aircraft turned away, leaving a trail of smoke. It turned again, then its shapely nose abruptly snapped down and it went careering into the water with a great explosion of spray, disappearing from sight, leaving no sign of wreckage. As far as Everett could see, not one of the seven-man crew escaped. He circled over the spot, but there were no dinghies, no figures trying to swim in the rough water. He told the ship what had happened. The ship acknowledged the signal, congratulating him on his success and wishing him good luck.

What the wireless operator meant, Everett knew, was, Try not to kill yourself when you come down. A laudable sentiment, one with which he had no argument. The questions remained: should he attempt to ditch the Hurricane close to a friendly ship, or should he bail out and hope that the same friendly ship would be able to pluck him from the ocean? He preferred the idea of bailing out, but it proved trickier than he had anticipated. The aircraft didn't want to let him go. Twice he tried to jump; twice the Hurricane angled down, trapping him in his cockpit. Everett decided to ditch after all. He remembered what the other MSFU pilots had said about ditching a Hurricane, and about the likelihood – more properly, the virtual inevitability – of the radiator beneath the fighter's belly acting as a scoop and sending the Hurricane head over heels into the sea, with the open cockpit canopy slamming forward and jamming. He knew that the only solution to the problem would be to stall the fighter just above the water so that it made contact at the lowest possible speed.

He began his approach. The airspeed indicator needle trembled as it fell. It seemed to know that Everett was on the perilous brink of a stall. He could feel the controls becoming spongy. The water blurred beneath him, just a few short feet away. He kept raising the nose to stretch out the approach, shaving off a few miles per hour with every movement of the stick. Tail well down. Nose angled nicely. The sea was like an endless highway below him. Now the Hurricane wanted to swing away to the left. He caught it, made it go straight. The tail wheel struck first. It snapped the nose down and the fighter hit the sea, coming to a soggy halt immediately. It felt as if he had flown into solid ground. Dazed, he heard the Hurricane's structure crumpling around him. But he was alive. And conscious. And in imminent danger of being drowned. He released his harness and clambered out of the cockpit and into the dinghy automatically released from the wing. A whaler from the destroyer *Wanderer* came into view as the Hurricane went down. In a few minutes he was aboard *Wanderer*, shaking hands, grinning, revelling in being alive.*

The CAM-ship fighter pilots (usually two to a ship, working twelve-hour shifts) were given remarkably little training in the difficult business of bringing their aircraft safely down in the sea. The reason was simple: there was no one to teach them. It was, in fact,

---

* Everett won a DSO for his victory over the Condor. He lost his life a few months later in a crash during a ferry flight.

more a matter of luck than judgement. Flaps down, nose up, the pilots were told, and try to put her down along a swell rather than at right angles to one. It was sensible advice, but it didn't prevent a number of fatalities. Sometimes the impact of the landing knocked the pilot unconscious; sometimes the Hurricane went down like a stone, taking the pilot with it. Pilots were required to pack their own parachutes and dinghies. After a few plunges into swimming pools in flying kit, they were considered ready to face a singularly uncertain future at sea.

Thirty-five merchantmen became CAM-ships. They proved moderately successful in action, shooting down seven Condors, with dozens more being scared away. While CAM-ships couldn't win the Battle of the Atlantic, they became a useful tool at a critical time, a stopgap until the introduction of a more effective idea, the Merchant Aircraft Carrier, otherwise known as the MAC-ship.

The first MAC-ship started life as a German vessel, *Hannover*, a merchantman of eight thousand tons, captured early in 1940. In a shipyard, she underwent a transformation; her superstructure was cut away, to be replaced by a flat steel deck some four hundred feet long. Renamed *Empire Audacity*, she was no beauty. Utilitarian in every respect, she looked as if she had been cobbled together from spare parts − which, in a way, she had. Pilots accustomed to fleet carriers were dismayed by the postage-stamp flight decks, and pictured horrific scenes of Sea-Hurricanes running off the ship after a "go-around" and plunging into the ocean.

Empire Audacity was completed in June 1941. She went to sea carrying a few Swordfish and six fighters, not the Sea-Hurricanes originally envisaged, but Grumman Martlets (later renamed Wildcats) instead. The American-built fighter had a similar performance to the Hurricane, but was notably tougher; not for nothing was the Grumman company, the principal supplier of fighters to the U.S. Navy, known as the Grumman Iron Works. While the Hurricane carried eight machine guns, they were of .303-inch calibre. The Wildcat carried six .50-inch guns (later cut to four to enhance the aircraft's performance). Although the Wildcat's landing gear was narrow, it was exceptionally muscular, and regularly shrugged off heavy-landing shocks that would have demolished lesser gear. Aircraft on the first MAC-ships had to be rugged. They spent most of their working lives on deck, lashed down, battered by ferocious gales and regularly drenched in saltwater.*

∾

Fritz-Julius Lemp, who had achieved worldwide notoriety when he sank the passenger ship *Athenia* on the first day of the war with Britain and France, lost his life at about this time. He had been on patrol for three weeks and had sunk one freighter. Now, south of Iceland, on the morning of May 9, 1941, he rendezvoused with U201, commanded by Adalbert Schnee. A sizable convoy of about forty ships sailed nearby.

Communicating by signal flags, the two U-boats agreed to attack, submerged, in daylight. Lemp, the senior, went first. He sank two freighters, *Esmond* and *Bengore Head*. Schnee attacked thirty minutes later and sank another freighter, *Gregalia*. After this promising beginning, Lemp and Schnee had the misfortune to run into one of the new escort groups organized to protect convoys against U-boats. This group consisted of nine vessels, including the British destroyer *Bulldog*, the flagship. *Bulldog* immediately attacked Lemp's U110 in company with an elderly ex-U.S. Navy destroyer, *Broadway*, and a corvette, *Aubrietia*. Depth charges exploded all around U110, wrecking instruments and controls, and causing serious, potentially fatal flooding. The ballast tanks blew, sending the crippled sub to the surface. Scrambling up to the conning

---

* All servicing had to be done on deck, since the ships had no hangars. Later MAC-ships and the superior escort carriers incorporated some hangar space, which made life easier for the fitters, riggers, electricians, and other maintenance personnel. *Empire Audacity*'s deck had only two arrester wires to bring aircraft to a halt after landing, compared with half a dozen on the average fleet carrier.

tower, Lemp stared in wide-eyed horror at the British destroyers heading straight for his boat, guns ablaze, clearly intending to ram. Lemp didn't hesitate. He gave the order to abandon ship, instructing his engineering officer to open the ballast tank vents. For some reason, perhaps the overwhelming demands of self-preservation, the order was never carried out. The vents remained closed, although no one realized it at the time. Compounding the problem, the radio man forgot about the top-secret coding device known as Enigma and associated code information. Both were his responsibility: to rescue or to destroy. He did neither. There is some evidence to suggest that Lemp knew of the radio man's failure and that he attempted to swim back to the sub to make sure that the data would not fall into the enemy's hands. But the crippled U110 had drifted too far; Lemp couldn't reach it. Besides, a boarding party from *Bulldog* was at that moment heading for U110. Some U-boat veterans claim that the British shot Lemp as he struggled in the water, others say that he threw up his arms and disappeared beneath the swirling surface, a suicide aware of the shame he had brought on his name.

A boarding party, under the command of a remarkably gallant twenty-year-old RN sub-lieutenant named David Balme, jumped from their tender to the deck of the U-boat. Firearms at the ready, the sailors spread around the deck, ready to shoot any German who might attempt to interfere. To their astonishment, they found the U-boat deserted, with all lights burning brightly. Balme was keenly aware that the sub might have been packed with explosives and that a timing device might be ticking away the last few seconds before it all went up. But he didn't hesitate. Taking half a dozen men with him, he went below and proceeded to ransack the vessel of any charts, manuals, and equipment that looked useful. The sailors formed a human chain to convey the items up to the deck. Balme found the Enigma equipment plugged in, apparently in use when the crew had abandoned ship. Unfamiliar with the device, Balme thought at first that it was some form of typewriter; but it looked as if it might be important, so he sent it up the hatch to be taken off.

Addison Baker-Cresswell, commander of *Bulldog*, attempted to tow U110 to Iceland, but after about a hundred miles, the submarine's stern suddenly sank; her bow rose dripping out of the water. She paused, upended, her bow vertical as if taking one final look around. A moment later, she disappeared into the depths. U110 was lost but her treasure trove of secrets was safe, including the working naval (as distinct from Luftwaffe or army) Enigma, code books of incalculable value, charts, and technical books and diagrams on an extraordinary range of subjects. During the investiture at which awards galore were handed out to the participants, including Balme, who got the DSC, and Baker-Cresswell, who got the DSO, King George VI remarked that the operation was probably the single most important event in the war at sea.

The German public was told that Lemp had died a hero's death, but surviving U-boat men were bitterly critical of him for allowing an Enigma machine to fall into enemy hands.

The device that Balme had captured was a vastly more complex version of an enciphering machine developed in the 1920s to "scramble" text for business communications. The "unscrambling" could only be accomplished by another Enigma. The system depended on a vast array of settings determined by notched wheels and rotors. The invention of a Dutchman, Hugo Koch, the Enigma concept proved difficult to sell on the commercial market. Koch eventually had to transfer the patents to a German, Artur Scherbius, who went ahead with the construction of a prototype. He exhibited it at the 1923 Congress of the International Postal Union. A brochure described the benefits of the machine in terms the Nazis would have understood: "The natural inquisitiveness of competitors is at once checkmated by a machine which enables you to keep all your documents, or at least their important parts, entirely secret without occasioning any expense worth mentioning. One secret, well protected, may pay the whole cost of the machine."[2]

Scherbius had no more commercial success than Koch. But by now, political developments determined Enigma's future. Hitler had just come to power. Soon, it was announced that the Wehrmacht had taken up the machine, rating it sturdy and simple to operate and service. If captured, it could not be operated without knowledge of the keying procedures. The Germans bought several more Enigma machines and modified them, adding enormously to the number of alternatives for each letter in a communication. The Germans were positive that Enigma was impossible to break. Hitler trusted it implicitly, and before long, it was in general use throughout the armed forces of Germany.

Their confidence was, perhaps, somewhat misplaced. Major Harold Lehrs Gibson of MI6 reported from Prague at about this time that two Polish mathematicians had made considerable progress in deciphering Enigma's transmissions, or at least those of the commercial version. Gibson's report excited much interest in British cryptanalytical circles, and later the French succeeded in penetrating the military model, with the help of a traitor, dubbed "Source D," an officer of the Reich's principal cryptanalytical bureau, who made himself known to the French Embassy at Berne in the summer of 1937. Source D produced a secret instruction manual and various helpful documents. These were copied and returned, with payment. The French produced an Enigma replica.

The following year, Major Gibson, the British intelligence man in Prague, had another sensational report: a Pole calling himself Lewinski was offering more intimate knowledge of Enigma. The price: ten thousand pounds, plus a British passport and French visas for himself and his wife. Lewinski, an engineer and mathematician, claimed to have worked on Enigma for the Germans. British Intelligence sent two men to Warsaw to interview him. They were Alfred Dilwyn Knox, Britain's leading cryptanalyst, and a rumpled mathematical genius named Alan Mathison Turing. They met Lewinski at the Madame Curie Museum in Warsaw, and it was soon apparent that the Pole possessed detailed knowledge of

Enigma. The British arranged for Lewinski and his wife to move to Paris. There, comfortably ensconced in a Left Bank flat, Lewinski set to work to reproduce Enigma. He did an excellent job; the model he produced was about twenty-four inches square and some eighteen inches high, contained in a simple wooden box connected to two electric typewriters. The transfer of a plain-language signal to cipher text presented few problems. Armed with the book of keys, the operator selected the key for the time of day, the day of the month, the month of the quarter, and typed out the message on the left-hand typewriter. The machine enciphered the message and typed it out on the right-hand typewriter. The recipient – as long as he possessed the relevant keying information – simply reversed the process to obtain the original message.

Bletchley Park, some fifty miles northwest of London, was the world's first centre for the breaking of machine-enciphered messages. In 1939 (when it was known as the British Government Code and Cipher School), its staff numbered some 150; by the end of 1942 about 3,500 people worked there; by war's end, the complement had soared to 10,000. The sprawling Victorian mansion was soon augmented by dozens of small wooden huts plopped down all over the extensive grounds. Hut 3 accommodated what was known as "The Bomb," a forerunner of the modern computer, a vastly complex apparatus created for the sole purpose of matching the electrical circuits of Enigma to facilitate decryption. "Its initial performance was uncertain," writes Anthony Cave Brown, "and its sound was strange; it made a noise like a battery of knitting needles as it worked to produce the German keys. But with adjustments, its performance improved and it began to penetrate Enigma at about the same time as the Germans prepared to attack Poland."[3]

The curious thing is that the Poles seemed to have had absolutely no foreknowledge of the attack, despite the ability of British intelligence to read the Germans' secret ciphers. But failure to act upon intelligence is common in war. When the Germans burst through the borders of France, Belgium, and the Netherlands, they achieved total tactical surprise, yet scores of Enigma messages had warned of the forthcoming invasion. The same sort of failure was apparent in Norway and later in the Soviet Union. Overall, perhaps, it may have been just as well; such failures only reinforced the Germans' complacent belief in the inviolability of the Enigma system.

In May 1940, it became imperative to evacuate Lewinski and his wife from France, and MI6 flew into Orly, near Paris, to transport them to London.

After which the Polish couple disappeared. The rumour mill placed them in Australia or Canada, but no official word has ever been forthcoming.

In February 1941, during a commando raid on the Lofoten Islands in Norway, a British destroyer, *Somali*, fought off a determined attack by a diminutive German trawler. Eventually, the destroyer sent the smaller vessel out of control onto the beach. The destroyer's signals officer went aboard the wreck. He found the Enigma keys for that month as well as several rotors. It was treasure beyond price for the boffins at Bletchley. Now they could read current messages without wasting time trying to determine what keys had been used. They could also read older messages; it was a unique opportunity to check their work.

"Ultra" was the name given to highly secret intelligence produced by the decryption of signals enciphered in Enigma machines – including a great variety of signals pertaining to the Battle of the Atlantic. The pursuit and destruction of the German battleship *Bismarck* might never have taken place without the efforts of Alfred Dilwyn Knox and Alan Mathison Turing, who had first investigated Enigma. By early 1941, the brilliant Knox was fighting a hopeless battle against cancer. Unable to make the journey to work at Bletchley Park, he stayed in bed at his home at Hughenden in the Thames Valley. There he did much of the decryption involved in the battle with *Bismarck*. Making the task particularly difficult was the Germans' use of a special battleship cipher. "Although he failed to crack the cipher (which was not cracked by any other agency either), he did manage to unbutton Luftwaffe and diplomatic orders associated with *Bismarck*'s sortie," writes Anthony Cave Brown. "It was these orders that revealed *Bismarck*'s position on the night of May 26/27, 1941, after she had escaped her shadowing cruisers and her location was unknown to the Admiralty."[4]

Knox's ill health became a matter of national importance. Churchill offered to make a destroyer available to transport Mrs. Knox and her husband to the warmth of the Caribbean – at a time when destroyers were worth their weight in gold to the British. It was all in vain; Knox couldn't be moved. Churchill then asked his personal physician, Lord Moran, to arrange for special medical treatment. But Knox died on February 27, 1943. His passing went unreported in the press. It had to; it was the price of being involved with Ultra.

The eccentric Turing took over Knox's job as the Battle of the Atlantic approached its climax. The pressure of the job seemed to crush the last reserves of nervous energy in the man. He became progressively more eccentric, mumbling for hours at a time in his room at the Crown Inn, Shenley Brooke End. He never had a haircut; he let his clothes become dirty, transforming himself into the archetypical eccentric professor.

6

AMERICA MOVES CLOSER TO WAR

"The condition of man . . . is a condition of war of everyone against everyone"
– Thomas Hobbes

A FUNDAMENTAL CHANGE had taken place in the Nazi attitude to the naval war. The humiliating loss of *Bismarck* and the abysmal failure of the battle cruisers *Scharnhorst* and *Gneisenau* to wreck the Allied Atlantic supply system destroyed the last vestiges of Hitler's faith in big surface ships. As far as he was concerned, the U-boat was the only naval weapon that had demonstrated war-winning potential. Thus, Dönitz's status in the Third Reich began to increase – as Raeder's declined. Of even greater importance, America moved a step closer to war. For months, President Franklin Roosevelt, now in an unprecedented third term in office, had been sending encouraging messages to Prime Minister Winston Churchill, much to the annoyance of some members of the British Cabinet, who wanted greater control over the transatlantic exchanges. The big worry was the U.S. ambassador to the Court of St. James, Joseph Kennedy. An ambitious man of notoriously malleable morals, Kennedy made little attempt to hide his dislike of the British; he was confident that Britain would soon go down to defeat. It was hardly surprising, then, that the Cabinet wanted to keep Kennedy from seeing as much of the important transatlantic traffic as possible – no easy job, considering Kennedy's position.

Churchill kept telling the U.S. president that America would inevitably find itself at war with Germany. Roosevelt was of the same mind, but kept his thoughts to himself. Churchill often claimed that Roosevelt said his intention was to wage war but not declare it. In the summer of 1941, Roosevelt found circumstances outmanoeuvring him when a U-boat, U652, fired a torpedo at the U.S. destroyer *Greer*, an elderly four-stacker similar to the famous fifty transferred to the RN the previous year. The reason for the attack by the twenty-four-year-old commander, George Werner Fraatz, appears to have been that a Hudson from 269 Squadron of RAF Coastal Command had spotted the sub but had been unable to attack before the submarine crash-dived. Ten miles to the south, *Greer* was en route to Iceland with mail and supplies for the American forces there. The Hudson informed *Greer* of the U-boat's presence. At that uncertain period of the war, the American skipper, Laurence H. Frost, was authorized to defend his ship but not to mount an unprovoked attack on any German vessel. Possibly Frost saw the encounter as a good way to train his crew. He may have intended to maintain contact with the U-boat until the British arrived; then again, the U-boat commander may have identified *Greer* as one of the fifty four-stackers supplied to Britain. In any event, Fraatz fired a torpedo at her, the first attack by a U-boat on an American warship. That torpedo missed *Greer*, and so did a second. Now the American ship went on the offensive, dropping depth charges near U652, but causing no serious damage. Admiral Ernest King, the U.S. Atlantic Fleet Commander, was angered by Frost's failure to pursue the U-boat more aggressively, and, equally, his failure to call in additional ASW (anti-submarine warfare) forces.

But Roosevelt was pleased. The incident gave him a perfect

opportunity to complain of the German outrages. Unprovoked piracy, he called it. Soon U.S. ships sailed under a new "shoot on sight" policy, enabling them to defend themselves against any Axis submarine that threatened the freedom of the seas. In one of his famous "Fireside Chat" radio broadcasts, Roosevelt pointed out in his winning way that you don't wait until a rattlesnake has bitten you before you crush him.

The *Greer* incident occurred at a convenient time for Roosevelt. The U.S. Navy was preparing to escort its first fast convoy, Halifax 150, from Canada to Iceland. Righteous indignation was an effective way to counter any criticism that might be brewing in Congress or elsewhere.

The world continued to become increasingly dangerous. In late June, Germany shook the world by invading the Soviet Union, in direct violation of the infamous 1939 non-aggression pact between Hitler and Joseph Stalin. The onslaught was of staggering proportions, involving 3.6 million Axis troops, 3,500 tanks, and 2,700 aircraft. Facing the Germans, the Soviet forces had about three million men with ten to fifteen thousand tanks and about eight thousand aircraft, although few were a match for those of the Luftwaffe. Eventually, nearly ten million troops were involved in one of the titanic campaigns of the war.

Initially, it appeared that nothing could stop the Germans, and most experts expected the battle to be short-lived. The Germans advanced at a furious rate, taking enormous numbers of prisoners. Soon the Soviet troops recovered from their shock and began to display the dogged spirit of invincibility that their allies came to admire so much. They shook the Wehrmacht with a series of counterattacks that quickly grew in strength, defying the prognostications of the experts who had already written off the U.S.S.R. Britain's cryptographers at Bletchley Park contributed mightily by breaking the Enigma key used by the Germans on the Eastern Front – although the information presented to Stalin was in disguised form to conceal and protect its source. Becoming allies did little to pierce the veil of suspicion over every aspect of relations between east and west.

Soon Britain was sending sizable quantities of aid, a huge additional burden for the available merchant shipping. The first Russia-bound convoy left Britain in August 1941. At first, losses in the convoys were not particularly serious, but heavy weather and, later, ferocious cold, as well as persistent attacks by German U-boats and aircraft, inflicted crippling losses on the Allied convoys. While Allied sailors seemed willing to accept the considerable risks of the Arctic convoys to assist a gallant ally, they were disappointed and mystified by the cool reception they received in the Soviet Union. But if the Russians were generally hostile and suspicious, so was the West. Indeed, on the day of the invasion, Churchill had broadcast: "No one has been a more consistent opponent of Communism for the last twenty-five years. I will unsay no word I have spoken about it. But all this fades away before the spectacle which is now unfolding."

The German–Soviet war cost the lives of some ten million Soviet servicemen and women; about three million Germans died in the conflict, representing approximately three-quarters of the Third Reich's fatal casualties.

In August 1941, Bletchley Park broke the Germans' naval Enigma. It was a triumph. Now virtually all instructions to U-boats could be read by the British. But such intelligence had to be handled with care; if U-boats were intercepted and sunk in large numbers, Dönitz would realize that his code had been broken and he would quickly organize a totally new system. For the moment, then, the plan was simply to keep convoys out of trouble as much as possible by rerouting them clear of the U-boats. At the same time, the Admiralty decided to capture or destroy the supply ships that provided the U-boats with fuel. The first to be attacked was the 10,000-ton tanker *Belchen*. The cruisers *Aurora* and *Kenya* hit her while she was refuelling U93. The tanker sank, but U93 escaped. Later in the day U93 rescued fifty survivors from *Belchen* and took them to Lorient. Four other supply ships were attacked, including the 9,000-ton tanker *Gedania*, captured by the destroyer *Marsdale* after a pitched battle on the tanker's deck. The German vessel yielded a remarkable number of top-secret documents. So did the weather-reporting trawler *Lauenburg* when captured by a boarding party from the destroyer *Tartar*.

From mid 1941 to the end of the year, U-boat crews found remarkably little action in the North Atlantic. Dönitz logged the lull in traffic as "striking." He directed Wilhelm Kleinschmidt in U111 to patrol the ice pack area off Newfoundland. Possibly, he reasoned, the British were sending their convoys far to the north. Kleinschmidt had little luck. A few days later, U203 encountered a convoy four hundred miles south of Greenland. Dönitz, delighted by the prospect of easy pickings after such a drought, ordered the sub to shadow the convoy while other U-boats were brought in. The convoy, consisting of forty-nine ships and known as Halifax 133, was one of the first to be provided with escorts for the entire voyage, and was known as a "clear across" convoy. A recently formed Canadian escort group was to take the convoy to 35 degrees west; a British escort group based in Iceland was then to shepherd the ships to 20 degrees west. For two days, U203 shadowed the convoy, while other U-boats made a beeline for the ships like sharks scenting blood. U203 sank a Norwegian freighter, then U371 sank another Norwegian freighter, *Vigrid*.

The Canadian escort group hardly covered itself with glory in the encounter, dropping dozens of depth charges to no avail, and failing to communicate efficiently. The Canadians, though eager, had received insufficient training for their demanding job. Moreover, most of their ships had no radar or, at best, had equipment inferior to that in British escort ships. U556, under the command of Ritterkreuz-holder Herbert Wohlfarth, attacked the convoy in

the early hours of June 27. A British corvette, *Nasturtium*, picked up
the sub on her sonar and fired off depth charges. Two more British
corvettes, *Celandine* and *Gladiolus*, joined in but couldn't obtain
echoes. Had the original contact been simply wishful thinking?

Nasturtium was adamant that the first Asdic contact had been of
excellent quality. Then *Gladiolus* announced a contact.

Depth charges churned the sea into a frenzy. A large patch of
oil appeared. Although encouraging, this was by no means proof of
a kill. When under attack, the Germans often released oil, hoping
that the attackers would think they had scored a kill and go on their
way. The British corvettes didn't fall for it. U556 was in serious
trouble. Flooding had damaged the boat's controls. Wohlfarth
decided that his only means of escape lay in surfacing and attacking the corvettes, hoping to slip away in the confusion. He blew
tanks and surfaced, almost hitting *Gladiolus*, which was dropping
her few remaining depth charges. One landed on the submarine's
deck but rolled off. The three corvettes opened fire as soon as U556
surfaced, hitting the conning tower and killing some of the crew.
Wohlfarth quickly assessed his position as hopeless. He gave orders
to scuttle. In the meantime, *Gladiolus* launched a whaler with a
boarding party. But it was not to be a repetition of the Lemp affair.
When British sailors boarded U556, they found the control room
flooded and the ship reeking with the stench of chlorine gas. They
didn't linger. *Gladiolus* picked up most of U556's crew. British
interrogators rated most of them as inexperienced and of indiffer-
ent quality. It was an interesting and encouraging development.
Dönitz's service appeared to be running out of "supermen."* Moreover, results of the attacks on Halifax 133 were far from impressive.
The U-boats had sunk six ships, totalling 38,000 tons, and damaged
two tankers. But in the process they lost three U-boats. Dönitz was

---

* At this period Allied opinion of the typical U-boat crew began generally to
decline.

alarmed. How could the British know so much about the movements of U-boats? Might there be a security leak?

On July 1, 1941, some four thousand U.S. Marines set sail from the United States in four troopships, bound for Iceland. Seventeen warships, including the veteran battleships *Arkansas* and *New York*, two light cruisers, and thirteen destroyers, escorted the troopships. En route to Iceland, one of the destroyers came upon a lifeboat from the Norwegian freighter *Vigrid*, sunk by U371 nearly two weeks before. The fourteen survivors included four Red Cross nurses.

Arriving at Reykjavík harbour on July 7, the Americans immediately set to work to build bases. Iceland's potential in the antisubmarine war was about to be realized. Within a few weeks, the U.S. Navy's Patrol Wing 7 had taken up residence with PBYs (Catalinas to the British, Cansos to the Canadians) and Martin PBM3 Mariners, some thirty-six aircraft in all. RAF Coastal Command had three squadrons (209 flying Catalinas, 269 with Hudsons, and 330, a Norwegian squadron operating Northrop N3PB single-engined floatplanes, which looked more like sport aircraft than the others, but did useful work). Accommodations took the form of Nissen huts half buried in the earth and anchored down with hawsers. Such precautions were necessary in a land that frequently had to endure winds of 120 mph.

In August, a 269 Squadron Hudson crew spotted a U-boat south of Iceland. Unfortunately, due to a mechanical fault, the plane's depth charges couldn't be released from their underwing racks, and the U-boat disappeared in a rain squall. About an hour later, another 269 Squadron Hudson came on the scene. Squadron Leader James H. Thompson was at the controls. He spotted a second U-boat, U570. Thompson dropped four 250-pound depth charges set to detonate at fifty feet. His judgement was superb. Two of the charges straddled the U-boat, almost turning it over as they exploded.

Inside the metal hull, conditions became nightmarish. The lights went out; the instruments failed. The inexperienced crew panicked. Someone yelled that seawater had got into the battery and that chlorine gas was filling the boat. The crew rushed forward into the control room. But someone had slammed the control room hatch and shut down the ventilation system. The aft section of the boat was isolated. Attempting to escape, the skipper, Hans Rahmlow, called for full speed from the electric motors and "hard down" on the bow planes. The order couldn't be obeyed; battle damage had wrecked the controls.

Having dropped his supply of depth charges from his Hudson, Thompson had to resort to the aircraft's rifle-calibre machine guns. The Hudson's crew kept up a steady fire. On the fourth run over the target, Thompson was astonished to see what appeared to be two white "flags" held by members of the U-boat crew, one in fact a shirt and the other a white board. They were giving up the fight! Circling warily, Thompson called for assistance. A Catalina from 209 Squadron based at Reykjavík arrived to escort the sub to Iceland. Thompson had to return to his base at Kaldadarnes, Iceland, while a small flotilla of vessels including destroyers hurried to the scene to foil any attempt by U570 to scuttle.* It was a choppy, windy day and the sea was rough, complicating the process of boarding. To the surprise of the British, the German crew seemed quite willing to surrender; they appeared to be demoralized and exhibited none of the fighting qualities for which the U-boat men had become famous.

The weather became progressively worse as darkness crept over the scene. The following morning, S. R. J. Woods, skipper of the British destroyer *Burwell*, decided to hold the German crew hostage while he towed the sub to Iceland. Communicating by signal lamp with Rahmlow, Woods was told that U570 was sinking.

---

*   At Kaldadarnes, Thompson attempted to land in a vicious crosswind and ended up in a swamp. The crew was unhurt but the Hudson was badly damaged.

Woods didn't believe it. He ordered Rahmlow to send half the crew below and blow ballast tanks. If any attempt was made to scuttle or to destroy secret documents, said Woods, he would leave the Germans to their fate. While this dialogue was in progress, a bizarre incident occurred. One of the Norwegian Northrop floatplanes from Iceland appeared and, ignoring the Allied warships, dropped two bombs near U570. They missed, but they had an electric effect on Rahmlow. Suddenly becoming cooperative, he took the proffered messenger line and agreed to secure it. But as the steel cable snaked across the boisterous sea, the hemp line broke. Woods, believing that the Germans had sabotaged the line, ordered a burst of machine-gun fire over the enemy sailors' heads. Unfortunately, it was too rough for accurate shooting. The burst from the machine gun went wildly astray, hitting five of the U-boat's crew, although none fatally. After that, the Germans were willing, even eager, to surrender.

Woods agreed to take the wounded men aboard *Burwell*, and Rahmlow blew ballast and fuel tanks in an attempt to calm the turbulent waters long enough to transfer his wounded to the British destroyer. Conditions made it impossible, so Woods ordered Captain H. O. L'Estrange of the trawler *Kingston Agathe* to attempt the transfer, since his vessel was the more manoeuvrable. A four-man boarding party from the trawler scrambled into a tethered raft, eventually getting aboard U570. They lost no time looking for the sub's Enigma, but it was nowhere to be found. Then they began the task of transferring the crew. According to American intelligence reports, the first men to leave U570 were its officers and not the wounded. Rahmlow, Berndt, the first watch officer, and Erick Mensel, the engineer, led; the five wounded men followed, apparently highly critical of their officers' action.

At this point in the unusual proceedings, the Canadian destroyer *Niagara* arrived astern of U570 and shot lines to the German sailors, instructing them to come aboard. These instructions seemed to complicate an already confusing situation. Since they had originally been ordered by Woods to remain on their ship, the Germans were understandably reluctant to disobey him. But a German-speaking petty officer convinced them of the wisdom of obeying the order. Soon they were scrambling aboard the Canadian ship. The towline held while the battered U570 was towed to Iceland. It arrived at about 1900 on August 29. A British crew took over and sailed her to Barrow-in-Furness, where she underwent thorough testing and some time later she went into service with the RN as HMS *Graph*.

U570's crew was interrogated by the British in London, who again noted the youth, inexperience, and general incompetence of the men. The four officers went to an officers' POW camp in the Lake District, where fellow prisoners excoriated them for their "cowardice." Bernhard Berndt, the watch officer, later hatched a bizarre plan to "rescue" U570 from nearby Barrow-in-Furness and destroy her. He succeeded in escaping from the camp, but a Home Guard unit caught him and shot him dead. Dönitz described the whole sorry business as "a depressing event," postulating that Rahmlow must have suffered from gas poisoning that rendered him temporarily incapable of command.

~

By mid 1941, the war had been raging for almost two years. Incredibly – and frustratingly – RAF Coastal Command had so far failed to sink a single U-boat in the Atlantic. But a change in the Command's fortunes was imminent. In June, U-boats had sunk fifty-seven ships; significantly, however, only six of them had been attacked within a radius of 350 miles of a Coastal Command base. U-boat skippers quickly learned that the greater the distance from a Coastal Command base, the less likely were attacks from the air. One thought dominated the minds of Allied naval and air force personnel: If only there could be a string of such bases from the British Isles to the North American coast, the U-boats would be almost impotent, and what had become one of the war's most serious problems for the Allies would be solved.

In September 1941, 120 Squadron RAF began to operate from Nutt's Corner, Northern Ireland. The unit was the first in the RAF to fly the new four-engine Liberators, known as B-24s in the American service. The full-bellied Liberators looked awkward on the ground. They taxied with a sort of waddle and seemed firmly affixed to *terra firma* during most of their takeoff runs. But they were ideally suited to the job of long-range anti-U-boat patrol. By the standards of 1941, the Liberator was an advanced aircraft. The self-sealing material had been stripped from its fuel tanks, creating more capacity and reducing weight. One British test pilot described it as "an amply powered cartload of bricks."[1] It was one of the first aircraft that had to be "motored" until it touched down, at a rate of descent managed by carefully judged applications of power. The Liberator had to be flown off the runway when the air speed indicator indicated the right speed. If pulled off the ground too soon in a heavily loaded state, it had an alarming habit of "getting stuck," gaining neither speed nor height. Its cockpit/flight deck was a revelation to pilots accustomed to flying Blenheims and Ansons; no one had ever seen so many switches and levers gathered in one place before.

The new aircraft inspired the usual crop of rumours. A favourite was that it had been declared totally unacceptable by the Americans, so they were fobbing them off on the British and Canadians. The British and Canadians wished that were true, for they quickly discovered what a thoroughly excellent aircraft the Liberator was. It could carry a heavy load of bombs or depth charges and had an impressive range. It rapidly became the most useful aircraft on long-range patrol duties, regularly striking out to a radius of seven hundred miles or more. Aircrew were delighted with the Liberator, seeing it as meeting most of the maritime squadrons' needs.

But now everyone wanted the Liberator. Thus began an unseemly struggle between the American air force, the RAF and the RCAF, and various other Allied units, all pleading for B-24s. From being a thoroughly suspect new type, the Liberator was now in demand in almost every theatre of war.

The PBY Catalina was another successful American design from the same company that produced the Liberator. For the Allies, it met an urgent need at a particularly difficult time. The Catalina (the Canadian-built amphibian version was known as the Canso) had first flown in the mid 1930s. It represented a major step forward from the ancient biplane Stranraers that still equipped many of the Coastal Command and Eastern Air Command units of the RCAF. It had an excellent range, but it was slow and lightly armed, a shortcoming which cost many lives in attacks on U-boats.

In the summer of 1941, Coastal Command studied the problems of anti-submarine warfare and came up with some valuable recommendations. For example, that the best chance of inflicting serious damage was to attack while the submarine was still on the surface, or at least within fifteen seconds of submergence; the movements of the boat were too unpredictable for the explosives to have any effect if the sub was any deeper. Existing depth settings of 100 to 150 feet on aerial depth charges were consequently obsolete. The ideal, for destroying a surfaced submarine, would be a depth charge set for twenty-five feet, but detonators then in use could be set no shallower than fifty feet.[2]

One possible solution was to use stronger explosives. It took some months, but eventually the contents of the depth charges changed from Amatol to Torpex, making them 30 to 50 per cent more powerful. At the same time, a new detonator was developed, the Mark XIII, although, disappointingly, its minimum setting of thirty-four feet was still too deep to take care of a fully surfaced U-boat. Moreover, the depth charges still tended to "plane" over the water after impact, and something had to be done to prevent the formation of air bubbles that delayed the action of water pressure on the pistol. Eventually, the depth charges incorporated the Mark XIII Star detonating pistol, and a break-away tail section and concave nose spoiler to prevent "planing." But the squadrons had to wait until mid-1942 for these vital modifications to be implemented on the production line.

Now, with two years of practical (and often frustrating) experience, Coastal Command issued new instructions for attacks on U-boats. Coastal recommended patrols at up to five thousand feet in clear conditions (although few pilots flew that high, since they were all too conscious of the necessity of getting down low to drop their depth charges before the U-boats dived) and close to cloud ceiling in less than perfect conditions. On sighting a U-boat, the aircraft were instructed to dive as rapidly as possible and drop all depth charges, except, that is, for the Liberators, which could carry very heavy weapon loads. Surprise was vital. To that end, coastal patrol aircraft shed their matte black undersides. Experience had shown that U-boat lookouts were less likely to spot aircraft with white undersides than those painted black.

By now, about half of Coastal Command's anti-submarine aircraft carried ASV Mark II radar. It was a step forward, but only a short step. The equipment was subject to bewildering echoes, principally from the sea. It was of little use at night, the U-boat's favourite time for action. It tended to produce promising echoes from icebergs and assorted flotsam and jetsam, leading to countless attacks that were a total waste of time and effort. Even if the echo was "good," the aircrew invariably experienced problems within the last couple of miles of the sub. In the darkness, attacking aircraft often overshot their targets, because the aircrew couldn't see them, and because the target would abruptly disappear from the radar screen when the aircraft got close.

It was a vexing problem. Just how vexing may be judged from the fact that in the autumn of 1940, Air Chief Marshal Bowhill, commander-in-chief of Coastal Command, felt obliged to ask the units under his command for any bright ideas anyone might have for the more efficient killing of U-boats, particularly at night.

The most promising response came from Squadron Leader Humphrey de Verde Leigh, a personnel officer in Coastal Command. A pilot in the First World War, Leigh had flown many anti-submarine patrols and had experienced the frustrations of searching for the elusive underwater craft. Locating the U-boat had become considerably easier since the introduction of ASV radar; nevertheless, the difficulties of the last mile or two of the approach remained. The target simply dropped off the radar screen, leaving the aircrew literally in the dark. Leigh suggested mounting a ninety-centimetre searchlight in the nose or belly of a Wellington bomber. He specified the Wellington because he knew that several had been equipped with an extra motor and a heavy current generator to become the DWI Wellingtons used to explode magnetic mines. Leigh explained it all in a paper: "The electrical generating equipment used in the DWI Wellingtons . . . consisted of either a Gipsy Queen engine and a 90 kw generator or a Ford V-8 engine and a 35 kw generator, either of which would give ample power for the searchlight . . . mounted in a swivel ring to allow at least 20 degrees downwards or sideways movement. The 15 cwt 90 cm Army type searchlight as at present used for ground defence gives an effective beam of about 5,000 yards with 2 degrees dispersion. It is suggested that a searchlight of not less than this power . . . would be most suitable for this purpose."[3]

Bowhill liked the idea. The boffins at the Royal Aircraft Establishment at Farnborough were less enthusiastic. They claimed that the type of searchlight specified by Leigh would be far too big to fit into a Wellington's turret – and did their best to interest Bowhill in experiments carried out in 1928 with towed flares.

Bowhill dismissed their suggestion out of hand, and ordered Leigh to work full time on his idea. Leigh soon abandoned the idea

of using the ninety-centimetre military searchlight, instead specifying the naval twenty-four-inch, or sixty-one-centimetre, light.
This could be built into a retractable mounting and lowered
through the aperture in the floor of the Wellington's fuselage originally intended for the long-abandoned "dustbin" ventral gun position. The very successful Frazer Nash hydraulic-control-system
gun turret was adapted to operate the searchlight.

By March 1941, a Wellington was ready for flight trials. Technicians installed the vital ASV radar. The RN provided a submarine so
that the trials might be as realistic as possible. After some disappointing trial runs, Leigh himself decided to operate the light that would
bear his name. Leigh occupied the bomb aimer's position, and in a
matter of minutes after takeoff he was watching the sea skimming
beneath him. The run-up to the target was about to begin.

The ASV radar picked up the submarine without difficulty. One
mile away from the target, Leigh switched on his light. He left it
on and found it quite simple to hold the beam on the target, clearly
illuminating it. More trials followed. A naval observer noted that
crewmen on the "target" subs could not hear the approaching aircraft until the last moments of the attack. The Leigh light seemed
certain to enjoy a successful future.

But a totally unexpected development threw a cloud of doubt
over the entire project. A group captain by the name of Helmore
had developed an airborne light to illuminate enemy bombers
during night raids over Britain. Helmore and Leigh had approached
the question of electrical power from totally different angles.
Leigh's light needed ten and a half kilowatts of electrical power,
whereas Helmore's was thirteen times as powerful and required so
much power, the batteries took up the whole bomb bay of a twin-
engined Douglas Boston. Leigh positioned his light below the aircraft fuselage, so that the operator's eyes were some six feet above
the top of the four-degree-wide beam – later widened to twelve
degrees – which could be steered from the nose of the aircraft.

Helmore's occupied the whole of the nose of the aircraft, so that the pilot had to look along the length of the actual beam, which was very wide and fixed to point straight ahead of the aircraft.[4]

In June, Air Chief Marshal Joubert took over Coastal Command. The Leigh light was in jeopardy. Joubert ordered Leigh to return to his duties as Assistant Personnel officer. "After some two months I found, as I do not mind admitting, that I had made a mistake," Joubert later stated. "I found out that the Helmore Light was unnecessarily brilliant for use against U-boats and otherwise unsuitable. I then came to the conclusion that Leigh's light was preferable."[5]

Leigh found himself transferred once more to full-time employment on his light. Now, with the enthusiastic approval of the likes of Joubert and others, it was time to finalize the design. The job took several months. The motor-driven generator system was too large and too heavy; a battery of seven standard 12-volt batteries, trickle-charged by a generator powered by the Wellington's engines, did the job equally well; after all, the light would have to burn for only the final thirty seconds of an attack.

This new version of the Leigh light installation weighed some six hundred pounds. It went into production, but eighteen crucial months had elapsed between Leigh's original suggestion and the first use of the device on operations. At best, the device illuminated the target U-boat superbly, simultaneously dazzling its gunners and spoiling their aim. At worst, it dazzled the aircrew, leading to catastrophic crashes into the sea.*

~

---

* Toward the end of the war, a Canadian pilot, John Brooks of Toronto, was still undergoing operational training over the North Sea when his ASV operator picked up a target. It seemed to be a good opportunity to practise the use of the Leigh light. Flying at low level, Brooks approached the target and at the appropriate moment switched on his Leigh light – to be confronted by the sight of *Queen Mary*, her immense hull filling his windshield. For an electric moment, he pictured himself crashing full tilt into the Allies' most valuable troop carrier. Applying full power, Brooks just managed to drag the sluggish Wellington over the huge ship's mast-tops.

Although his U-boats were still wreaking havoc on the North Atlantic, Dönitz was by no means complacent. The incursion into Icelandic waters, initially so promising, had proved to be a costly failure, with three U-boats lost (one sunk, one captured, and one badly damaged) and no Allied ships sunk. Hitler had promised huge increases in U-boat strength, but as yet there had been little improvement in the output of the yards. The reasons were primarily a chronic shortage of skilled shipyard workers and Hitler's desire to reinforce the U-boat strength in the Mediterranean. Dönitz, still concerned about the possibility of security leaks, decided that henceforth U-boats would be referred to in official communications by the surname of the skipper rather than a number; for example, U-Wohlfarth rather than U556. But Dönitz's worries went deeper. There had been disquieting signs of a slump in morale among some of his U-boat crews. Allied anti-submarine measures were slowly but surely becoming more effective. U-boat casualties were mounting. Would morale continue to slide? It was a possibility that had never concerned him before, but it concerned him now. At the same time, the British worried about their lacklustre record of U-boat kills. If the Germans went into vastly increased production of U-boats, a difficult situation might well become catastrophic.

7

OPERATION DRUMBEAT

"Strength lies not in defence but in attack"
– Adolf Hitler

IN THE EARLY HOURS of October 31, 1941, U552, under the command of Erich Topp, spotted a fast convoy heading east. It was Halifax 156, consisting of forty-four ships escorted by five American destroyers. Topp aimed for a four-stack destroyer, *Reuben James*, firing two torpedoes. One hit the destroyer on the port side. It was a fatal blow. The ship broke in two. The bow sank immediately; the stern remained afloat for a few minutes, enabling the other destroyers to pick up forty or so of the 160-man crew. The rest were lost. *Reuben James* had the melancholy distinction of being the first U.S. Navy vessel sunk by the Germans in the Second World War. The sinking generated angry words from Harold R. Stark, Chief of Naval Operations, who declared that America was already at war, whether the country knew it or not. President Roosevelt used the incident to further his case for the repeal of the Neutrality Act.

Despite the sinking of *Reuben James*, the Atlantic became notice-
ably quieter in the last weeks of 1941. There were several reasons.
First, the German High Command had ordered twenty U-boats to
be diverted to "special duties"; eight of these were to escort the
battleship *Admiral Scheer* on a sortie into the Atlantic, six were to
escort prize ships, raiders, and blockade runners, and six were to be
transferred to the Mediterranean theatre. Predictably, Dönitz considered such activities a complete waste of his force. Weren't his
resources already severely strained? Why transfer U-boats to the
Mediterranean? It was a backwater in comparison with the Atlantic.
He flew to Berlin to discuss the matter with Admiral Raeder – a
virtually pointless trip, since he gained no concessions of any
significance. "In a series of discussions and a lengthy exchange of
teleprinter correspondence with Naval High Command," he
reported, "I did my utmost to persuade them to accept my point
of view."[1] (A few months later, Arthur T. "Bomber" Harris, the
chief of RAF Bomber Command, would be equally frustrated and
infuriated when ordered to divert many of his precious bombers to
Coastal Command for anti-submarine patrols.) But the period was
not without its positive aspect for Dönitz. German code-breakers
had penetrated the RN's main operational code and were well on
their way to breaking the naval code used jointly by Britain,
Canada, and the still-neutral United States for convoy operations.
Intensification of British anti-submarine activities in Icelandic
waters and in the Northwest Approaches led to Dönitz concentrating his U-boats westward toward Greenland. In these waters,
the U-boats were far less likely to encounter ASW aircraft, Hudsons
or Catalinas, from Iceland. This was the notorious Air Gap, an area
in which the U-boats were almost guaranteed no interference by
Allied aircraft because of the distance to the nearest bases.

In November, about 850 merchant ships crossed the Atlantic
with few losses. The following month saw a sudden rise in tension
in the Far East, with reports of an anticipated Japanese landing

in Malaya, and then on December 7 the Japanese attack on the U.S. naval base at Pearl Harbor. The United States no longer had any choice but to enter the war. Intensely relieved to have the Americans as active allies, Churchill declared that he had never before felt so certain of eventual victory. His euphoria was short-lived. On December 10, Dudley Pound, the First Sea Lord, telephoned him with dire news. As Churchill later recalled, "His voice sounded odd. He gave a sort of cough and gulp, and at first I could not hear quite clearly. 'Prime Minister, I have to report to you that the *Prince of Wales* and the *Repulse* have both been sunk by the Japanese, we think by aircraft.'"[2]

On the 11th, Germany and Italy declared war on the United States. The news was not unwelcome to Churchill, who had been beset by nagging fears that the Americans might be totally involved with the Far East and cut back on aid to Europe. What the average German thought about being at war with the United States can only be guessed at. The Third Reich never indulged in opinion polls. No doubt many citizens privately thought Germany's declaration of war to be extraordinarily ill-timed. In Russia, the amazing advance of the German armies had been stayed, at least temporarily, by a combination of savage winter weather and stubborn resistance by Soviet troops.

It could be argued that the Americans were, from a naval point of view, already waging war against Germany. Hadn't they occupied Iceland? Weren't they daily escorting Atlantic convoys? Weren't they arming their merchant ships, firing at German vessels without compunction? And weren't they sending immense quantities of war supplies to Britain and the Soviet Union? Without apparently giving much thought to the longer view, Hitler came to the conclusion that war with America was in fact precisely what his countrymen and allies needed. And a striking victory by Dönitz's U-boats would be just the thing to start it all off.

～

Just after Christmas, 1941, the British mounted a commando raid on Norway. It was a two-pronged assault, on Vest Fjord, running into Narvik, and against the island of Vaagso, near Alesund. The action ran into trouble en route to Norway when one of the troopships experienced mechanical trouble and had to abort. The raid on Vaagso was successful, however, with several enemy merchant ships sunk or captured.

The commando raid was one of a number undertaken during this period. The British desperately needed some positive news for their allies and their general public, for this was a time when the Axis powers seemed to be winning almost every battle on every front. The commando raids were proof that the British were fighting back – successfully. Newsreel audiences thrilled to the sight of steel-helmeted Tommies leaping from landing craft with revolvers, rifles, and machine guns at the ready. The grainy, undoubtedly genuine footage told the story of the entire action, from grinning black-faced commandos giving their weapons a last polish and check, to battle scenes punctuated by umpteen bullets darting about like high-speed fireflies, and finally, sullen German prisoners being marched off to interrogation and POW camp. The message was plain: Soon these troops and countless comrades would be swarming ashore in even greater number, ready to kick the Germans out of Occupied Europe.

Hitler was convinced that if the invasion came, it would be in Norway. Thus the commando raids on Norwegian targets were of particular concern to the German leader. Following the raid on Vaagso, he ordered U-boats to Norwegian waters, even suggesting that some might be permanently stationed there to help protect the area against an assault. Again the order for deployment of U-boat forces came at an unfortunate time for Dönitz. He had just been putting the finishing touches on details of his forthcoming attack on shipping in North American waters, operation Paukenschlag (Drumbeat). But ever the loyal Nazi, Dönitz swallowed his disappointment, resolving to do the best he could with the forces at hand. At that time, he had ninety-one operational U-boats. Of these, twenty-three were in the Mediterranean, and three more were under orders to proceed there. Six were stationed west of Gibraltar, four were deployed along the Norwegian coast. Dönitz observed, "Of the remaining fifty-five available, sixty per cent were in dockyard hands undergoing repairs prolonged by shortage of labour. . . . There were only twenty-two boats at sea and about half of these were *en route* to or from their operational base areas. Thus, at the beginning of 1942, after two and a half years of war there were never more than ten or twelve boats actively and simultaneously engaged in our most important task, the war on shipping, or something like a mere twelve per cent of our total U-boat strength."[3]

Dönitz believed that a successful U-boat assault on the American East Coast would be even more important to the Axis cause than the attack on Pearl Harbor. Like that spectacularly successful operation, it would reveal the glaring inadequacy of American defences. Besides, the last few months of 1941 had been less than triumphant for the U-boats. A mere 62,000 tons of shipping had been sunk, the lowest toll since May 1940. Dönitz urgently needed a major triumph.

Hitler approved Operation Drumbeat – but with a mere half-dozen Type IX boats, half the number Dönitz had originally been counting on. The submarines ran into frightful weather on their trip west. U701 lost its first watch officer, who went on deck without a safety belt and vanished into the angry sea. A winter hurricane a few days later produced waves as high as houses, according to Peter Cremer, skipper of U333: "They struck the boat like an avalanche and swept away the few things they could seize on. Fenders and lines under the outer casing disappeared, supports cracked like matchwood. The boat listed up to 60 degrees – as the pendulum in the control room showed – so that it seemed one could plunge one's bare hands in the water, then righted itself like a self-righting doll, owing to its low centre of gravity, only to tip over immediately to the other side. . . . The U-boat literally climbed the mountainous seas, plunged through the wave crests, hung for a moment with its stern in the empty air and plunged down the other side into the trough of the waves. When it buried its nose, the screws in the stern seemed to be revolving in the air. The stern dropped down, the screws disappeared in the maelstrom and the exhaust broke off with a gurgle. In the hard thumps, U333 shuddered in every frame member like a steel spring."[4]

On the far side of the Atlantic, little was being done to prepare for the possibility of a U-boat attack. Much criticism has been directed at the American in charge of this area of operations: Admiral Ernest J. King, the tough, vitriolic commander of the American Fleet. Like many mid-westerners, King distrusted the British – and most Europeans – and disdained what he perceived as their foppish manners and snobbish attitudes. They weren't the straight-talking, no-nonsense individuals he knew and trusted. It has been said that he refused to organize convoys along the American coast simply because the British had advised him to do so. But the story is improbable; King was an intelligent commander and unlikely to risk his sailors' lives on a whim. He did, however, possess a violent temper, and he created strong and lasting impressions among many people. The American naval historian Samuel Eliot Morison described him as "spare and taut, with piercing brown eyes, a powerful Roman nose and deeply cleft chin . . . a sailor's sailor. . . . He had no toleration for fools or weaklings . . . and was more feared than loved . . . a hard, grim, determined man."[5] One of his daughters confirmed the stories about his temper, declaring, "He is the most even-tempered man in the Navy. He is always in a rage."[6] King declared that an inadequate convoy escort was worse than no escort at all. From the start, he maintained that if it was a question of using available escort forces to protect troopships or merchant ships, he would always favour the former. He followed this dictum throughout the war. King faced the same shortage of escort vessels that plagued the RN. The U.S.

Navy was fighting a two-ocean war and was not adequately prepared on either front.

On the second day of the new year, the Admiralty in London issued warnings of a forthcoming U-boat offensive, the information having come from Enigma decrypts. Canadian maritime squadrons at Dartmouth, Sydney, Gander, and Torbay, together with USN aircraft from Argentia and USAAF aircraft from Gander, increased their patrol activity but encountered no U-boats. In addition, B-17, B-18, and B-25 bombers flew patrols from Langley Field, Virginia, Mitchel Field, New York, Westover Field, Massachusetts, and, after mid January, Bangor, Maine. The aircrews weren't trained for anti-submarine warfare, and none of the crews had received training in ship recognition. It wasn't at all certain that over the threatened sea-lanes they would know a U-boat if they came upon one.[7] Augmenting the bombers was the U.S. Army's First Air Support Command. It sounded impressive but wasn't, the force consisting of only about a hundred single-engined observation planes. Some likened the First Air Support Command to Joffre's flotilla of Paris taxicabs that brought reinforcement to the Marne in September 1914; in truth, it was less useful, for in addition to the pilots' lack of training in their demanding job, their aircraft could patrol for no more than an hour or two before running out of fuel.

By mid January, the first of Dönitz's U-boats had reached North American waters. U123 was under the command of the highly regarded Reinhard Hardegen, who would become one of the top-scoring U-boat skippers of the war. He spotted the British freighter *Cyclops* about a hundred miles southeast of Cape Sable, Nova Scotia. Two torpedoes sent her to the bottom with a hundred of her 181-man crew. U123 went on her way without pausing to assist the survivors struggling in the frigid ocean. Hardegen was obeying orders; Dönitz had expressly forbidden any U-boat to stop and pick up survivors. They were engaged in a struggle to the death, and no thought or action should deflect from that purpose: "Rescue no one and take no one with you," Dönitz had commanded. "Have

no care for the ships' boats. Weather conditions and the proximity
of land are of no account. Care only for your own boat and strive
to achieve the next success as soon as possible. We must be hard in
this war. The enemy started this war in order to destroy us, therefore nothing else matters."[8]

On January 19, a Digby of 10 Squadron RCAF attacked U84,
commanded by twenty-five-year-old Horst Uphoff. The Digby
pilot, Flight Lieutenant E. M. Williams, approached from a little
over a thousand feet. But only one depth charge fell away, because
a crew member had forgotten that all the depth charges had to be
released manually due to problems with the electric release mechanism. Another U-boat slipped away to safety.

Most of the Allied shipping travelling to the United States and
Canada sailed in convoy to about longitude fifty-five degrees west,
then dispersed, the ships proceeding individually to their destinations. The U-boats saw easy pickings here, since initially there was
little attempt to provide escorts, and those that were used tended
to be poorly armed U.S. Coast Guard cutters. Many of the ships
sunk were oil tankers, most of them going down close to the coast,
in the shallow waters of the continental shelf. The tourist areas of
Florida and Georgia quickly became favourites of the U-boat
crews, because the Americans seemed to make every effort to facilitate their work. No matter that their nation was at war, the hotels
and clubs along the coast were still brightly lit. Seen from the U-
boats at sea, they made a superb backdrop, the glow nicely silhou-
etting the Germans' prey. Local authorities were reluctant to order
any reduction of the illumination; after all, such action might have
an adverse impact on the all-important tourist trade. The result was
bizarre; while thousands of Americans relaxed on the beaches and
sipped cocktails, men suffered death and terrible injuries nearby.
Often, holiday-makers witnessed sinkings in horrific detail. The oil
tankers were particularly vulnerable. A single torpedo hitting a
tanker could convert it in a matter of moments into a grisly ball of
fire, with fuel-fed flames billowing high into the balmy southern

skies. On one tanker, several crewmen climbed up the masts in an effort to get away from the merciless fire. But they had nowhere to go; they were still clinging desperately to the mast when the flames reached them. All perished. Even if crewmen succeeded in jumping off burning tankers, they were often immolated by fires blazing on the surface. And fuel oil didn't have to be burning for it to be fatal; with thousands of gallons floating on the ocean's surface, it was hard not to swallow some of it. Ingesting just a few mouthfuls was lethal.

The U-boat crews who went north into Canadian waters also did well. Twelve U-boats were involved, ten Type VIIs, plus two of the longer-range Type IXs. They encountered ferocious weather, with blizzards battering the boats, and ice encrusting their super-structures and upsetting the submarines' balance.

U130, a Type IXC commanded by Ernst Kals, took up position in the Cabot Strait, between Newfoundland and Cape Breton. On January 12, a crystal clear and very cold morning, a Bolingbroke bomber took off from Sydney, Nova Scotia, with Sergeant R. L. Parker of 119 Squadron RCAF at the controls. Parker spotted the sub and lost no time in attacking. He dropped two 250-pound bombs. Both missed. Five more Bolingbrokes arrived on the scene. They enjoyed no more success than Parker had. U-boat radio messages warned of enemy air activity but described the airmen as "not dangerous because of inexperience." Early the following morning, still in the same area, Reinhard Hardegen's U123 sank two freighters, the first ships to be sunk by U-boats in Canadian waters. All were sailing independently rather than in convoy.

On January 13, three Type IX U-boats reached their assigned positions: U123 near the eastern tip of Long Island, U125 off New Jersey, and U66 off Cape Hatteras, North Carolina. Reinhard Hardegen, the skipper of U123, sank the 9,600-ton Panamanian tanker *Norness*, after which he took his crew for a sightseeing trip along the coastline, close enough to glimpse the shimmering lights of New York harbour. In the early hours of the following morning,

Hardegen spotted the British tanker *Coimbra* en route to Halifax. Minutes later, the 6,768-ton vessel erupted in a ghastly fireball clearly visible from the shore. Thirty-six men died; only six, all wounded, were rescued. Hardegen's sinking of the two tankers set off a flurry of activity: aircraft, blimps, and a variety of small craft set off, bursting with good intentions but sadly, like the others, lacking in experience of the difficult craft of sub-hunting. Hardegen slipped away to the south, convinced by his experiences that the U.S. Navy "was a paper fleet and that its commanders were either incompetent or negligent, or both."[9]

On the night of January 18/19th, Hardegen's U123 arrived off Cape Hatteras to join U66, commanded by Richard Zapp. The U-boat men could scarcely believe their eyes when they saw the number of ships in the area, all brilliantly lit and all without escorts. Zapp torpedoed the 6,600-ton tanker *Allan Jackson*. Thirty-five of the forty-eight-man crew burned to death in the furious blaze that swept the vessel. Shortly after one the following morning, Zapp spotted a sizable ship, a merchantman or troopship, he thought. The single-funnelled vessel displayed no lights, which, Zapp reasoned, probably indicated it was on some war-connected mission. The ship, the 12,000-ton *Lady Hawkins* of the Canadian National Steamships line, was one of five "Lady" ships built in the late 1920s for trade with the Caribbean. They were popular vessels, their only shortcoming being a tendency to roll viciously in heavy weather; at such times, their crews dubbed them "The Drunken Ladies."

Lady Hawkins had left Halifax on the 16th, calling at Boston. She had 212 passengers, almost all of them civilians, and a crew of 109. She was zigzagging at fifteen knots. On the 18th, nearing Cape Hatteras, Huntley O. Giffin, the somewhat orotund captain of the ship, had told his chief officer, Percy Kelly, that no submarine would ever get him. He had made the remark many times, apparently never thinking that he might be tempting providence. Kelly wished the captain would keep his thoughts to himself. After a final check of the ship, Kelly went to bed. At about 0130, the ship staggered, shuddering, rocked by two powerful explosions. Awakened from a deep sleep, Kelly ran from his room; the air reeked with the stench of explosive. All the ship's lights had gone out. There was no doubt that *Lady Hawkins* was sinking. Kelly scrambled up the companionway to the deck, where dozens of frightened passengers milled about in the darkness. The crew struggled with lifeboats that had been damaged when the torpedoes struck. One lifeboat upturned as it slid down to the sea, emptying its passengers in a nightmarish jumble. Confusion and terror punctuated every moment.

Percy Kelly found himself in the water. "I swam to a boat and hung on to the grab lines for what seemed an eternity. My hands began to lose their feeling and I thought my time had come. I was ready to let go when Bill Burton, the ship's carpenter, pulled me into the boat."[10]

As the senior surviving officer, Kelly took charge, going back to help other passengers to escape from *Lady Hawkins*. "Soon I was helping save others from a sea of slimy fuel oil. We pulled them in until no more could be taken. Then I had to give the agonizing order to pull away; the sinking ship was on her beam ends and we dared stay no longer."

Forced to abandon dozens of passengers and crew, Kelly says, "The cries of the people in the water rang in my ears for years." *Lady Hawkins* slid beneath the surface. She had lasted precisely twenty-five minutes after the torpedoes struck her. Now the only reminder of her existence was a few boxes, odd bits and pieces, and the bobbing heads of scores of people who less than half an hour before had been sleeping peacefully in their beds. Kelly counted the passengers before him, many of them writhing in agony as they retched up fuel oil. There were seventy-six in a thirty-foot boat designed to carry sixty-three. The lifeboat's rudder was missing. Water kept slopping over the sides. Kelly was all too aware that if a stiff wind came up, the boat would turn turtle. The survivors told each other that they would soon be picked up; after all, the

American coast was only a few miles away. But Kelly knew better; it could take as long as two weeks to reach dry land, he calculated. A practical sailor with a lifetime of experience behind him, he organized his motley crew of civilians, servicemen, and merchant sailors, specifying who had to bail, and when. He fashioned a makeshift rudder from an oar, and sorted out precisely how much food and water the boat carried and how much he could allocate to the passengers.

As a pale, wintery sun rose the next morning, he handed out breakfast: half a biscuit and a dipper of water. At midday, everyone had a mouthful of condensed milk measured out in the metal cap from the bottom of Kelly's flashlight. The day passed uneventfully. As evening approached, the survivors got another meal: another dry biscuit and a little water, a repeat of breakfast. Now the long hours had to be endured, with nothing to look at but each other and the endless sea. During a teeth-chattering night of chilly winds and wet clothing, a barman from the ship became the hero of the moment by announcing that before abandoning *Lady Hawkins* he had rescued a bottle of rum. "I told them that here was our life-saver and everyone must share," Kelly recalls. "Each was to take a very small mouthful, neat. I implored them to be fair. When the bottle reached me, the last person, there was one very small mouthful left. How wonderful it tasted! I felt it go through my entire body, even my toes."

The days dragged on, a weary, unbroken procession of them, utterly tedious yet fraught with terror. At first, hopes were high; everyone watched and listened for the sight or sound of a ship or plane. But hope quickly faded, and with it the will to live in some of the individuals. Passengers began to die, quietly, one after the other. Kelly remembers: "The burials from the small lifeboat, such a dot on a large expanse of water, were conducted with care and reverence. We said a prayer as each body was lowered over the side."

By now, everyone's strength was almost gone. Many of the passengers and crew were in need of medical attention. Despair had dulled their eyes. As night fell, the survivors settled down to sleep, or to die, for many seemed to have abandoned thoughts of rescue.

Kelly dozed, only to be awakened by a shout from the seaman at the rudder. He bellowed, with surprising strength, "A ship! A ship!"

Yes, there *was* a ship. But was it a mirage? Incredibly, it turned out to be the real thing: a magnificent sight, a magical sight, the steamer *Coamo*, bound for Puerto Rico. Boats came down, splashing into the sea, crewmen reached out to the chilled, feeble occupants of the lifeboat. Kelly made sure his passengers were taken care of, then he relaxed, letting the responsibility roll off him like an enormous burden. He was taken to a stateroom, helped out of his clothes and into pyjamas, and put to bed.

"I remember closing my eyes and in a hazy sort of way trying to say a prayer of thankfulness. Then I began to cry . . ."

Kelly's passengers were the only ones to survive the sinking of *Lady Hawkins*. Nearly 250 died in the other boats, most of them never found. Kelly was awarded the OBE (Order of the British Empire) for his gallantry and skill during the tragedy.

The Type VII U-boats continued to patrol the Newfoundland and Nova Scotian coasts – and continued to experience equipment failures. Erich Topp, commanding U552, sank the 4,000-ton British freighter *Dayrose*, but of the five torpedoes he launched, only two hit their target; the others missed or failed because of mechanical problems. On the 17th, Topp had another frustrating day; he attacked a freighter escorted by two armed vessels. Three torpedoes failed. The next day, near St. John's, Newfoundland, he spotted the American freighter *Frances Salman*. Manoeuvring into a good position for attack, Topp launched three torpedoes – all of which missed or malfunctioned.

Despite the many technical problems encountered by the U-boat crews and the consistently awful weather, the first major assault on North America by Dönitz's crews had to be rated a striking success, claiming about a quarter of a million tons of shipping. And not a single U-boat had been lost. One reason for this resounding success was that, on February 1, the Germans had effected a major change in their use of Enigma by introducing a fourth "wheel" for their communications with U-boats in the Atlantic and Mediterranean. It was an unexpected blow for Bletchley Park and brought to a halt the decryptions of signals between BdU and the U-boats, an interruption that lasted several months. At the same time, B-Dienst mastered the British Naval Cypher No. 3. The achievement was to have far-reaching effects.

Dönitz was gleeful, noting in his war diary that the defences encountered to date were generally weak:

> The coast was not blacked-out, and the towns were a blaze of bright lights. . . . The lights, both in lighthouses and on buoys, shone forth, though perhaps a little less brightly than usual. Shipping followed the normal peace-time routes and carried the normal lights. Although five weeks had passed since the declaration of war, very few anti-submarine measures appeared to have been introduced. There were, admittedly, anti-submarine patrols, but they were wholly lacking in experience. Single destroyers, for example, sailed up and down the traffic lanes with such regularity that the U-boats were quickly able to work out the time-table being followed. They knew exactly when the destroyers would return, and the knowledge only added to their sense of security during the intervening period. A few attacks with depth charges were delivered by American patrol vessels; but the attackers did not display the requisite perseverance, and the attacks were abandoned too quickly, although quite often, thanks to the shallow water, they stood a good chance of succeeding. The aircraft crews employed on anti-submarine work were also untrained.[11]

Hardegen became the star of Operation Drumbeat, sinking eight ships, totalling 53,360 tons. He noted in his war diary, "It is a pity there weren't a couple of mine-laying boats with me on the night I was off New York, to plaster the place with mines! And if only there had been ten or twenty boats with me here tonight! They would all, I am sure, have had successes in plenty. I have sighted something like twenty ships, some blacked out, and a few tramps. They were all sticking very close to the shore."[12]

One incident tarnished the glory of the U-boats' North American incursions. On his way back to France, Peter Cremer, skipper of U333, came across a solitary freighter. He closed to four hundred yards, submerged, to look her over. Definitely British, Cremer decided, and sank her with his last two torpedoes. As the first torpedo struck home, the ship sent out an SOS, identifying herself as the British ship *Brittany*. In fact, she was the German blockade runner *Spreewald*, with a cargo of rubber and tin, plus eighty-six British prisoners. The loss of the valuable strategic materials infuriated Dönitz. A court-martial seemed to be in store for young Cremer. On February 2, however, the *Spreewald*'s survivors were found in three lifeboats and three rafts. Then the full story came out. In addition to sailing disguised as a British ship, *Spreewald* was not where she was supposed to be at the time of the encounter. Cremer was acquitted.

~

In early 1942, atrocious weather severely affected the production of U-boats. "Over the winter," wrote Dönitz, "nearly one hundred boats coming off the ways or in various stages of workup were to be immobilized – frozen at dockside or otherwise delayed for three to four months. The majority of the seventy-eight boats commissioned in the months of November 1941 to February 1942, inclusive, did not leave the Baltic for seven or eight months. . . . Examples: Commissioned on November 22, 1941, U438 sailed from the Baltic on August 1, 1942. Commissioned on December 11, 1941, U600 sailed on July 14, 1942. Commissioned February 26, 1942, U611 sailed on October 1, 1942." [13]

What of Germany's battleships? Since early in 1942, the warships *Scharnhorst, Gneisenau,* and *Prinz Eugen* had been in France. By their mere presence they had tied down a great deal of British strength. The RAF had attacked the ships on many occasions, losing forty-three aircraft and 247 airmen and succeeding in inflicting only minor damage. On February 12, 1942, the ships sailed out of Brest harbour, making a dash north for Germany to prepare for setting out into the Atlantic. The breakout came as no surprise to the British; tipped off by Ultra, they had been expecting it for months. Contingency plans had been drawn up amid intense secrecy. Indeed, secrecy was taken to absurd limits on some stations; aircraft took off with their crews uncertain about what they were supposed to attack. The British had convinced themselves that the Germans would attempt the "dash" through the Channel at night. The Germans anticipated this, and headed through the straits in daylight. Thereafter, nothing seemed to go well for the British. When a squadron of torpedo bombers took off to engage the German ship, only a few of them were armed. The plan was to pick up torpedoes at another base, but it turned out to be snowbound. Then the promised fighter escort for the torpedo bombers failed to materialize. Six Swordfish, led by Lieutenant Commander Eugene Esmonde, who had led the gallant attack on the battleship *Bismarck* the previous year, attacked the Germans on their own. This operation was a catastrophe.

"Not one of the Swordfish escaped," wrote Adolf Galland, who commanded the German fighter escort, and who spoke of the "death-defying courage" of the naval aircrews. [14]

The other attackers fared little better. But on their way up the Channel, both *Scharnhorst* and *Gneisenau* hit recently sown British mines. The damage to *Gneisenau* was minor; *Scharnhorst*'s damage was more extensive, involving a gun turret and her turbo-electric motors and putting her out of action for a year. Although the two battle cruisers were in dock, undergoing repairs, the OKM (*Oberkommando der Marine* – naval supreme headquarters) decided to proceed with the transfer of *Prinz Eugen* and *Admiral Scheer* to Norway. They set sail, but near Trondheim encountered a "pack" of four British submarines. One of them, *Trident*, fired a salvo of three torpedoes at *Prinz Eugen*, blowing off thirty feet of her stern and forcing her to limp back to Germany. She became a training ship and never sailed in action again.

Oddly, both the Germans and British regarded the "Channel Dash" as a disaster. The British might have felt more charitable about it had they known that, because of the Dash, the Germans had cancelled plans for a foray into the Arctic and kept *Tirpitz*, *Admiral Scheer*, and *Hipper* in Norwegian waters as protection against the invasion that Hitler was sure would soon come.

～

The German navy continued to enjoy better fortune in the Western Atlantic. Halifax, Nova Scotia, became the focus of operations for ace U-boat skipper Heinrich Lehmann-Willenbrock, commander of U96. On February 23, he attacked the British merchant ship *Empire Union*. No. 2 Coast Artillery at Dartmouth, Nova Scotia, sent a single-engined Westland Lysander observation aircraft to investigate. The Lysander headed south for about twenty minutes. "We were flying parallel to a Catalina until we passed over a freighter coming up the coast," logged Sergeant R. H. Smith, the wireless operator/air gunner. "We went on beside the Catalina for another ten miles, then it climbed and turned to sweep back the way it had come. We turned and followed back to the freighter, then turned and headed into the setting sun." At this point the Lysander's two-man crew spotted the submarine. "The periscope was clearly visible, also a swirling around what was possibly the conning tower. As we approached, the submarine started to go under so that it was invisible for the last thirty seconds of our run on it. We passed over the spot where it had disappeared and dropped the depth charges. No air bubbles or oil observed."[15]

Smith and his pilot, Flying Officer Humphreys, had carried out an exemplary attack in an unlikely anti-submarine aircraft and were unlucky not to have sunk or seriously damaged U96. The Canadians were still using fifty-foot settings on their depth charges, which Coastal Command's long experience had shown to be too deep. New Mark XIII pistols with a depth setting of thirty-five feet were just now arriving at Eastern Air Command – another example of how the Canadians had to make do with inadequate equipment yet were expected to produce good results.

Operation Drumbeat's second wave of U-boats arrived off the North American coast in March. Six Type IXBs and twenty Type VIIs had orders to patrol south from New York. None entered Canadian waters. One of the Type IXs was Reinhard Hardegen's U123, which had been notably successful earlier in the year. En route to North America, Hardegen came across two heavily loaded tankers sailing alone. He sank the first, the 7,000-ton U.S. tanker *Muskogee*, with a single torpedo. He couldn't be so economical, however, with his second target, the 8,100-ton British tanker *Empire Steel*. Hardegen launched four torpedoes. The tanker erupted in a huge bonfire, but the ship's crew managed to get at least part of the conflagration under control. They continued to fight the fire as Hardegen and his crew watched. Finally, after some five hours, the tanker broke up and sank. None of the crew survived. A few days later, on March 26, Hardegen closed in on what appeared to be a disappointing target: a 3,000-ton tramp steamer. In fact, the ship was *Atik*, a well-armed American Q-ship engaged in anti-submarine patrols off the east coast. *Atik* lowered two lifeboats as if the crew were abandoning ship. Simultaneously, dummy bulwarks fell away, revealing a gun. It opened fire, and depth charges and machine guns joined in. Hardegen very nearly came to grief; he lost one member of his crew, a midshipman, hit by gunfire.

On March 30, Hardegen reached Cape Hatteras in bright moonlight. During the next two days, he attacked three ships, but technical problems plagued him and he had no success. Heading further south, he attacked two tankers off St. Simon's Island, Georgia. Both ships erupted in fireballs but were later salvaged and returned to service. In the early hours of April 9, Hardegen sank the 3,400-ton refrigerated ship *Esparta*, before heading still farther south. In the dangerously shallow waters off St. Augustine, Florida, he spotted the 8,100-ton tanker *Gulfamerica* bound for New York on her maiden voyage. She carried ninety thousand barrels of fuel oil. Hardegen fired one torpedo and blew the tanker and her crew to bits, an action witnessed from start to finish by horrified onlookers on the shore.

Hardegen was startled by the vigorous reaction of Army and Navy aircraft. Considerable numbers of B-25s and PBYs came roaring out from shore, as did the destroyer *Dahlgren*, and *Asterion*, sister ship of *Atik*. Flares illuminated the burning tanker, giving the grim scene an incongruously festive air. Hardegen crash-dived – and immediately hit the bottom of the shallow underwater shelf, a mere sixty-six feet down. The destroyer *Dahlgren* sped to the attack, got a good sonar contact, and launched depth charges, battering the U-boat with massive explosions. The head valves burst. Air went bubbling up to the surface.

Damage to U123 was serious: one engine down, head valves bent, most of the batteries out of action, hydroplanes damaged, shafts and possibly screws bent too. Amazingly, however, the American destroyer had passed over the U-boat twice without launching any more depth charges. Trapped in their sub, the Germans wondered how the American sailors could fail to see them, or to understand that they were a sitting duck. Proof of the enemy's abysmal lack of experience and training, concluded Hardegen.

Now he had to face an unavoidable fact. To give his crew a chance at survival, he had to surface and surrender – and scuttle the boat. He never thought he would have to take such a step, but there was no choice. Or was there? In a moment he had changed his mind completely. He wasn't going to abandon the boat, damn it. He and the crew were going to save it!

Working furiously, they patched the boat up as best they could. They did a remarkable job, considering their lack of facilities and equipment. Cautiously, the U-boat rose to the surface. The crew had heard no noise from the destroyer for some time. It might mean that the enemy had gone. It might mean, on the other hand, that it was sitting, waiting. But the Germans found nothing except two aircraft dropping flares five miles away. U123 limped away to deeper water where the crew rested and made more emergency repairs. It had been a nerve-wracking experience. Late on April 12, Hardegen was ready to resume his patrol. Off Cap Canaveral, he sank the 2,600-ton freighter *Leslie* with his last torpedo, later sinking another freighter, *Korsholm*, with his deck gun.

At last he headed home to a hero's welcome at Lorient, where he was greeted by Dönitz and Raeder. Then came the ultimate accolade: a vegetarian dinner with Adolf Hitler himself.

The March/April wave of U-boats had cut a swath through Allied shipping in North American waters. The six Type IXs sank twenty-nine ships, among them thirteen tankers. The twenty Type VIIs sank forty-six ships, including twelve tankers. On this second wave of the operation, the U-boats were refuelled and supplied with provisions by a U-boat tanker, U459, one of the big so-called Milchkuhe (Milk Cows) which had recently come into service. The process was complex and wearying – and the U-boat crews had little or no training in its complexities. Things went badly from the start. The weather was too rough and accidents were numerous, including "hose leakages caused by poor manoeuvring, by repeated passing-over of hoses, by inept handling on deck (chafing and tearing because of lack of chafing mats . . .) or through hooks on the diving planes. While the hoses were being passed over, one boat fouled the hoses with its forward hydroplanes, tore the hawser and both hoses away and, when this was cleared, let go the whole equipment." For the crews, the tricky operation in mid ocean was exhausting, requiring, for example, "the provisioning of four boats in a period exceeding sixteen hours in one day; on another day, working eight to ten hours with lifeline attached, with seas and breakers constantly washing over them."[16] Nevertheless, refuelling at sea permitted longer cruises for the U-boats.

Despite the U-boats' success, Allied anti-submarine equipment was becoming an increasingly dangerous fact of life for the German crews. On April 10, U85, under the command of Eberhard Greger, sank the 4,900-ton Swedish merchantman *Christina Knudsen*. Three days later, the U-boat lay in wait for more prey off Bodie Island, to the north of Cape Hatteras, North Carolina. A few minutes after midnight, an American destroyer, *Roper*, got a radar contact, not an unusual happening in these busy waters. But then sonar (an acronym derived from Sound-Navigation Ranging, the U.S. version of Asdic, eventually used by all the Allies) picked up the sound of fast screws. Now U85 was in trouble, for *Roper* had recently been equipped with British-built Type 286 radar – at a time when most Germans believed that such sets were too bulky and too delicate to be carried aboard small ships such as destroyers.

Greger, unable to dive in the shallow waters, decided to run for it. *Roper* set off in pursuit. With the USN ship steadily gaining on him, Greger fired his stern tube. The torpedo missed, just, passing *Roper* on the port side. Believing he was about to be rammed, Greger turned hard to starboard. He ordered the crew to prepare to abandon ship.

Roper switched on her twenty-four-inch searchlight, opening fire with her deck guns. The American sailors, now at point-blank range, saw the Germans running along the U-boat's deck. Some said they thought the enemy sailors were going to man their deck gun. They intensified their fire.

U85 started to sink by the stern. About forty of her crew were left struggling in the water, many pleading with the Americans to save them. Ignoring the pleas, *Roper* cut a path through the cluster of bobbing, splashing men, then condemned them to death by dropping eleven depth charges set for fifty feet. All the remaining men from U85 died, either sliced by *Roper's* propellers or blasted by her depth charges.

The Cape Hatteras area was no longer a happy hunting ground for the U-boats. Anti-submarine patrols by ships and aircraft made every venture through these waters dangerous in the extreme. On April 30, U333, commanded by Peter Cremer, was some three hundred miles east of Jacksonville, Florida. During the afternoon, Cremer spotted the modern double-hulled British tanker *British Prestige*. He tracked her until dark, then fired two bow torpedoes. Both missed. Cremer submerged, reloaded, then rose to the surface – whereupon the tanker rammed him, probably unintentionally. The collision seriously damaged U333, twisting her stern, rendering the two port torpedo tubes useless, wrecking the bridge and the attack periscope. Cremer couldn't have been blamed if he had abandoned the patrol there and then; but he still worried about his misadventure with *Spreewald*. Another unfortunate episode and he might acquire a reputation as a bad-luck skipper, a pariah. Infinitely worse, he might lose his command.*

Cremer was determined to repair U333 somehow. He and his crew put forth a superhuman effort, and incredibly, a few days later, U333 was back in action. He sank the American tanker *Java Arrow* – or thought he had. In fact, the tanker was salvaged and returned to service. The same night, Cremer spotted a Dutch freighter, *Amazone*. Two torpedoes sent her to the bottom. A couple of hours later on that noteworthy night, an American tanker, *Halsey*, appeared, heading north with a cargo of naphtha and fuel oil. Two

---

* Such worries preyed on the minds of some U-boat skippers; one, Peter Zech, CO of the Type IX boat U505, became so distressed by his mediocre performance on patrol that he shot himself to death during a depth-charge attack in October 1943. His boat was later captured and is now on permanent display at the Museum of Science and Industry, Chicago, Illinois.

of U333's torpedoes hit her. She blew up in a gigantic fireball. But vengeful defence vessels now put in an appearance. A U.S. Coast Guard ship fired a number of depth charges. The force of the explosions "slammed U333 into the sand at sixty-five feet, froze her hydroplanes, and caused other external and internal damage."[17] Then came the first vessel's sister ship and the Coast Guard cutter *Vigilant*. It appeared that the redoubtable Cremer had perhaps run out of luck. In fact he still had some left. U333 crawled along the bottom like a gargantuan reptile, struggling to reach deeper water. Cremer's patience and fortitude were rewarded. After some fifteen hours of torment, the boat and its crew struck out into the Atlantic. The boat had taken a cruel beating but it was able to make its way east, leaving its frustrated pursuers far behind.

Cremer was a singular individual. A lesser man might have been content to nurse his damaged boat back to base, but Cremer still considered himself on patrol. During the dark, rainy morning of May 10, five hundred miles east of Florida, he encountered the 5,200-ton British freighter *Clan Skene*. He fired his last two torpedoes. The ship went down in moments. At last, Cremer set off for home.

On hearing of Cremer's remarkable voyage, Dönitz awarded him the Ritterkreuz. Cremer's first patrol to America had ended with a court-martial, his second with a blaze of glory.

In the same month, Hans-Dieter Heinicke in U576 came close to sinking one of the world's most famous ships, *Aquitania*. The liner was part of an American troop convoy consisting of seven transports escorted by the battleship *New York*, the light cruiser *Brooklyn*, the brand-new escort carrier *Avenger*, and fourteen destroyers, as well as air patrols. The ships were to join another troop convoy, consisting of four troopships; in all, the combined convoys carried nineteen thousand troops. Heinicke surfaced and reported by radio to Dönitz. Then one of his diesel engines broke down.

Dönitz was not optimistic about the chances of intercepting the valuable convoy with its numerous escorts. There were four Type

VII boats heading for American waters; but they were six hundred to a thousand miles away from the convoy. It was a long shot, Dönitz realized, but he had to try. The target was just too attractive. In fact, Heinicke did manage to repair his diesel; he regained contact with the convoy as the two elements combined. The story could so easily have ended in the destruction of *Aquitania* and other transports, with the death of countless troops. It didn't happen. What Heinicke described as a strong air escort forced him to submerge, and he soon lost the convoy. Aircraft were becoming increasingly important in the battle.

Although the second wave of U-boats in North American waters sank forty-six ships, including twelve tankers – close to a quarter of a million tons in all – the Allies could take a certain comfort from the fact that the average sinking per patrol had declined, from 3.2 ships for 18,651 tons during the first "Drumbeat" operation, to 2.3 ships for 12,097 tons during the second.

~

At a conference in Washington in April 1942, the British, Canadians, and Americans made a concerted effort to integrate their handling of intercepted Axis messages. One of the British delegates was Rodger Winn, a former barrister, who, though crippled by polio, enjoyed a highly successful career in the RN. He had been in charge of U-boat tracking since mid 1941 and had acquired an uncanny ability to second-guess Dönitz and other senior officers who comprised the BdU (a term often used to refer to Dönitz himself). Winn travelled to Washington to meet Admiral King and to persuade him to institute convoys and set up a U-boat tracking room similar to the British Admiralty's Combined Operations and Intelligence Centre.

Given King's well-known antipathy to the English and their institutions, a stormy meeting was predicted. It didn't happen. Winn presented his case in the logical, step-by-step manner that one might expect of a successful barrister. King was impressed (indeed, he and Winn enjoyed cordial relations for the rest of the war). Shortly after this meeting, King declared that he had always been in favour of convoys, although he could not resist a dig at the British by claiming that the U-boat bases on the French Atlantic coast should have been bombed into rubble when Dönitz first made moves to occupy them. On this point King was correct; "Bomber" Harris related in his memoirs how frustrated he had been when he was instructed, at the instigation of the Admiralty, "to devastate the two French towns of Lorient and St. Nazaire. These ports on the Atlantic coast of France were the two main U-boat bases used in the Battle of the Atlantic; admittedly, the German occupation of them constituted an extremely serious menace to our sea communications, so if bombing could have deprived the enemy of their use, there would have been every reason to direct a good deal of our effort against them. But the Germans knew the facts as well as we did, and had taken due precautions. The U-boat shelters, the only worthwhile target in the two ports, were covered with many feet of reinforced concrete and were without question proof against any bombs we had at that time. . . . I protested repeatedly against this hopeless misuse of air power on an operation which could not possibly achieve the object that was intended."[18]

Although the new alliance between the United States and Britain worked well, the Americans often seemed unsure about Canada's status as a fully independent nation of the British Commonwealth, since "in appearance and practice, the RCN was virtually indistinguishable from the RN. Not surprisingly, then, Canada and the RCN came under 'British Empire and Colonies' in the USN's filing manual. Americans preferred to deal with Commonwealth naval issues through the British Admiralty Delegation in Washington."[19] On a personal level, however, relations between the neighbours were generally excellent. Frank Curry, a seaman on the corvette

Caraquet, recalls the kindness and generosity of the Americans when his ship had to put in to Baltimore, Maryland, for a refit:

> Right from the start, we Canadians were treated as guests and given first-class treatment and every privilege in the book. Nothing was too good for us, and after the rough life on the *Caraquet* and the austerity of Canadian naval bases, we felt we were in paradise. While our ship was dismantled and put back together, we moved to living quarters ashore. . . . The first shock came when we entered the mess hall for our first American meal. There were lineups of American sailors, but an officer insisted that we go to the front. . . . There followed an even bigger surprise – the food. It was beyond our dreams to see the array of delicacies at every meal, served on china. . . . We Canadians must have looked like half-starved refugees plunked down in a land of plenty as we ate our way through. . . . We were overwhelmed by the generosity of the American sailors, and by their respectful interest in us. Many of them had yet to see active service and were impressed at how we had managed to survive years of service in the North Atlantic on our small ships.[20]

It had taken some eighteen months of development and testing, but the Leigh light was at last ready for operational use. Five Wellingtons of RAF Coastal Command had been equipped with the device. On the night of June 4, Squadron Leader J. H. Gresswell of 172 Squadron picked up an ASV contact. He had found an Italian submarine, *Luigi Torelli*, in the Bay of Biscay. But Gresswell quickly discovered that using the Leigh light was not without its problems. On his first approach, he failed to catch even a glimpse of the submarine. Too high, he decided. He turned around for another run. The submarine crew saw him and apparently took him for a

German aircraft, firing recognition flares. Gresswell approached for the second time. Lower . . . lower. The radar guided him unerringly to the target, and the Leigh light provided the all-important last-minute glimpse of it. Aided by bright flares, Gresswell straddled the submarine with 300-pound Torpex-filled depth charges. He thought he had destroyed her, but, badly damaged, *Luigi Torelli* managed to limp to Spain. The Italians' German allies were dismayed when they heard about the incident. Apart from the effectiveness of the new light, it proved that the British had equipped their aircraft with high performance radar equipment, something the Third Reich's experts had repeatedly declared them incapable of doing. Dönitz demanded a radar detector, a device to warn surfaced U-boats that airborne radar was operating in the vicinity. A French company had initiated research on just such a device shortly before the war; the Germans ordered a prototype, to be ready in a few weeks. The French delivered on time – and the device proved highly successful. The so-called Biscay Cross was a diamond-shaped antenna made of wood which could be mounted on a U-boat's bridge while the vessel was surfaced. Dönitz was enthusiastic, and wanted all his U-boats equipped with the device immediately.

Under the command of Karl Thurmann, U553 slid quietly through the Cabot Strait into the Gulf of St. Lawrence on May 8, 1942. It was the first time an enemy warship had sailed into Canadian waters since the nation had ceased to be a colony seventy-five years earlier. In all, four U-boats penetrated Canadian territory in this period: U553, U432, U558, and U213, a minelayer, which had the job of landing an agent at St-Martins, New Brunswick.

The Gulf of St. Lawrence is some 250 miles across at its widest point. Plans had only been drawn up for the defence of the inland sea less than a year before the outbreak of war. For the first few months of the war, the only air cover for the area was a detachment of six porky, single-engined Northrop Delta floatplanes flown by the RCAF. No one took the danger from U-boats very seriously since the development of Asdic. But it soon became apparent that conditions in the Gulf were peculiarly hostile to the device. Strong currents, uncommonly powerful tides, and widely varying temperatures from the layering of salt and fresh water – all combined to make clear Asdic echoes almost impossible to obtain.

In early 1940, a modest naval presence consisting of light vessels had been organized in the Gulf area. Patrols by aircraft were supposed to locate the targets, then the naval vessels would attack them. There were actually a considerable number of military aircraft based nearby, at Gander, and in Goose Bay, Labrador, and Sydney, Nova Scotia. In addition to the operational squadrons in the area, both Canadian and American, there were various training schools, part of the British Commonwealth Air Training Plan. The schools had about 150 Ansons – each of which was capable of carrying a bomb load of five hundred pounds, as well as a contingent of trained and student aircrew. But coordination between the forces was inept, with communications often dependent on the none-too-reliable commercial telephone service.

On the evening of May 10, 1942, a USAAF B-17 from Gander, Newfoundland, spotted U553 and attacked her, doing some damage. It apparently didn't occur to the local American commander, Major General C. G. Brant, to pass on this news to No. 1 Group, RCAF. Relations between Brant and the RCAF commander, Air Commodore C. M. ("Black Mike") McEwen, had never been particularly warm. Now they deteriorated. McEwen complained, with justification, that he had to find out about the incident for himself. Also assisting in the surveillance were the unpaid civilian volunteers of the Aircraft Detection Corps (ADC). Like most amateur sub-hunters, their enthusiasm far outweighed their usefulness; besides, if they obtained any useful information, the ADC people would undoubtedly have run into all sorts of problems in getting through to the authorities. On the Gaspé shore between Ste-Anne-des-Monts and Fox River, there was no telephone service. And even the telegraph line had extremely limited capabilities, with offices some twenty miles apart.

None of the aircraft spotted the U-boat. The following night, the U-boat sank the steamers *Leto* and *Nicoya* north of the Gaspé coast. The presence of a German U-boat in the Gulf of St. Lawrence galvanized the Canadian service into action. U553 kept the Gulf in an uproar until the end of May. But all the commotion didn't lead to a single further sighting of the elusive submarine.

The crisis came at a delicate time in Canadian politics. The conscription issue still simmered. In the broadest terms, English-speaking Canadians tended to believe that Canada should support Britain in its struggle for survival. The *Québécois* considered it none of their business and they consistently opposed conscription. As far as they were concerned, *les Anglais* were enjoying a booming economy because of the war. The same couldn't be said of the *Québécois*. To the English-speaking majority, this view seemed unpatriotic, smacking of downright treason. It was an argument that would last as long as the war.

Prime Minister Mackenzie King believed that the presence of German U-boats in Canadian waters would convince French-Canadians that "the war was not a remote affair, and that Canada could not limit its contribution." And at the same time, the naval minister, Angus L. Macdonald, announced in the Commons the loss of the two steamers in Canadian waters. He had little choice; the news was spreading like wildfire.

Heinz-Otto Schultze, commanding U432, arrived in Nova Scotian waters in mid May. He sank the 325-ton fishing trawler *Foam*, from Boston. Schultze received instructions from Dönitz's headquarters at Kerneval to join U588 and U213 and patrol an area two hundred miles southeast of Cape Sable to seek a major convoy thought to be in that area. The three U-boats found no convoy, but encountered many ships sailing alone. Viktor Vogel, commanding U588, sank two merchantmen; Schultze sank a British freighter before returning to the Cape Sable area to take over from Thurmann, by now low on fuel and provisions. Amelung von Varendorff, in U213, chased a freighter for eight hours, then fired three torpedoes, all of which missed. On his return to France, he received a frosty reception from Dönitz. Two months later, he was killed in action.

Other U-boats headed into U.S. and Bahamian waters. U455 sank the seven-thousand-ton tanker *British Workman*, before turning for home; en route, she sank another tanker, *George H. Jones.* Venturing further south, the U-boats encountered stiffening resistance, with large numbers of aircraft patrolling the coastline. In April, ships had gone down at a rate of about one a day off the U.S. coast, and even heavier losses were anticipated. But in the first seventeen days of May, not one merchantman was lost in the so-called Eastern Sea Frontier. The rest of the month saw only four vessels sunk. Dönitz lost one U-boat, the Type VII U352, commanded by Hellmut Rathke. Thirty miles south of Cape Lookout, Rathke had seen the Coast Guard cutter *Icarus*, en route from New York to Key West to join the coastal convoys then being organized. The two vessels spotted each other almost simultaneously. Rathke fired first. But the torpedo was defective. It dived straight into the ocean floor and exploded, shaking up *Icarus* and her crew. Despite the shock, the Coast Guard crew responded vigorously. In a matter of minutes, five depth charges straddled U352, seriously damaging the boat and killing one officer. On the bottom at 114 feet, Rathke held his breath, hoping the Americans might be convinced that he had been sunk. But no such luck. More depth charges came thumping into the water and exploding, punishing the fragile hull with massive blows, fracturing welds and breaking pipes. Rathke decided to surface and scuttle. It was easier said than done. As U352 broke surface, *Icarus* met her with a hail of fire from her 3-inch bow gun. U352 went down. Thirty-three German survivors were taken into

Charleston, South Carolina, the first U-boat men taken by the Americans. Thirteen other men died with their boat.

Another of Dönitz's U-boats met with better success in the Gulf of Mexico. U125, under the command of Ulrich Folkers, probed the area southwest of Cuba. He startled everyone by sinking nine ships in rapid succession, including the 8,900-ton American tanker *Mercury Sun*, and an even larger Canadian tanker, the 12,000-ton *Calgarolite*. Captain Tom Mountain of *Calgarolite* later reported that his ship was torpedoed some 120 miles south of the Isle of Pines, Cuba, bound for Colombia. Two torpedoes hit the vessel on the starboard side, whereupon the crew clambered into lifeboats. The U-boat surfaced, shelled the tanker until she sank, then took off without making contact with the crew. Captain Mountain's lifeboat reached Cuba four days later; the other got to Mexico in three. The crew suffered no casualties.

The longer range Type IXC/40 boats, U506 and U507, in company with the Type VII U753, soon entered the Gulf. They quickly scored victories. Harro Schacht, the skipper of U507, sank the American tanker *Federal*. Then Erich Würdemann in U506 torpedoed the Nicaraguan freighter *Sama*. Dönitz had ordered both Type IXs to head northwest across the Gulf to the mouth of the Mississippi. An attractive volume of traffic could be expected; but the big U-boats had to proceed with caution in those shallow, muddy waters with their dangerous currents. Both Würdemann and Schacht had the bad luck to be spotted by patrol planes. Both their subs sustained damage but survived.

Schacht had a remarkably successful patrol. He sank the American freighter *Norlindo*, after which he courteously provided the survivors with cigarettes, lime juice, and cake. The following night he sent two tankers to the bottom, following this exploit by sinking an American freighter *Alcoa Puritan*. In his impeccable English, he wished the fifty survivors good luck as they set off for shore in their lifeboat. During the course of the next two days, he sank the Honduran freighter *Ontario*, and a Norwegian freighter, *Torny*.

RENOWNED CARTIER DESIGNER
ALFRED DURANTE
PRESENTS THE MANY LOOKS OF LOVE

Genuine love deserves to be recognized with genuine beauty—especially one with a Cartier heritage. Hand-crafted in solid sterling silver enhanced with a layer of rhodium plating for shine and beauty, this 3-in-1 design glitters with 33 genuine white topaz stones! Each band is engraved to create the expression, *"I Love You Today, I Love You Tomorrow, I Love You Always."* The centre ring features a round topaz solitaire accented with 3 stones on either side. The top and bottom bands each shimmer with a row of topaz—for a total of over 2 carats of brilliance! Wear the centre ring alone, pair it with a band or wear all three stacked to express your perfect love!

This Alfred Durante design is an exceptional value at $129.00*, payable in 3 *interest-free* payments of $43.00 backed by our 120-day money-back guarantee. Send no money now; just mail the Priority Reservation today!

1000010564-N6A4L6-BR01

BRADFORD EXCHANGE
PO BOX 5290 PS B CSC
LONDON ON N6A 5T5

CANADA POST
POST CANADA

POSTES
CANADA

Postage paid
if mailed in Canada
Business Reply Mail

Port payé si posté
au Canada
Correspondance-
réponse d'affaires

1682167

01

**bradfordexchange.ca/
StackingLove**

THIS IS NOW... THIS IS ALWAYS...
THIS IS FOREVER

- Alfred Durante

3 Rings in One!

Over 2 Carats of
Genuine White Topaz

Solid Sterling Silver

I Love You Today
I Love You Tomorrow
I Love You Always

I Love You Always
Topaz Stacking Ring

THE HERITAGE OF CARTIER CRAFTSMANSHIP...
EXCLUSIVELY FROM THE BRADFORD EXCHANGE

ALFRED DURANTE

ORDER TODAY AT
BRADFORDEXCHANGE.CA/STACKINGLOVE

Erich Würdemann also took U506 to the mouth of the Mississippi, from May 11 to May 20. He put in a spectacular performance, sinking four tankers and a freighter. The U-boats then headed for home, their skippers confident of a warm welcome by Dönitz. On the way, Würdemann sank two British freighters by gun east of Florida, making his total eight ships sunk and three large tankers damaged.

The single Type VII U-boat in the Gulf of Mexico was U753, commanded by thirty-four-year-old Alfred Manhardt von Mannstein. It was von Mannstein's second patrol, the first having been less than a success; he was rammed and badly damaged by a British ship.

The Gulf of Mexico proved to be a successful hunting ground for the determined young U-boat skipper during the two weeks he spent there. On May 19, he nearly came to grief when he was rammed by a merchant ship. The deck gun was wrecked, and von Mannstein was fortunate to be able to slip away. Over the next few days, however, he sank the American freighter *George Calvert*, and, after failing to sink a British schooner and an Erie-class gunboat, used five torpedoes to sink the 6,600-ton Norwegian tanker *Hamlet*.

En route for home, U753 was crossing the Bay of Biscay late in the afternoon of June 23 when she was spotted by a Whitley VII of 58 Squadron, RAF Coastal Command. The Whitley's captain, Flight Sergeant W. Jones, ordered an immediate attack. It was his and his crew's second operational patrol, but their performance was worthy of veterans. They released their depth charges about five seconds after the U-boat submerged. The ocean erupted; huge mushrooms of spray blossomed, then fell away. The aircrew watched. Several patches of oil appeared, stains on the surface that spread like the reproduction of some grisly amoeba. A moment later the U-boat itself emerged, water streaming off its deck and conning tower. The crew scrambled out on deck and manned the deck guns. In reply, the Whitley's front and rear gunners kept up a steady fire with their rifle-calibre machine guns and saw several crew members fall in the conning tower and on the deck. U753 then disappeared at a steep angle. Confident that the sub had been sunk, the airmen congratulated each other. Good show! Fine shooting! Every man aboard the Whitley would have been surprised – and disappointed – to learn that U753 was in fact able to limp home to the Atlantic coast of France.*

The attack on U753 was one of several incidents in the Bay of Biscay during June 1942. Dönitz revised his instructions to U-boat skippers crossing the Bay. In the past, he had been content to leave it up to individual skippers to take appropriate action when attacked. Most had preferred to remain on the surface, relying on lookouts during the day to warn of approaching aircraft. At night, they had been fairly safe, but now the Leigh lights on many Coastal Command aircraft had made their nocturnal journeys more perilous. Dönitz decreed that until further notice, U-boats were to cross the Bay of Biscay submerged, surfacing only for brief periods at night in order to recharge their batteries. It was not a popular order; and most U-boat officers saw it as a temporary measure. When the U-boats were equipped with the Metox detectors, they would have ample warning of approaching aircraft. Moreover, Dönitz intended to arm his U-boats so that they could successfully take on enemy aircraft; they would all be armed with much heavier armament, including twin 37-millimetre, and batteries of 20-millimetre, rapid-fire guns.

A few days later came the first sinking of a U-boat by a Leigh light-equipped aircraft, a Wellington VIII of 172 Squadron. The aircrew, commanded by Pilot Officer W. B. Howell, an American

---

* Repairs took several months. A little over a year later, the U-boat went down with all hands, destroyed by a Sunderland of 423 Squadron.

in the RAF, picked up a radar contact at seven miles. About a mile from the target, they switched the light on, revealing a Type IXC U-boat rolling gently on the surface. Four depth charges straddled the boat. When the water settled, the aircrew saw that the water around the submarine had become uncommonly dark. U502, commanded by Jürgen von Rosenstiel, sank with all hands. Six days later, Howell and his crew attacked another Type IXC U-boat, U159, again using their Leigh light. The U-boat skipper, Helmut Witte, ordered his gun crew to shoot out the aircraft's Leigh light. The gunners, blinded by the intense glare, couldn't obey. U159 escaped but suffered damage.

The loss of oil tankers around the American east coast furrowed many Allied brows. In all, 129 had been sunk since Operation Drumbeat was launched in January. The losses came at a difficult time, for efforts were being made to stockpile immense quantities of petroleum products for future operations, most notably the invasion of Europe. Making the situation infinitely worse, some fifty British tankers had to be transferred to the Indian Ocean to support operations in the Far East. The British asked Washington to "lend" them seventy tankers of 10,000 deadweight tons each. It is a reflection of the amazing strength of the American industrial base that this request was not only met but exceeded: 684,000 deadweight tons for Britain, 170,000 for Canada – and this at a time when the United States had been suffering serious losses of tankers. A few months later, the British asked for another "loan." This time, the Americans responded with the equivalent of forty tankers – 400,000 deadweight tons.

Dönitz's U-boats continued to savage Allied convoys in the Atlantic and elsewhere. Rodger Winn, the ex-barrister in the Admiralty's U-boat tracking room, came up with disturbing figures, estimating that the Germans had built 355 U-boats, of which seventy-five were believed to have been sunk. New U-boats were coming off the lines at the rate of fifteen to twenty-five a month. Some four hundred U-boats should therefore be operational by the beginning of 1943, he claimed.

The U.S. Army Chief of Staff, George Marshall, wrote Admiral King a scathing letter, criticizing the admiral's reluctance to use convoys and declaring that the U-boat sinking off the Atlantic seaboard had reached a level that could threaten the entire war effort.

8

WINNING AND LOSING

"Hit hard, hit fast, hit often"
– Admiral William F. "Bull" Halsey, USN

IN JUNE 1942, the British Prime Minister journeyed to the United States. Winston Churchill looked forward to his meeting with President Roosevelt, the first since the Japanese attack at Pearl Harbor. But humiliating news awaited him at the White House. Tobruk had fallen. Some 33,000 British and Commonwealth troops had been defeated by about half that number of Axis troops led by the redoubtable Rommel. The fall of Tobruk crushed Churchill; indeed, it was a heavy blow for the British on every level. The *Manchester Guardian* had this to say: "Norway could be forgiven as a scratch affair; Dunkirk followed the defection [*sic*] of our allies; the first Libyan failure was due to a human error of judgment and to the diversion of forces to help the forlorn hope in Greece; Hong Kong, Singapore, Java were an almost inevitable sequence after our gamble of Eastern unpreparedness had failed. But Libya as the ordinary man sees it is another matter. Here at least we were supposed to be strong. . . . The Government will have to put itself in the place of the workers who find that after they have worked so hard and so long their production is thrown away in the field, battered by superior weight, or left as booty to the enemy."

It seemed not improbable that the government would fall. That it didn't was almost entirely due to the persuasive tongue of the prime minister.

In Washington, the so-called Argonaut Conference lasted until June 27, the two principal subjects for discussion being shipping losses and the devastating military setback in North Africa. With characteristic generosity, the Americans offered emergency aid, including an armoured division (commanded by George S. Patton, Jr.), three hundred brand-new Sherman tanks, minus engines, and one hundred new 105-millimetre self-propelled anti-tank guns.

The three hundred engines for the tanks were loaded on the 6,200-ton freighter, *Fairport*. Escorted by two cruisers and seven destroyers, the convoy left New York on July 13. Three days later, U161, a Type IX U-boat commanded by Albrecht Achilles, spotted the convoy. Achilles attacked, sinking *Fairport* with her valuable cargo. On hearing of this, Roosevelt immediately ordered three hundred more engines to be sent to North Africa.

～

Horst Degen, skipper of U701, had reason for satisfaction. Off Cape Hatteras, he had encountered the fourteen-thousand-ton American tanker *William A. Rockefeller*. A U.S. Coast Guard aircraft circled above. Disregarding it, Degen attacked. He stopped the tanker with a single torpedo, and the crew began to abandon ship. Depth charges came thumping down from the Coast Guard aircraft but did no serious damage; a Coast Guard cutter launched seven more, all to no avail. Degen slipped away to safety. He waited until nightfall, then returned to find the tanker dead in the water. One more torpedo sent *William A. Rockefeller* to the bottom. It was the culmination of a highly successful patrol for Degen. Nine ships had gone down to U701 for an eminently satisfactory sixty thousand tons. There would be a warm welcome in France on the boat's return.

Degen surfaced shortly after 1300 hours to air out the U-boat. The vessel reeked; stale, fetid air saturated every inch. He and three other officers served as lookouts. No other vessels or aircraft could be seen, and the pleasant early summer sun made the occasion almost festive. U701 exchanged its foul air for fresh, after which Degen gave orders to dive.

At that precise moment, the first watch officer spotted the aircraft. It was an A-29, the USAAF's version of the RAF Hudson, part of the 396th Medium Bombardment Squadron based at Cherry Point, North Carolina. The skipper, Lieutenant Harry Kane, had seen U701 on the surface a few moments earlier. Flinging the hefty twin-engined bomber into a steep turn, he alerted his four-man crew. They prepared three 325-pound depth charges as the noise of the engine rose and the aircraft seemed to tremble with eagerness to get to grips with the U-boat. U701 had already slipped beneath the surface as Kane roared overhead at about fifty feet. He could see the long and slender form of the U-boat sliding effortlessly through the water like some huge fish. Kane released his depth charges. His timing was superb. He straddled U701; one depth charge fell astern, the other two landed on the sub, one on either side of the conning tower. A text-book performance.

Seconds later, the D/Cs exploded, completely wrecking the U-boat, flooding it aft of the conning tower. The crew abandoned ship, Degen leading some of his men through the conning tower while eighteen more made their way out through the bow torpedo-room loading hatch. Seven of the crew of forty-three were lost. Kane circled the area for about two hours, dropping lifejackets and a dinghy, until a shortage of fuel compelled him to return to base. A Coast Guard cutter attempted to rescue the survivors, but by the time it arrived on the scene, the local currents had swept them away. Not until July 10, three days after the sinking, were seven survivors found. Among them was the captain,

Horst Degen. His was the first U-boat to be sunk by an aircraft of the USAAF.

The following day, a USAAF B-18 picked up a good radar contact at first light; it was U157, a new Type IX. The B-18 dropped depth charges, but apparently did no serious damage. For the next forty-eight gruelling hours, U.S. sea and air forces hunted U157. During the night of June 12/13, air force B-18s got a promising radar contact. The Coast Guard took over, dropping a series of depth charges. They succeeded in sinking U157 with all hands.

U158, under the command of Erich Rostin, was heading home, all her torpedoes expended, when she encountered the four-thousand-ton Latvian freighter *Everalda* near Bermuda. Using his deck gun, Rostin stopped the ship, took her captain prisoner, and sent a party on board to scuttle her. Afterwards, Rostin was incautious enough to inform the BdU of his triumph. Several British installations picked up the message and plotted a fix. This was relayed to a U.S. Navy Mariner flying boat on patrol. The Mariner pilot, Richard Schreder, found the U-boat in a matter of minutes. Below him, members of the submarine's crew lay sunning themselves on deck — a most unusual state of affairs, particularly with Bermuda little more than one hundred miles away; most U-boats maintained meticulous lookouts and kept crew members off the deck as much as possible so they could dive quickly if enemy aircraft or ships appeared. Going straight in to the attack, Schreder dropped two bombs and two Mark XVII depth charges, set to explode at shallow depths. Even as the U-boat's crew were hurling themselves below deck, the depth charges landed. One hit the bridge, becoming wedged in the superstructure. As the German sailors clamped down their hatches, they probably congratulated themselves on a lucky escape. None realized that the submarine was taking the depth charge along, firmly lodged in the superstructure. At the critical depth, the D/C exploded. It blew an immense hole in the hull, sinking the boat at once with all hands. Rostin, the captain, had been awarded the coveted Ritterkreuz only two days before. Although not widely known to the German public, he was a highly successful skipper, having sunk a total of seventeen ships in his two patrols to the Americas.

A few days later, another U-boat crew had an unusual experience. U68, commanded by Karl-Friederich Merten, fired five torpedoes at two large freighters inbound from Panama. Two torpedoes missed their targets but hit other ships, the British freighters *Ardenvohr* and *Surrey*. Both began to sink.

Merten fished one survivor out of the water and learned that *Surrey* had been loaded with five thousand tons of dynamite. While the man spoke, *Surrey* slipped beneath the surface, and a moment later the entire cargo blew up in a monstrous eruption that tossed U68 clear of the water. Crashing back with an enormous splash, the submarine temporarily lost her engines and compasses. The crew were winded and bruised but, remarkably, uninjured. While the crew attended to the diesels, Merten received a report of another ship in the vicinity, the British freighter *Port Montreal*. Undeterred by his close call, he set off in pursuit. Unable to catch up with his prey, he tried a long-range shot. To his astonishment, it scored a direct hit, sending *Port Montreal* to the bottom.

By late summer 1942, Dönitz's Atlantic U-boat force had grown significantly. Now it numbered 124, with the recent addition of twenty-six Type VII boats and twelve of the longer-range Type IX U-boats. In addition, three of the valuable U-tanker boats were added to the fleet, promising even longer cruises for the U-boats and their crews. Few U-boats ventured close to Newfoundland and Nova Scotia in the second half of 1942, because Dönitz shifted his main effort into mid-ocean waters. At this point, the notorious Air Gap in the mid Atlantic still existed, although Coastal Command in Britain and Iceland, and No. 1 Group in Newfoundland, were working to extend their coverage of this critical area. Coastal Command aircraft pushed patrols and escorts westward to about six hundred miles from their British and Icelandic bases, while aircraft of No. 1 Group in Newfoundland ranged eastward to somewhat lesser distances. According to the RCAF official history, "The intervening 'air gap' ran in a funnel shape from its neck in the north, where air patrols from Newfoundland and Iceland left a relatively short distance uncovered, broadening to the south where a great expanse of ocean lay beyond the limits of land-based aircraft."[1]

This was the U-boats' favourite hunting ground. In the first half of 1942 they had succeeded in sinking 505 Allied ships, most of them sailing independently in U.S. waters. This major loss cost the Germans a mere eleven U-boats. The Germans' campaign in American waters had, it seems, caught the Americans at first totally by surprise, and with no convoys along the eastern seaboard, awful losses resulted. But in time the implementation of the coastal convoy system and specialized training of ASW crews made it much harder for the U-boats to operate.

Several U-boats ventured north into Canadian waters in mid 1942. Ernst Vogelsang in U132 slid unseen through the waters of Cabot Strait between Nova Scotia and Newfoundland on the night of June 29. He steered directly for the mouth of the St. Lawrence River. On the evening of July 5, he took up position off Cap Chat, some 250 miles northeast of Quebec City. He waited for Convoy QS 15, en route for Sydney, Nova Scotia. Sure enough, the ships appeared during the early hours of July 6. Vogelsang fired five torpedoes. Three missed, probably because of technical problems, but two struck a pair of freighters, which sank. Vogelsang remained in these waters for some time, sinking the British freighter *Pacific Pioneer* in early August. Kurt Diggins, commanding U458, sank the British tanker *Arletta*. Hans Oestermann (U754) and Dietrich Lohmann (U89) had to be satisfied with more modest victories: a 260-ton American trawler, *Ebb*, and a 54-ton trawler, *Lucille M*. Lohmann took the unusual step of apologizing to the eleven survivors of this small Canadian vessel, explaining that he was under orders and "had to obey." It was Lohmann's only victory during his seventy-seven-day foray into American waters.

Dönitz considered his performance deplorable and transferred him to other duties.

The corvette *Drummondville* depth-charged U132 without any apparent results. Incredibly, the primitive communications in the area kept word of the attack from reaching shore authorities for some six hours. At Mont Joli, Quebec, a telephone call from the naval detachment at Rimouski precipitated hasty action by 130 (Fighter) Squadron. The unit had a number of P-40 Kittyhawk fighters temporarily based at the base, which were hastily refuelled and armed; four took off into the darkness with Squadron Leader Joseph Chevrier in the lead. He never returned. It seems probable that he experienced engine trouble and crashed into the sea near Cap Chat. In every way it was an unhappy episode; particularly distressing were the reports later circulated accusing the aircrew at Mont Joli of being drunk and happily engaged in all manner of debauchery when the alert was received. Adelard Godbout, the Quebec premier, warned that the population of the province was bewildered and inadequately informed about what the German submarines were doing; rumours spread like wildfire. Godbout added that he had heard from "reliable sources" that two men had landed from a submarine and had attacked the wireless station at Mont Joli airfield.

The story was totally unfounded. But such fantasies were inevitable when official sources failed to tell people what was happening. In the meantime, the air defence of the east coast had to be maintained. The Newfoundland squadrons continued to watch over the Strait of Belle Isle; 117 Squadron flew three Cansos from Gaspé; at Mont Joli, the 113 Squadron detachment patrolled in its Hudsons. In narrow channels and other confined waters, however, air patrols were of limited value, as demonstrated by the attacks on convoys LN6 and SG6 late in August. LN6 was a convoy of modest size sailing from Quebec City to Goose Bay; SG6 consisted of a cluster of American ships sailing from Sydney to Greenland escorted by the U.S. Navy and at the time of the attack, a 10 Squadron Digby. The American troopship *Chatham*, being faster than the other ships in the convoy, was given permission to forge ahead of them, under escort. U517, commanded by Paul Hartwig, torpedoed her in broad daylight on August 27. Thirteen of her men died. Hartwig and Dietrich Hoffmann in U165 sailed down the Belle Isle Strait, looking for more prey. In the early hours of September 3, Hartwig encountered two more small convoys, heading in opposite directions. He sank the 1,800-ton Canadian laker *Donald Stewart*, loaded with aviation gasoline and bulk cement intended for new runways at Goose Bay, Labrador. Three corvettes and a minesweeper appeared, seeking revenge. Hartwig evaded them without difficulty and was soon lost to sight in the foggy Gulf of St. Lawrence.

There was no shortage of prey. Hoffmann spotted an eight-ship convoy travelling from Quebec to Sydney, with an escort of a corvette, a minesweeper, two motor torpedo boats (MTBs), and an armed yacht, *Raccoon*. Hoffmann spent the next twenty-four hours attacking and shadowing the convoy. He sank two ships, a Greek freighter, *Aeas*, and the 358-ton *Raccoon*. Hartwig rejoined him on the afternoon of September 7 – and promptly sank three more of the convoy's ships. The convoy's four remaining escorts seemed utterly confused by the rapid succession of events and took no action. Fortunately, a Hudson of 113 Squadron appeared on the scene. The pilot, Pilot Officer R. S. Keetley, spotted U165 and swooped down from four thousand feet about twenty miles south of Anticosti. But he was too high. The U-boat dived. Keetley claimed a victory over U165, but in fact he had inflicted no damage on the sub. Interestingly, Hoffmann complained to the BdU that the "intense" air activity was making it difficult to inter-cept convoys.

A few days later, Hartwig in U517 caused a sensation by sinking the corvette *Charlottetown* in daylight watched by onlookers on shore. On September 15 and 16, the two U-boats intercepted a twenty-two-ship convoy. A Canso of 117 Squadron was patrolling overhead but didn't spot either German submarine. Hartwig sank two ships. Later, with air cover now the responsibility of a Canso of 5 Squadron, Hoffmann sank two more. Eleven ships sunk in two weeks was a bitter blow, particularly since not one U-boat had been sunk.

For about a week, the Germans seemed content to lie low, and on September 25, Paul Hartwig in U517 reported "constantly strengthened" air patrols. He spoke from personal experience. A Hudson of 113 Squadron (temporarily based at Chatham, New Brunswick), had attacked U517 the previous day. Hartwig was lucky that a blown fuse prevented the dropping of more than one depth charge. Near midnight, another 113 Squadron Hudson with Flying Officer M. J. Belanger at the controls caught U517 by surprise and shook the boat with two massive explosions close astern.

Earlier in September, Convoy ON127 sailed from Britain, escorted by C4 Group, an all-Canadian force, except for one RN corvette. Two destroyers led the group: *Ottawa*, under the command of Lieutenant-Commander C. A. Rutherford, and *St. Croix*, commanded by Lieutenant-Commander A. H. Dobson. The other corvettes in the group were *Amherst*, *Arvida*, and *Sherbrooke*.

The convoy and its escorts ran into the thirteen U-boats of the *Vorwarts* (Forward) wolfpack and were startled by the sudden torpedoing of *Elizabeth van Belgie*, *F. J. Wolfe*, and *Svene* on the 10th of September in a submerged attack. U96 was the U-boat responsible. Dobson ordered *Ottawa*, *St. Croix*, and the RN corvette *Celandine* to hunt down the assailant; he instructed *Sherbrooke* to stand by the damaged vessels, later ordering the corvette to sink *Svene*, which could not continue. Meanwhile, *F. J. Wolfe* had difficulty maintaining her position in the convoy and was eventually sunk by *Sherbrooke*. A similar fate befell *Elizabeth van Belgie*. *Ottawa* took up a position to the rear of the convoy, anticipating the appearance of a shadowing U-boat.

St. Croix moved to the van of the convoy. She quickly picked up an Asdic contact one thousand yards ahead. A matter of minutes later, the tanker *Empire Oil* took a torpedo on her starboard, followed by another on her port side. The destroyers and corvettes scurried about the convoy, seeking Asdic echoes. They found none. *Celandine* returned to the convoy, the destroyers picking up *Empire Oil's* survivors. Before they could return to the convoy, another ship, *Marit II*, had been torpedoed. Later that day, *Fjordaas* also took a torpedo, this one from U218. Both ships managed to stay afloat. It was a busy night for the escorts. *St. Croix* drove off one U-boat, *Arvida* another; both *Amherst* and *Ottawa* attacked Asdic contacts without observing any results. At this point, *Celandine's* radar broke down.

The convoy lost another ship, *Hindanger*, the following day, torpedoed by U584. Again it was a case of a ship being badly damaged but remaining afloat. *Amherst* later sank her. With the strength of the escort force sadly depleted, the convoy suffered more losses; U211 torpedoed *Hektoria* and *Empire Moonbeam*. Not long afterward, *Daghild* took a torpedo and sank. The convoy was being decimated.

Early on the 12th, Dobson placed his four remaining escort vessels forward of the convoy, but, despite the presence of U-boats in clear weather, he failed to employ his destroyers on wide-ranging sweeps on either beam of ON127.

The worst seemed to be over when, on the 13th, the dreaded Air Gap was passed; the first aircraft from Newfoundland appeared, driving off most of the shadowing U-boats. As darkness fell, the convoy received more escorts, the RCN destroyer *Annapolis* and the RN destroyer *Witch*. The crew relaxed; the worst was over. Or was it? Shortly after midnight, a torpedo fired by the Type VII U-boat, U91, commanded by Heinz Walkerling, slammed into the destroyer *Ottawa*. *St. Croix* hurried to her assistance and found her grievously damaged – much of her bow had been blown away, although she did not appear to be in immediate danger. A few minutes later, a second torpedo hit *Ottawa*, striking her just forward of "A" gun. Her back broken, she sank quickly. She took with her 141 of her ship's company.

On the 14th, the arrival of aircraft from Newfoundland effectively ended the battle. It had cost the convoy eight ships sunk, four damaged. One U-boat was slightly damaged.

～

A few days earlier, U156, a Type IXC U-boat, had launched two torpedoes at the twenty-thousand-ton armed Cunard White Star liner *Laconia* in the South Atlantic 250 miles northeast of Ascension Island. One missile hit the liner forward, the other amidships. *Laconia* sank some ninety minutes later, taking her captain, Rudolph Sharp, to his death. The ship had been carrying 1,800 Italian prisoners of war and 269 British and Polish military personnel. According to some accounts, when the ship began to sink, the Polish troops guarding the Italians refused to unlock the hatches, and even those prisoners who did succeed in getting to the deck were denied entry to lifeboats, held back at bayonet point. Hundreds of prisoners, some with lifejackets, many without, splashed around the sinking ship, desperately seeking help in the shark-infested waters.

Werner Hartenstein, captain of U156, ordered his crew to pick up as many of the survivors as possible. He also contacted Dönitz, who ordered seven U-boats to the scene to assist in the rescue operation. Hartenstein's crew fished some four hundred grateful survivors from the water, squeezing 172 Italians and twenty-one British men and women into the narrow confines of U156. The rest went into lifeboats. Hartenstein wanted to arrange a temporary cease-fire with the Allies; he requested permission from Dönitz, then went ahead, not waiting for a response. On September 13, a day after the sinking, Hartenstein broadcast the following message in English: "If any ship will assist the shipwrecked *Laconia* crew, I will not attack her, providing I am not attacked by ship or air force. I picked up 193 men. 4 degrees – 52" south. 11 degrees – 26" west." He signed it, "German submarine." After this, he cruised among the survivors, redistributing the loads in lifeboats and doling out food and water. Hartenstein's rescue operations lasted two days; then U506 and U507 arrived on the scene.

Hartenstein continued his good work, apparently believing that a truce had been arranged. None had.

The Americans had recently established an air base on Ascension Island. Eighteen P-39 fighters and five B-25 bombers were based there; they had the latest ASW depth charges and bombs, but the aircrews had not been trained in anti-submarine activities. Moreover, Hartenstein's message had not been picked up by the base.

Early on the morning of September 15, five U.S. aircraft in transit from Ascension Island to Accra flew over the scene. One dropped down to a lower altitude for a closer look. Whereupon all three U-boats opened fire, claimed the American airmen. The U.S. aircraft escaped without damage and made off.

The following morning, a B-24 Liberator from Ascension Island appeared. The pilot, James D. Harden, was ordered to attack the U-boats. Harden dropped three depth charges without effect. Then he dropped bombs, one of which exploded among the lifeboats, capsizing one and flinging its occupants into the sea. A final run saw two more bombs hit the water close to U156. Harden reported that the sub had capsized and claimed it as a "kill"; in fact, the U-boat suffered only minor damage and resumed its patrol.

Dönitz was infuriated by the Allied action, believing it to have been a deliberate contravention of an accepted cease-fire agreement. He lost no time in issuing the following order: "All attempts to rescue the crews of sunken ships will cease forthwith. This prohibition applies equally to the picking up of men in the water and putting them aboard a lifeboat, to the righting of capsized lifeboats and the supply of food and water. Such activities are a contradiction of the primary object of war, namely, the destruction of enemy ships and their crews."[2]

At about this time, the RCAF at last sank its first U-boat. Squadron Leader Norville Everett Small, known to everyone as "Molly," was one of Eastern Air Command's outstanding airmen, and at the time one of the few regulars in the air force. His career spanned many years. He had joined the RCAF in the 1920s, as a mechanic, and later became an NCO pilot. He left the service for a few years in the 1930s, flying for a commercial operator, but on the outbreak of war, he rejoined with the rank of pilot officer. In June 1942, he had taken over command of 113 Squadron, a bomber reconnaissance unit. The following month, he took off in a Hudson to investigate reported U-boats southeast of Cape Sable. His crew consisted of the observer/navigator, Pilot Officer G. E. Francis, and two wireless operator/air gunners, Sergeants R. A. Coulter and D. P. Rogers. He approached the area at three thousand feet, each member of the crew staring intently into the haze that clung to the sea's surface like gossamer.

And there it was. Long, low, a dull grey monster: U754, just as reported! She seemed to be stationary in the water. A sitting duck! Small told his crew to prepare to attack. The airmen acknowledged. Small eased the twin-engined bomber into a dive. The whole enterprise depended upon whether the U-boat could be reached before its crew saw the Hudson.

Incredibly, the German sailors seemed unaware of the plane's presence. As the aircraft approached, they continued to chat, no doubt boasting to each other what they were going to do the moment they got back to France . . .

Suddenly an arm pointed in the Hudson's direction. Small could imagine the warning voices, strained, harsh with alarm. It was as if a still photo had suddenly become a movie run too quickly. Like tiny parasites on the back of some prehistoric monster, the sailors sprang into action, dashing for cover, hurling themselves at the hatches. In a moment, just as Small was pulling out of the dive, the U-boat's deck cleared – almost magically, it seemed.

The four 250-pound Mark VII depth charges fell away, angling down at the U-boat. Small had judged his drop perfectly. The D/Cs smacked into the water all around the U-boat, just as it disappeared beneath the surface. The water swirled as if gathering strength. Then erupted. Great bursts of water marked the spot where each depth charge had landed.

Small circled, watching, waiting.

One of the gunners opened fire as U754's conning tower reappeared. Then disappeared. In a moment, huge air bubbles came popping to the surface. The ocean shook as a heavy underwater explosion rocked it. Masses of oil, ugly dark stuff, rose to the surface, spreading, staining the sun-dappled water.

Small continued to circle, watching intently. But the ocean revealed nothing more. U754 had gone to the bottom with every member of her crew.*

~

Dönitz wanted better air cover for his U-boats, particularly over the increasingly dangerous Bay of Biscay. He went to see Göring, but the plump Luftwaffe commander-in-chief shrugged regretfully. The Eastern Front had priority – the Führer had decreed it. Dönitz persisted. He wasn't asking for hundreds of aircraft, just a couple of dozen or so. He added that the Führer would support the action, because, as he had noted several times, the U-boat had so far proved itself by far the most effective weapon in the Kriegsmarine, and he would not like to hear that many of them were being destroyed heading for their home ports after highly successful patrols.

The meeting took place at Göring's opulent headquarters in East Prussia. Dönitz was never comfortable in Göring's presence;

---

*   Small won the squadron's first DFC. Tragically, he was killed in a flying accident a few months later.

overdressed, perfumed, the air marshal seemed to be the antithesis of the ideal Nazi. He apparently spent far more time on his magnificent art collection than on the running of the air force. Morale in the Luftwaffe was said to be slipping – and was it any wonder? In spite of this, however, the fact remained that Göring was still the Führer's favourite, probably the next head of state should the unthinkable happen. One had to tread with care.

Eventually, Göring agreed to order the Atlantic Air Command to initiate long-range patrols by powerfully armed Junkers 88C fighters over the Bay of Biscay. Based at Kerlin Bastard and Merignac, the Ju 88s were formidable adversaries, capable of making short work of a Catalina or Hudson. Predictably, the British countered with patrols of even more heavily armed Beaufighters, later Mosquitoes. Some fierce battles ensued when enemy patrols ran into one another.

Although anti-submarine squadrons did not produce "aces" in the same way that fighter patrols did, one star performer emerged in the latter weeks of 1942. He was Terry Bulloch, an Ulsterman who had flown Ansons and Hudsons earlier in the war and had succeeded in shooting down a Heinkel 115 seaplane. Unlike most of his contemporaries, Bulloch did not find anti-submarine patrols a bore. He revelled in the chase and kept thinking up ways to increase the odds for the attackers. He trained his crew as thoroughly as did his adversaries, the U-boat skippers. He was determined not to waste any opportunity to score a victory over a U-boat. Bulloch's big chance came when he was posted to 120 Squadron, based at Reykjavík, Iceland, the first RAF unit equipped with the new Consolidated B-24 Liberator. The Liberators flown by 120 Squadron at that time were Mark Is originally built for the French; their fuel tanks were of the non-self-sealing-material variety, holding 2,500 gallons. Not long afterward, the first depth charges with twenty-five-foot settings became available. Coastal Command's instructions to aircrew called for them to drop depth charges in a straddle *across* the U-boats' path. The practice troubled

Bulloch; it meant that a large proportion of the D/Cs dropped fell in the water, either short of or beyond the target. Bulloch decided that the only satisfactory way of dropping D/Cs was along the length of a U-boat. "You really had to get within ten or twelve feet of its pressure hull to do any damage with depth charges. They used to go down to twenty-five feet; they were set hydrostatically by a fuse. So you had to get the U-boats either on the surface – which was difficult, because if they spotted you they'd be down in sixty seconds – or just below it. If it was lower than twenty-five feet it would give them a bit of a shock, but do very little, if any, damage."[3]

Bulloch's first victory came on October 12, 1942. He set off to escort an Atlantic convoy and picked up a radar echo shortly after noon. Five minutes later, the Liberator crew spotted a U-boat. Bulloch attacked. His six depth charges landed in a remarkably tight cluster around the target. Any one of them would probably have been fatal; the combined effect of them all exploding was devastating. U597, a new Type VII boat, commanded by twenty-eight-year-old Eberhard Bopst, disintegrated and disappeared from view. None of the crew survived.

Bulloch spotted another U-boat shortly after this success. He attacked but two depth charges "hung up," and he had no option but to return to base.

Experiments by the RAF's 120 Squadron were demonstrating the remarkable potential of the B-24. Mark V aircraft, minus the rubberized self-sealing material from the wing tanks, but plus auxiliary tanks, became known as Class "A" VLR Liberators. Class "B" conversions were mainly Mark III Liberators with extra fuel tanks in the bomb bay, but without dorsal or tail turrets. Armour and most of the aircraft's oxygen equipment were removed to increase range.

All was not well in Canada's Eastern Air Command, according to officers visiting from Britain. Wing Commanders S. R. Gibbs and P. F. Canning, RAF, had recently spent eight months advising the USAAF on every aspect of operational control, the creation of combined operations rooms, and the establishment of an anti-submarine force on the lines of RAF Coastal Command. The visitors felt that the Canadians should be more offensive in their anti-submarine operations. Also, it was necessary to streamline their organization; they should create a combined services (air force and navy) headquarters. An earlier visitor from RAF Coastal Command, J. P. T. Pearman of Coastal's operational research section, pointed out that most of Eastern Air Command's flying was within two hundred miles of base. Attacks tended to be delayed until U-boats had reached focal areas of trade. In October, Commander P. B. Martineau, RN, a staff officer from Coastal Command HQ, completed a lengthy advisory tour in North America and reported, with scant regard for Canadian sensibilities, "Generally speaking, the Eastern Air Command is a very long way behind any other place I visited either in Canada or the United States."[4] Martineau emphasized the need to adopt Coastal Command's "Offensive Tactics," instead of sticking with the practice of escorting convoys whether they were threatened or not. The RAF had abandoned such tactics eighteen months before.

Martineau was far from impressed by the knowledge of the aircrews of Eastern Air Command, rating them as poorly informed about the latest techniques of anti-submarine warfare, that is, the tactics promulgated by Coastal Command. He had a point. Eastern Air Command had tended to treat the Coastal Command bulletins on ASW as just more bumph in a war buried in it. Few aircrews read the material; most rarely even saw it. No senior Canadian officer, except the highly successful Squadron Leader "Molly" Small of 113 Squadron, seemed to believe that these missives might actually help them do their jobs more efficiently. The RCAF official history remarks, "Martineau blamed the senior officers of Eastern Air Command for this general lack of leadership, and with that it is hard to disagree."[5] In answer to criticisms concerning the pilots and aircrew, Air Vice Marshal A. A. L. Cuffe, commanding Eastern Air Command, pointed out — no doubt with some asperity — that the command was still being "bled" of experienced pilots, their replacements often coming straight from operational training units. A spot check in mid–October revealed that only eighty-nine of the establishment of 135 bomber reconnaissance aircraft were on strength. Nine were allocated to training duties. Only fifty or so of the remaining aircraft were available for operations on the east coast. Cuffe declared, not unreasonably, that he had too few aircraft to do a good job of training or operations. The irony was, however, that the shortage of aircraft might have been largely eliminated had the Command adopted Coastal Command's offensive methods, which, experience showed, saved countless hours of flying. In October 1942, Eastern Air Command began using these tactics off the Newfoundland coast, protecting convoys by means of sweeps along parallel tracks fifty miles on either side of the mean line of advance, fifty miles to the rear, and one hundred miles ahead. The late afternoon or early morning hours were preferred; at such times, the U-boats were usually manoeuvring their way out of combat or preparing for the night's attacks. Results were encouraging.

Criticism from Coastal Command was also directed at the RCN. At this stage in the war, about half the escorts operating between New York and Britain were Canadian. Yet Canadian ships still sailed with radar and other ASW equipment markedly inferior to that of their British and U.S. counterparts. Equally important, the Canadians had been hastily and inadequately trained. By mid-1942, scarcely a third of the sixteen thousand men serving at sea were adequately trained by any naval standard. Three-quarters of them were men of the Royal Canadian Naval Volunteer Reserve, who had been rushed into service to man the corvettes, Bangors, and various smaller craft, and fight off the U-boats as best they could.

The Americans were far less active in the North Atlantic at this time than they had been before Pearl Harbor, vast numbers of escort vessels having been transferred to the Pacific, leaving the British and Canadians to look after the convoys. Although many of the British ships were becoming elderly, some dating back to the

First World War, they were equipped with the latest in ASW technology. The Canadian ships weren't. Most had operated without radar for about a year after the RN vessels were equipped. Even though the Canadians now had radar, it was outdated and generally inferior to that carried by RN vessels, most of which had by that time converted from earlier sets to equipment operating on a wavelength of only ten centimetres. It was an extraordinary advance, made possible by the British development of the cavity magnetron in 1940, which in turn made possible the vastly improved radar introduced by the Allies. This version of ASV, the Mark III, was a revelation. It could detect convoys at a range of forty miles and surfaced submarines at twelve miles. It would, when produced in sufficient numbers, become the definitive ASV radar. Moreover, the Germans' Metox receiver could not detect its signals.

Few Canadian ships enjoyed the benefits of ASV Mark III. As usual, the Canadians had to wait at the back of the line until the needs of the British and Americans had been met. Confusing the situation even more was that an almost bewildering flood of innovations in anti-submarine warfare began to appear. Although no one questioned their value, their use necessitated intense retraining of crews – with the Canadians falling steadily behind in the technical race. The severe lack of technical specialists in the RCN continued to have serious ramifications. At the same time, the preparations for the North African landings (Operation Torch) made further inroads into the North Atlantic escort fleet.

In the fall of 1942, the Royal Navy became downright vociferous in its criticism of the Canadians. On December 17, Churchill suggested to Prime Minister Mackenzie King that the Canadians be withdrawn from the crucial mid-ocean run and instead escort the Britain-to-Gibraltar run so that they could be fitted with various items of new equipment and, equally importantly, undergo intensive training. The proposed demotion sent shockwaves through the RCN. The original plan was for the groups to be transferred for a maximum of four months; in the event, only three groups were transferred, and these only for eight to ten weeks. Within a few weeks, the furor over the withdrawal of the Canadian groups had been forgotten. The Canadian ASW vessels had at last been equipped with the latest radar, HF/DF (high frequency direction finding), and other equipment. In general, that was the extent of it; little retraining took place, but there can be no doubt that the exercise was worthwhile; in March 1943, the RCN took over responsibility for convoy and anti-submarine operations from the U.S. waters south of Nova Scotia to the limit of Western Approaches' control east of Newfoundland, maintaining control until the end of the war.

In the last months of 1942, the Germans began modifying their U-boats, adding platforms for anti-aircraft weaponry aft of the conning tower, called "bandstands" or "winter gardens." The deck-mounted guns had largely disappeared, since most merchant ships were in convoy when attacked and the torpedo was the weapon of choice for the U-boats. Allied aircrews soon noted how vigorously U-boats now responded to air attack. Several 20-millimetre guns were often installed on the bandstand with three or four 7.9-millimetre machine guns. Before long, even heavier concentrations of armament were crammed on to the limited spaces.

The steady increase in Allied air power concerned Dönitz deeply. It took little imagination to see that it could lead to a total denial of the Atlantic to his U-boats. A new type of U-boat was needed, one that could travel underwater at high speed for long periods without the need to surface and recharge batteries. Clearly, the current form of propulsion, diesel and electric power, was inadequate. A German scientist, Dr. Hellmuth Walter, had been developing a new U-boat propulsion system for several years.* Walter had focused his research on fuel of highly concentrated hydrogen peroxide and diesel oil. In 1940, an experimental submarine had

---

* At the same time he had been working on the revolutionary Messerschmitt 163 rocket-propelled fighter.

been built embodying Walter's system. It had promise, but, like the revolutionary rocket-propelled Messerschmitt 163 – on which he was working at the same time – it had to be treated with extreme care. The fuel was murderously unstable and would explode on encountering the tiniest morsel of dirt in the containers or in the vessel's pipes. In its present form it was hardly suitable for the rough and tumble of operations in the North Atlantic.

Work continued.

By the end of 1942, Dönitz's U-boats were still the Allies' most serious problem. But two factors overshadowed every effort made by Dönitz and his crews: the astonishing numbers of merchant ships constructed during this period, far exceeding the tonnage of ships sunk, and the continued expansion of Allied airpower.

9

TURNING POINT

"It's a long lane that knows no turnings"
– Robert Browning

JANUARY 1943. North Atlantic shipping losses had dropped significantly, not because of Allied ASW activity, but because of vile weather, some of the worst in living memory.

Early in the month, Grand-Admiral Erich Raeder travelled to Hitler's headquarters at Rastenburg, East Prussia. The sixty-seven-year-old sailor listened in silence as Hitler berated him and his navy. A few weeks earlier, a numerically inferior British force had defeated a German naval attack on a convoy to Murmansk in Russia, sinking a destroyer and severely damaging the heavy cruiser *Hipper*. Almost beside himself with anger, Hitler accused Raeder's sailors of cowardice and incompetence. He then demanded that Raeder scrap all remaining heavy ships. Although Raeder was given no opportunity to defend himself during the Führer's diatribe, he later sent a memorandum pointing out that scrapping the navy's major ships would only mean an immense naval victory for the Allies at no cost to them. The order was rescinded. But Raeder lost his job.

Dönitz succeeded him, becoming the new Oberbefehlshaber der Kriegsmarine, commander-in-chief of the navy, effective January 30. He intended, however, to remain commander of the U-boat force, despite his new duties overseeing the entire navy. Still frustrated by the inadequate production of U-boats, he lost no time in going to see Albert Speer, the minister of armaments and munitions. Instead of twenty new U-boats a month, Dönitz wanted, and was promised, forty. Soon, he was sure, he would have the necessary number of U-boats to defeat the Allies.

The same month, in Casablanca, Churchill and Roosevelt agreed that the defeat of the U-boats was still their number-one priority. On the last day of the meeting, the British Eighth Army entered Tripoli. It was sweet revenge for Churchill, who, during his last meeting with the American president, had received the humiliating news of Rommel's triumph at Tobruk. Good news emerged from Russia, too. The German Sixth Army had surrendered at Stalingrad.

But the Germans showed no inclination to surrender in the North Atlantic. Most U-boat crewmen believed it was the Allies who would soon throw in the towel, their war machine fatally weakened by the shattering losses at sea. It was just a matter of time, they told each other – just as the Allies were convinced that the Axis powers would soon collapse under the weight of British and American bombing. The governments on both sides did their utmost to propagate such beliefs; they were good for morale.

∿

The last half of 1942 had seen about three million tons of Allied shipping sunk in the Atlantic, a loss of lives and materiel that boggled the mind. On the other hand, Dönitz's losses of U-boats had risen sharply over the same period. Eighty-one German and Italian submarines had been destroyed, compared with only twenty-eight in the first half of the year. Significantly, about half the lost U-boats had been victims of attack from the air. Gradually, air power was becoming the most important weapon in the Atlantic conflict. Eastern Air Command, mindful of this trend, was ever conscious of the dreadful cost of the notorious Air Gap and made earnest efforts to increase the range of their aircraft. For example, under the direction of Squadron Leader N. E. ("Molly") Small, several of 5 Squadron's Cansos were stripped of any equipment that might be considered non-essential: extra guns, ammunition, and stores, amounting to some twelve hundred pounds. The weight-saving enabled the Cansos to operate about seven hundred miles from base. It didn't solve the problem, but it helped.

The best planes for the job were the B-24 Liberators, yet the Americans were still reluctant to provide significant numbers of them to the RAF and RCAF for maritime work. Why? It remains one of the major mysteries of the war that this situation continued to exist when the leaders of the free world kept stressing the absolute necessity of defeating the U-boats as rapidly as possible. Why not transfer a few hundred Liberators to coastal duties? The numbers were trivial in comparison with the legions of "heavies" employed daily in the bombing of Axis targets all over Europe and elsewhere.

Meanwhile, the patrols continued, the big broad-winged aircraft droning out to sea, sometimes searching for convoys that weren't where they were supposed to be, avoiding miscellaneous flak that occasionally welcomed any aircraft coming within range, no matter what its type or nationality. The price of patrol work was boredom: hour after hour of gazing at the grey ocean, searching for the merest hint of a wake or a periscope or sign of a lean hull slipping through the water, searching for prey. Fatigue made eyes play tricks. Pilots sometimes swerved to avoid a hill that had suddenly sprung up in the middle of the ocean. A flock of seagulls became a formation of Focke-Wulf 190 fighters; a cloud suddenly transformed itself into a bevy of dive bombers. The weather was the worst enemy. It could be counted on to change without warning. Many aircraft set out on patrol only to vanish over the sea. More often than not it was because of sudden alterations in the weather, unpredicted winds or the abrupt formation of a fog bank where the met man had predicted clear conditions. You treated weather with the utmost respect.

$\sim$

Commander P. B. Martineau, a staff officer from RAF Coastal Command, recommended the creation of a single authority to control anti-submarine operations on Canada's eastern coast. Particularly important, he said, was the setting-up of a single air force and navy operations room, a concept that had proved so successful in Britain. But in Canada, inter-service jealousies and resentments slowed the process. Canadian Air Vice-Marshal Cuffe, noting that several British area combined headquarters were located at some distance from naval dockyards, invited Rear-Admiral L. W. Murray, Commanding Officer Atlantic Coast, to move to Eastern Air Command's operations room. Murray responded that his broad responsibilities for naval operations and the control of merchant shipping made it impossible for him to do so. He in turn invited Cuffe to come to the dockyard. "Thus the manoeuvrings begun in 1939 continued, with positions now so entrenched that the vice-chief of the naval staff urged that the whole question had to be approached most tactfully," says the official history.[1] It hardly showed the services at their best. However, some progress was made in the coordination of ASW activities. In August 1942, J. O. Wilhelm, a physicist from the University of Toronto, had established an operational research centre at Air Force Head Quarters; Colin Barnes, another U of T physicist, organized an operational research centre in Halifax. Both centres produced analytical statistical reports on air operations, including studies of such specialized subjects as airborne radar, bombing accuracy, and sea/air radio homing. In so many ways, the war in the Atlantic was changing in character, becoming an increasingly technical conflict, a war of stratagems and secrecy as much as a war of machines and men.

In October 1942, No. 1 Group, Eastern Air Command (an operational sub-HQ, one of several formed during the war because of the difficulties of maintaining close control in distant and often desolate areas with poor communications) participated in the defence of two eastbound convoys, SC104 and SC107, which were intercepted by U-boat wolfpacks. The assistance provided to SC104 took the form of close escort by aircraft at about a thousand feet, which accomplished little. SC107, however, had aircraft flying much higher, covering nearby areas where U-boats had been reported. In other words, the recommended Coastal Command approach was at last employed by Eastern Air Command.

By the end of the month, the thirteen U-boats of wolfpack *Veilchen* had taken up station on the Grand Banks. In addition, three Type IX U-boats, U520, U521, and U522, were south of Newfoundland, bound for the Halifax and St. Lawrence areas. This gathering of U-boats gave Eastern Air Command an excellent opportunity to test the new tactics.

In the early afternoon on October 30, 1 Group sent two Hudsons from 145 Squadron at Torbay on an anti-submarine sweep ahead of SC107. Three hours later, close to the limits of their fuel, they spotted a conning tower breaking surface. Flying Officer E. L. Robinson began his attack at two thousand feet. He dropped four 250-pound Mark VIII depth charges, bracketing U658, lifting its stern forty degrees. When it thumped back on the surface, large oil slicks and air bubbles appeared. The U-boat, commanded by Hans Senkel, went straight to the bottom in two thousand fathoms.*

Shortly before nightfall on the same day, a Digby of 10 Squadron was on its way back to Gander after an anti-submarine patrol. Quite unexpectedly, the crew spotted a U-boat 115 miles due east

---

*   Robinson won a DFC for the exploit. He died in a flying accident the following year.

of St. John's. The skipper, Flying Officer D. F. Raymes, dived from 3,200 feet, dropping four 450-pound Mark VII depth charges. After the explosions had subsided, immense air bubbles and quantities of oil rose to the surface. U520 had been destroyed.

While these kills were encouraging, they did little to improve the fortunes of the convoy. Battling rain squalls and gusty winds, four Hudsons of 145 Squadron swept the track ahead of the ships. In mid afternoon, Pilot Officer L. T. Ross spotted U521. He attacked, but the U-boat slipped away to safety. The next day, two 116 Squadron Catalinas from Botwood, Newfoundland, made radar contact with the convoy in the early morning; the radar chose that moment to break down.

Soon afterward, U381 surfaced to send a sighting report to BdU. The message was promptly intercepted by the direction-finding operators in HMCS *Restigouche* and the rescue ship *Stockport*. More U-boats were on their way. At the same time, the weather was deteriorating by the hour; soon conditions became impossible for flying. Bereft of air support, the convoy pushed on, with another not far behind. The U-boats gathered, their crews tensed, experiencing the familiar amalgam of excitement and trepidation that has beset fighting men since time immemorial. On the night of November 1, they began the slaughter. It lasted until November 5, when Liberators from Iceland were able to operate. They drove the U-boats away, but fifteen of the convoy's forty-two ships had been sent to the bottom, with the attendant welter of death, injury, and hardship for the crews.

It happened so frequently that there existed a danger of it becoming taken for granted. Merchant shipping losses were regular occurrences: men blown to bits in catastrophic explosions, engulfed in fire aboard tankers, consumed by fuel-fed conflagrations on the ocean's surface, or suffering the slow, drawn-out agony of death by exposure and starvation in lifeboats. It was the daily account rendered by the war, and it was borne primarily by merchant sailors.

Relations between the RCAF and the U.S. naval and army air forces in Newfoundland became increasingly strained. It had to happen, given the top-heavy command structure that had been created and the divergent views on how anti-submarine operations should be conducted. The American Rear Admiral R. M. Brainard had USN and USAAF aircraft under his command, as well as 1 Group RCAF. Brainard issued "orders" to the navy units, "requests" to the USAAF units, and "proposals" to 1 Group RCAF. Rarely has a vital combat area been burdened by such a cumbersome system of communication. Exacerbating the problem was the fact that the Canadians were attempting to introduce the recommendations of RAF Coastal Command, which called for a flexible form of convoy support rather than the old, low-level escort. It had been proved effective in action in British waters; the RCAF was sold on the idea, and increasingly failed to respond to all Brainard's "proposals." "The matter came to a head on 12 November when 1 Group refused to supply air cover for [Convoy] SG12 as Brainard had asked because there were no submarines within 200 miles, according to NSHQ (Naval Service Headquarters) estimates."[2] Late in November, an incident occurred highlighting the weaknesses in the divided command. U518 attacked convoy ON145 some two hundred miles south of Placentia Bay. Dense fog prevented the U.S. aircraft based at Argentia from going out to escort the convoy. Three aircraft from Sydney, Nova Scotia, undertook an offensive sweep as far east as fifty-five degrees west; but the USAAF B-17 unit at Gander did not respond when asked to assist. Hardly surprisingly, the Canadians asked themselves why they did not assume responsibility for all anti-submarine work under one authority – and a Canadian authority at that.

In the final days of 1942, Eastern Air Command could look back on a highly significant year. One overwhelming factor was that the size of the U-boat force had grown out of all proportion. On January 1, 1942, the Germans had had twenty-two U-boats in the North Atlantic out of a total of 248 in commission. By

December, there were ninety-five U-boats in the North Atlantic out of a total of 582 in commission. The Battle of the Atlantic was turning into a sort of First World War Western Front of the sea, with both sides bringing in larger and larger forces, bent on a battle of attrition.

Were the Canadian crews of Eastern Air Command as good at anti-submarine operations as their counterparts in RAF Coastal Command? It is in fact misleading to compare them on this basis. For one thing, there were far more U-boats sailing the waters around Western Europe than there were in Canadian waters. The Canadian average of one U-boat sighting for every 134 aircraft sorties was only about a quarter of the Coastal Command ratio of one to thirty or forty; in 1942, U-boats in the Canadian zone averaged about one every forty thousand square miles.

Another crucial factor was that the weather was usually far worse off the Canadian coast than off the British Isles. Fog frequently disrupted air searches off the Grand Banks. Overcast conditions, so common in the waters off Canada and Newfoundland, made flying hazardous at low level. On some days it was almost impossible to calculate just how high an aircraft was, since atmospheric pressure is constantly changing and a long flight can see an aircraft's altimeter reduced to almost total uselessness unless it is constantly adjusted. The prevailing westerly wind was an implacable enemy; many aircraft ran out of fuel on long patrols because the winds had shifted and strengthened. Most aircrews rated the weather, with its treacherous ways and vicious temper, a far more dangerous enemy than the Germans. You could meet a German on more or less equal terms, but the weather often had you beaten before you started. Only with luck liberally mixed with humility could you survive that weather.

An additional obstacle facing the Canadians was questionable leadership. Instead of ensuring that crews made use of the latest techniques and systems, senior officers tended to be preoccupied with mundane day-to-day needs and the requirement simply to find enough men and equipment to fly the necessary number of sorties. A dearth of specialist knowledge compounded the problem. No one in senior command had any firsthand experience of anti-submarine operations. In November 1942 the RAF had suggested sending four senior Eastern Air Command pilots at a time on a four-week course with Coastal Command, to benefit from British expertise. The suggestion was not taken up.[3]

It was a frustrating time for the Canadians. To fulfill their mandate of anti-submarine activities in the Atlantic, they badly needed the VLR (Very Long Range) Liberators. Rather than go through the British, they tried a direct approach to the Americans. The Americans still said no, advising them to talk to the British. The need for the Liberators was becoming critical. The British converted some of the Liberators they had been using off the French coast to VLR configuration, but they still preferred to keep them on anti-submarine patrols in the Bay of Biscay. The British operational researcher P. M. S. Blackett calculated that Atlantic shipping losses could be reduced by a startling 64 per cent if the Air Gap could be closed.

Despite the encouraging developments, the period between November 1942 and March 1943 saw Allied shipping losses soar to their highest levels of the war. Shipbuilding broke every record and in fact surpassed losses at this time, but the rate of U-boat kills was still alarming. The Allied leaders planning the invasion of Europe were uncomfortably aware that Dönitz's U-boat force had suffered little in recent months; indeed, it seemed to be growing. The U-boats could wreck all the complex plans for the invasion of Europe that were then being formulated. No wonder the Allied leaders still placed the defeat of the U-boats at the top of their priority list.

In that fateful February of 1943, two young but highly experienced RAF Coastal Command officers visited Eastern Air Command. Their job was to study communications, aircraft control, and facilities. Sending such junior officers looked at first like a snub to the air staff in Ottawa. But in fact it would have been hard to find two more capable airmen. Squadron Leader Terry Bulloch, the British "ace" U-boat killer, and Flying Officer M. S. Layton, a Canadian navigator, were veterans of 120 Squadron RAF. Together, they had sunk two U-boats; both were members of the Distinguished Service Order; Layton also had a DFC. Their great value was that they saw EAC's problems through the eyes of successful operational airmen, not of staff officers. Bulloch and Layton were of the opinion that EAC should have been operating at least one Liberator squadron long ago. They were impressed by the quality of the RCAF aircrew, but less so by the communications. They noted that tactical intelligence from Coastal Command was not getting through to the crews who needed it the most. Only one squadron seemed to have absorbed Coastal's hard-won advice; hardly surprisingly, the unit in question was Small's 113 Squadron, probably the most consistently successful in Eastern Air Command. Its aircraft flew at the recommended search height of four to five thousand feet or just below the cloud ceiling. The white camouflage, now standard on Coastal Command aircraft, adorned 113's, but few others.

Radar had now been installed in most RCAF aircraft, which was a step forward, but crews now tended to rely too much on the equipment, the visitors claimed. Radar sets were on more or less continuously, so U-boats with search receivers often had more than enough warning to dive before the aircraft appeared. Lookouts in EAC aircraft usually scanned the horizon instead of diligently searching the area ten miles ahead; and when an attack took place, the EAC crews made insufficient use of photography. The Canadians still tended to escort convoys whether they were threatened or not, at the expense of offensive sweeps. In spite of some improvements, the Canadians were still the poor relations when it came to the supply of up-to-date equipment. In 10 Squadron, Digby crews were using homemade sights for dropping depth charges. Navigators had to rely on elderly compasses of questionable accuracy. Depth charges were outdated, as were marine markers, sextants, photographic and radio equipment, including R/T for communications with ships. Furthermore, the two visitors found that the Canadian airmen's operational clothing was inadequate. It astonished Bulloch and Layton that Cansos, notoriously chilly aircraft, were seldom equipped with electrically heated flying suits.

∾

By now, Dönitz had about one hundred U-boats in the Atlantic. More than forty operated in the mid-ocean "gap." They formed several groups. Group *Haudegen* had twenty-one boats situated to intercept convoys south of Greenland. Group *Landsknecht* lay in wait further to the east, with twenty boats. Early in February, Dönitz ordered ten boats from this second group to move west and form Group *Pfeil*. He then ordered Group *Haudegen* to move southwest, forming a line close to the Newfoundland Bank. He had distributed his forces effectively, but had placed many of the U-boats within range of the aircraft at Gander, Torbay, and Argentia. On February 4, Flight Lieutenant J. M. Viau of 5 Squadron attacked a U-boat, probably U414, with inconclusive results. Two days later, a PBY Catalina of the U.S. Navy and a Canso of 5 Squadron RCAF attacked another U-boat, believed to be U403. Neither attack resulted in a sinking, but they appeared to discourage other U-boats from venturing too close.

Fred Colborne of Calgary, Alberta, was the pilot of the 5 Squadron Canso. The attack took place some six hundred miles from the coast, in remarkably still conditions. The Canso approached at eighty-five miles per hour. "The only reason we caught the U-boat on the surface was because the crew didn't expect to see an aircraft that far out," remarks Colborne.[4]

February 1943 was a busy month for Colborne. On the 23rd, a westbound convoy reached the outer limits of 1 Group's area of responsibility. The convoy had had a rough passage, losing nine of its forty-eight ships. Two more went down the following day.

United States Navy PBY Catalinas had attempted to reach the threatened ships but found the range too great. Colborne came upon U604 on the surface about six miles ahead. Visibility was uncommonly good for the Atlantic in winter. He applied full power and put the nose down. Engines howling, the Canso dived from three thousand feet, pulling out at eight hundred feet. The U-boat was already preparing to dive. Colborne eased the controls forward, sending the Canso into a second steep dive. His co-pilot, Sergeant Duncan, activated the alarm signal and readied his camera to record the attack. Colborne remembers being sure he would never reach the U-boat in time. In a contemporary newspaper account, Colborne reported, "The telltale puff of smoke from the U-boat signaled the start of his crash dive. We were coming in too fast . . . too high. I cut the throttles and shoved her nose down and made the attack. Throttles on again . . . then the depth charges . . ."[5]

"The sub itself was very long and a dark greyish colour with a high conning tower," related the co-pilot, Sergeant Duncan. "It was traveling at about ten or twelve knots. We could see the front gun and part of the railing. Our captain pressed the button to release the depth charges . . . As we passed over the position a second time I took another picture of the air bubbles coming to the surface . . . We kept circling . . . an oil slick began to develop . . . bits of debris were floating on the water."

There seemed little doubt that the U-boat had been destroyed. The second engineer, Leading Aircraftman John Watson, declared colourfully, "The danger was all over and Hitler's little pet was blown to pieces."[6]

Colborne's navigator, Flying Officer W. P. Irving of Medicine Hat, Alberta, was so intent on taking pictures of the action that he nearly fell out of the Canso. Only quick work by Flight Sergeant Blain of Stockton, Manitoba, the wireless operator/air gunner, saved him. Blain was able to grab the navigator's legs and tug him back into the aircraft.

Despite the crew's enthusiastic reports, U604 survived the encounter, although it suffered serious damage. The captain, Horst Hoeltring, detailed his problems in some detail: "Both compressors torn off. Shafts displaced in axial direction. Diesel clutches are pounding hard. Main clutches cannot be fully disengaged. Main ballast tank V has 50 cm long crack. Tank vents air very rapidly."[7]

After a long and difficult journey, U604 reached Brest on March 9. Many weeks passed before the boat could be used operationally again.*

A few hours after Colborne's attack, Flying Officer Leo Murray of Winnipeg, the second pilot of another 5 Squadron Canso, spotted the wake of a U-boat some five miles away. He pointed it out to the skipper, Flying Officer D. G. Baldwin, who turned and dived. It was a humid day. As the Canso descended, Murray's binoculars clouded up. He lost sight of the U-boat's wake. Baldwin pulled out of his dive and climbed. The glasses cleared; the U-boat's wake became visible again. Not wanting to make a straight beam attack, Baldwin turned again, up the submarine's track. He dropped four depth charges – which were seen by the crew to land in a tight diamond pattern fifty to sixty feet ahead of the swirl left by the diving U-boat, later identified as U621.

In fading light, which made photography impractical, Baldwin turned for base, after updating the escort commander.† Again an apparently successful attack had failed to destroy its intended victim, although the damage to U621 put the boat out of action for some weeks. Both Colborne's and Baldwin's attacks had taken place at the limit of the Canso's endurance, underlining once more the need for VLR Liberators in this theatre of operations.

---

*   Colborne was awarded the DFC. He was one of Eastern Air Command's most experienced pilots, having invested his savings in flying lessons before the war. He soloed for the first time on the day Hitler invaded Poland. He survived the war.
†   Leo Murray was killed in a flying accident a little over a year later.

Again and again, poor coordination between naval and air forces resulted in U-boats slipping away to safety with Allied vessels and aircraft in hot but impotent pursuit. There was a tendency for naval and air staffs to issue instructions, relying on other services to carry them out. Canadian Wing Commander Clare Annis believed that "as matters now stand, each service is publishing a set of operational instructions and including in them their interpretation of the role the other service will play in the conduct of the joint operation of convoy escort. . . . Neither set of instructions carries executive authority in the other's Service. Each Service had depended on liaison with the other to ensure that their interpretation of each other's Service function will not conflict with its own ideas. This has resulted, it seems, in the issuing of two sets of orders which are neither complete in themselves nor even when combined. Moreover, as our control and administrative machinery now stands, it is necessary for the service wishing to introduce a new order or to alter an old one to raise a special memorandum and/or arrange for a special conference. This allowed for delay, oversight, misunderstandings and considerable inefficiency."[8]

One of a series of conferences took place at Argentia, Newfoundland, on February 26. This time the main item on the agenda was to find a way to improve the integration of USAAF operations with those of the U.S. Navy and the RCAF. Earlier in the month, the 25th Anti-submarine Wing of the USAAF had taken over control of the B-17s at Gander from the USN. While this may not have seemed to be a particularly contentious matter, it did generate some problems, largely because of the different ways the U.S. Army and Navy viewed their responsibilities. The Anti-submarine Command's mission was neatly summed up in its motto: "To seek and to sink." On the other hand, the USN and the RCAF saw their primary responsibility as the protection of shipping. For once, common sense prevailed. The USAAF representative announced that the Army would "join in on the change of mission to agree with yours."[9] However, although the Army did make a significant effort to support convoys, they had no aircraft with VLR capability.

At such meetings, the Canadians were invariably on the defensive, obsessed with the danger of letting even a modicum of control of their own forces slip away. They all suffered from the fear that the USN intended to impose operational control over Eastern Air Command. The RCN had launched a campaign to assume control of convoy and anti-submarine operations in the northwest Atlantic. The intention was to elevate the Commanding Officer, Atlantic Coast, to commander-in-chief status, superseding the American admiral at Argentia in all matters pertaining to trade defence. Now that the RCN was supplying nearly half of the escorts on the North Atlantic routes and all but a handful of USN warships had long since been withdrawn to go to the Pacific, CTF (Commander Task Force) 24's responsibility for convoy protection not only needlessly complicated command but offended Canadian sensibilities. At the time, there existed a profusion (some might say, a confusion) of eight American and Canadian operational authorities in control of the northwest Atlantic. After the Casablanca conference, however, a subcommittee of the Anglo-American Combined Staff Planners in Washington proposed a three-stage integration of command in the Atlantic. Air and sea anti-submarine forces in the eastern Atlantic would be under a British c-in-c; those in the western Atlantic under an American commander. Thus the stage would be set for the creation of a supreme command. Wing Commander Clare Annis, recently returned from the American capital, felt that there were "splendid opportunities" for Canada in the emerging situation, as long as the RCAF would agree to Eastern Air Command being under the RCN for operational direction. It was Annis's belief that the Americans might be willing to forego the installation of an American commander-in-chief if the Canadians were able to create a unified command (Admiral King, in fact, dispatched a signal to NSHQ and the Admiralty proposing the removal of the Argentia command from convoy operations). In addition, Annis felt that the USN and the U.S. Army would be more favourably disposed towards the allocation of Liberators to the RCAF.

In the meantime, at the end of March, a squadron of eleven B-17s joined the four already at Gander. In April, a squadron of B-24s arrived, although the aircraft were not modified to VLR standards and had a range of only 650 miles, little better than the RCAF's Cansos.

The RCAF, despite its chronic fear of becoming subordinated to a more powerful ally, now joined forces with the 25th Anti-submarine Wing of the USAAF, as well as the anti-submarine units of the USN, taking overall direction from the flag officer, Newfoundland Force, and the air and naval commanders-in-chief, Halifax. "By accepting naval direction," reads the official history, "the RCAF expected not merely to direct American Liberator operations, but to advance its own bid for VLR aircraft. Canadian airmen seized the opportunity afforded by the Atlantic Convoy Conference to raise the issue again at the highest levels. Just as the USN and RN were prepared at this time to support the Canadian naval case, both the RAF delegation in Washington and General Arnold had now accepted the reasonableness of the Canadian air force argument, but the RAF refused to support a proposal that would cut into British allocations from the United States, and Arnold, constrained by inter-service disputes with the U.S. Navy, refused to break previous agreements."[10]

A proposal to allocate to the Canadians a few of the Liberators going to the RAF met with a chilly reception from Sir John Slessor, the recently appointed c-in-c of RAF Coastal Command. Slessor could never rid himself of the traditional upper-class British belief that "colonials," though grand chaps in many ways, simply didn't have the breeding to make them as *sound* as the home-grown product. Apparently convinced of the inefficiency of Eastern Air Command, he declared himself in favour of the RAF taking on responsibility for the western Atlantic. Eventually, however, the

British did agree to letting the RCAF have a number of "their" Liberators straight off the production line.

By now, the shortage of Liberators had largely been overcome. Enormous production lines had been set up to manufacture the aircraft. Consolidated had two, in San Diego, California, and Fort Worth, Texas. Other companies busily turning out Liberators included Douglas in Tulsa, Oklahoma, North American in Dallas, Texas, and the Ford Motor Company at Willow Run, near Detroit, Michigan. Willow Run was the largest aircraft assembly operation in the world, with a production line one mile long by 440 yards wide. Although the vast operation had its problems, by mid 1944 it was turning out some five hundred Liberators a month.

The first RAF squadron to receive VLR Liberators was 120, and the RCAF's 10 Squadron based at Dartmouth, Nova Scotia, became the first Canadian unit to fly the type. By June 1943, 10 Squadron had completed its conversion from Digbys.

~

Early in March, the BdU brought in a new code for weather reports, which the cryptanalysts at Bletchley Park predicted would take two to three months to crack. At the same time, the staff at the Operational Intelligence Centre observed a remarkable increase in the volume of radio traffic between the U-boats and Dönitz's headquarters. Much of it concerned the increase in Allied air power over the Atlantic. Dönitz, for his part, regularly received not only the British signals and routing instructions sent to convoys, but also the U-boat situation reports transmitted to commanders of convoys at sea to provide them with the latest information on the whereabouts of U-boats. Dönitz was increasingly concerned about security. Had the Allies broken his codes? Repeated checks revealed nothing untoward. In his memoirs, Dönitz commented "That a widespread spy network was at work at our bases in occupied France was obviously something we had to assume. An efficient enemy intelligence service must in any case have been able to ascertain the distribution of U-boats among the various bases, the dates of their sailing and return to port, and also possibly the sea areas allotted to boats proceeding on operations. Our ciphers were checked and rechecked, to make sure that they were unbreakable; and on each occasion the head of the Naval Intelligence Service at Naval High Command adhered to his opinion that it would be impossible for the enemy to decipher them."[11]

Dönitz and his staff concluded that the Allies derived most of their data on U-boats from "very long-range airborne radar." He promptly ordered his boats to dive for at least thirty minutes if they became aware of radar transmission in their vicinity.

In the early spring of 1943, four large eastbound convoys, SC121, HX228, SC122, and HX229, found themselves in mortal combat with six wolfpacks. It became one of the biggest convoy battles of the war, some 150 heavily laden merchantmen, and their escorts, opposing close to fifty U-boats. The series of battles began with Convoy SC121, which ran into violent storms shortly after leaving New York. The convoy soon became scattered, whereupon the U-boats struck, harrying the disorganized remains of the convoy for four terrifying days. Thirteen ships went down, including *Bonneville* with the convoy commodore, Commodore R. C. Birnie, RNR. No trace of him was ever found.

Despite the best efforts of the escorts, most of which were American, not one U-boat was sunk. Convoy HX228 fared better, although the presence of one of the first escort carriers to be used in the Atlantic battle, the USS *Bogue*, could not have been a significant factor. The weather was so dreadful that the carrier was unable to fly off her aircraft; she had to take refuge in the middle of the convoy, another responsibility rather than an important new weapon in the battle against the U-boats.

The enemy now lay far to the north of the convoy. A few U-boats were able to make contact, but results were hardly impressive:

only four ships sunk for some 24,000 tons. U121, under the command of a highly successful young captain named Hans Trojer, nearly came to grief in the action. A snow squall spoiled Trojer's view of the convoy as it came near. Nevertheless he managed to slip between the escorts and fired at a large merchant ship. It blew up amid a shower of steel plates, which, Trojer reported, "flew like sheets of paper through the air."[12] Trojer then torpedoed another ship, a freighter, with lethal results. But debris clattered into his periscope. "The whole boat re-echoed with bangs and crashes," Trojer noted. His periscope became almost impossible to turn. Then it failed completely. Trojer was operationally blind. Heavy bits of wreckage kept crashing down on the submarine, creating a nerve-wracking din inside its steel body. Trojer heard the sound of a destroyer going overhead. He gave the order to dive as depth charges exploded nearby. U121 got away.

Four ships were lost in the engagement; two U-boats fell victim to the escorts, including U444, which had sunk the fourth ship. A British escort, *Harvester*, spotted the U-boat and sank her by ramming. The action badly damaged the destroyer, and she in turn was sunk by U432. Although the action was fast and furious, it was merely a curtain-raiser for the battles to come.

IO

THE BIGGEST BATTLE

"The harder the conflict, the more glorious the triumph"
– Thomas Paine

NEW YORK HARBOUR was jammed with shipping, ranging from weary old veterans, looking as if caked salt and rust held them together, to Libertys so new their paint seemed wet. The ships lay low in the water, groaning under the burden of war supplies, equipment of every description, foodstuffs, raw materials, high explosives, fuel, oil, tanks, guns, airplanes. Britain was becoming a vast depository of everything needed to win the war. In little more than a year, the Allies would invade the continent. It would be an operation involving enormous numbers and terrible risks. The still-recent disastrous "reconnaissance in force" at Dieppe in August 1942 had done nothing for anyone's confidence, with the possible exception of Adolf Hitler's.

But before the invasion could take place, the mountains of materiel had to be transported to England, the Allies' jumping-off point. The crews of the merchantmen had to walk – or crawl – over their deck cargoes to get from one end of the ship to the other. Shipping space had become fantastically valuable; fully equipped armies had to be transported with all their attendant service and supply organizations. The logistics were staggering. The moving would go on for months. Every ship lost meant that another ship had to be found for the job. Transportation was rapidly becoming the most important job in the war.

On March 5, shortly after seven on a chilly but not unpleasant morning, the merchant ship *Glenapp* pulled away from her wharf and into the North Hudson River, New York. Her master, Captain L. W. Kersley, and the Convoy Commodore, Captain S. N. White, stood on the bridge with the pilot. Ships moved out one by one, following *Glenapp* on the journey past Manhattan's skyscrapers. As the ramshackle armada passed through the Narrows between the Upper and Lower Bays, four Canadian escort vessels joined them: *The Pas, Blairmore, Rimouski,* and *New Westminster,* corvettes all. The ships and their protectors moved along the Ambrose Channel, which, as recently as that morning, had been swept for mines. At the Ambrose Light Vessel, the pilots disembarked. Now the ships began the lengthy process of getting into convoy formation.

Glenapp led the centre column. A cargo ship, *Historian,* and a tanker, *Benedick,* took their positions as leaders of the other two columns, after which the rest of the ships steamed up to take their positions. It was a time-consuming business; while it was going on, the weather deteriorated, with stiffening winds and the promise of worse to come. As night fell, squalls of rain swept across the stolid ranks of ships. Eventually, there would be 141 merchant ships; they would constitute two long-organized convoys, SC122 and HX229, and a third, HX229A, formed only in the last few days so as not to prolong the pressure on New York harbour. Freighters, tankers, refrigerator ships, bulk carriers, tank landing ships; eighty-one were British, twenty-nine were American, eleven Panamanian, seven Dutch, four Norwegian, three Icelandic, two Swedish, two Greek, one Belgian, and one Yugoslav. The ships' combined gross weight was nearly 900,000 tons. They carried some 920,000 tons of cargo: "170,000 tons of various petroleum fuels, 150,000 tons of frozen meat, 600,000 tons of general cargo such as food, tobacco, grain, timber, minerals, steel, gunpowder, detonators, bombs and shells, lorries, locomotives, invasion barges, aircraft and tanks."[1] It was the life-blood of the war, a tiny part of the immense volume of materiel that had to keep flowing across the Atlantic without pause.

The previous day, all masters had attended a convoy sailing conference at Battery Place, New York. Chairman of the conference was an American naval officer, Captain Reinicke. Most British merchant navy officers felt that Reinicke had far too much to say for himself, as did all navy types. "It was typical of all U.S. conferences which, in my opinion, were always overloaded with officers, each having something to say," remarks Captain W. Luckey of *Luculus*. "There was always an atmosphere of tension as though something sensational was about to happen at any moment. At the U.K. conferences, the atmosphere was that of calm; you were told the facts without any window-dressing and you left the conference feeling that all would go well during the voyage."[2] There were a few apologetic words about the shortage of escort vessels, but the masters absorbed it without comment; they had heard it all before. The latest information on U-boat strength raised some eyebrows. The masters noted pertinent data on clipboards or in nondescript notebooks. Eventually the meeting was over. The masters rose – middle-aged men, most of them, in civvies of excessive drabness – and with their sealed envelopes under their arms ("Not to be opened until at least twelve hours after departure"), they made their way back to their ships, not looking forward to what fate had in store, but relieved that the endless preparations were done at last.

One by one, the remaining ships steamed slowly into their allotted positions, like weary performers taking their places for the last show of the night. Crew members took a keen interest in just where their ship was positioned in the convoy. It had once been the rule that if you found yourself on the flanks of a convoy, you stood a better chance of being torpedoed than if you were in the middle. That rule no longer held in this era of nighttime attacks. Increasingly, the bolder U-boat commanders took their vessels past the escorts, right into the heart of a convoy, from where they could fire in every direction.

In many convoys, the position of a ship depended upon its destination. For example, the columns of ships on the port side of sc122 were mostly destined for Iceland, next were those heading for the north of Scotland to arrive at east coast ports. In the starboard columns were found those ships heading for South Wales and Bristol; they would break off and proceed independently when they neared their destinations.

It took some hours to form up the convoy's columns. Even then, the job was by no means done. More ships would be added when they reached Halifax, last stop before the ocean crossing.

The situation in the Atlantic in early 1943 had undergone significant changes. In addition to the promotion of Dönitz himself to commander-in-chief of the German Navy, control of the vital Western Approaches Command had gone to Admiral Sir Max Horton. Horton was well respected and well known by his enemy. Dönitz wrote in his memoirs, "Under the command of Admiral Horton, the British anti-submarine forces made great improvements, not only in material and technical means, but also and most particularly in tactical leadership and morale. As an outstanding submarine captain of the First World War and Flag Officer, Submarines, in the Second, Admiral Horton was better qualified than anyone else to read the mind of the German High Command and therefore to take those steps which would inevitably render more difficult the prosecution of our U-boat campaign."[3]

Horton had sunk the German cruiser *Hela* in September 1914, the first sinking of a German warship by a British submarine. At Western Approaches, he established his own style – and it bore little resemblance to that of his predecessor, the popular and personable

Admiral Sir Percy Noble. Horton, an autocratic individual, notoriously impatient and acid-tongued, spent most afternoons playing
golf, and most evenings playing bridge, but on countless occasions
he stayed up all night in pyjamas and dressing gown to attend to
problems at sea. Horton had hardly arranged his desk at Western
Approaches before he clashed with Rodger Winn, the brilliant ex-
barrister (and later, Lord Justice of Appeal), who ran the Submarine
Tracking Room. Horton's bombastic and overbearing manner
usually crushed any argument from juniors. Such tactics didn't
work with Winn. Maddeningly logical, never at a loss for just the
right word, he used his courtroom training to mount devastating
attacks when challenged. Horton had the good grace to concede
defeat after one notable altercation. Thereafter, Horton and Winn
enjoyed excellent relations.

For Dönitz, this was a critical moment. A realist with access to
every type of top-secret intelligence, he was far more aware than
the average German that the war, which was supposed to solve all
Germany's problems, was creating a spider's web of new ones.
Now everything teetered on the brink of catastrophe. In North
Africa, Rommel was on the run. The Allied strategic bombing
campaign had begun to have catastrophic impact on Germany's
cities. In Russia, Paulus had surrendered his Sixth Army at
Stalingrad. In the Far East, the momentum was steadily shifting in
favour of the Allies. Never had the cutting of the Atlantic lifeline
between North America and Britain been more important for
Germany. The Allies would soon attempt an invasion of the continent; no one with any knowledge of the war could doubt it. But
that invasion depended upon the continued supply of arms, supplies, and troops. Stop them in mid ocean and the situation would
be transformed.

The "situation room" in Dönitz's headquarters showed him the
position of every U-boat at any given moment, as well as that of
enemy naval units, as far as they were known. Dönitz's exceptionally capable deputy, Captain Eberhardt Godt, ran the facility,

keeping it up to date – no mean task with the complex and constantly changing situation on the oceans. Dönitz relied absolutely
on Godt and was never disappointed. Although his responsibilities
were much broader since he had taken control over the entire navy,
Dönitz maintained personal command of the U-boat service; he
frequently journeyed to the French Atlantic coast to meet returning U-boats and award medals. In March 1943, Dönitz still did not
have all the U-boats he wanted, but he believed his force was powerful enough to deliver a shattering blow to the Allies.

Western Approaches in Liverpool had designated B5 Group, one of
the most experienced, to escort SC122.* The senior ship was
Havelock, a Havant class destroyer, commanded by Commander
Richard C. Boyle, RN, a capable and seasoned convoy officer. His
group normally included two First World War destroyers, *Volunteer*
and *Warwick*. On this occasion, however, *Warwick* was absent for
repairs; her place was taken by a frigate, *Swale*, fresh from the
builder. In addition, the escort group had five British corvettes,
Pimpernel, *Lavender*, and *Saxifrage*, plus the Belgian-manned *Godetia*
and *Buttercup*.

The group had recently escorted a convoy from England and
run into some of the vicious weather so common that winter.
Upon arrival at St. John's, *Volunteer* had to go into dry dock with
leaking plates. The repair work was expected to be completed
within a day or two of the convoy's sailing. While annoying, this
delay was by no means catastrophic; with her brisk turn of speed,
Volunteer could be expected to catch up with SC122 in short order,
and the U-boats posed little danger in that area just east of
Newfoundland; there were too many aircraft and ships on patrol.

B4 Group was scheduled to take over Convoy HX229. It was
similar in makeup to B5. Another Havant Class destroyer of First

---

* All convoy escort groups were numbered and then allocated to convoys by
Western Approaches HQ months before their sailing dates.

World War vintage, *Highlander*, was the senior ship, under the command of Commander E. C. L. Day. Commander Day – nick-named "Happy," though never to his face – had commanded B4 Group for eighteen months and enjoyed a fine reputation; he was one of the best escort leaders in the RN. Unfortunately, his escort group was badly depleted. One of the destroyers, *Winchelsea*, was undergoing refitting; its replacement, *Vimy*, was in Iceland, having some repair work done. An ex-USN ship, *Beverley*, was the only destroyer available to the group. Six corvettes normally made up the group's complement, but for a variety of reasons, only four were available: *Abelia, Anemone, Pennywort*, all RN ships, and *Sherbrooke* of the RCN.

Somehow the indefatigable members of B-Dienst, the German cryptanalysis service that had broken the RN's naval cipher, did not realize that the third convoy, HX229A, had been formed, and never distinguished it from HX229. The creation of Convoy HX229A had necessitated the sending of an another escort group, the 40th, from Britain. Based at Londonderry, the 40th normally escorted convoys on the Sierra Leone run. It included three nine-hundred-ton sloops, *Londonderry, Aberdeen*, and *Hastings*, two ex-U.S. Coast Guard cutters, now named *Landguard* and *Lulworth*, and two frigates, *Moyola* and *Waveney*, all relatively new and well-equipped vessels, a startling contrast to the ancient destroyers and battered corvettes usually seen on the North Atlantic runs. It can have been no accident that this excellent group was selected to escort HX229A, for the convoy included merchantmen carrying particu-larly valuable cargoes. Commander J. S. Dalison was proud of his "Fighting Fortieth" as he called it, and lost few opportunities to sing its praises.

B4 was the problem group. Only one destroyer and one corvette would be ready to sail from St. John's on the appointed day, March 14. Although naval authorities were normally reluctant to modify the makeup of a well-established escort group, they had little choice in this case. The destroyer *Volunteer*, originally scheduled to rejoin B5 once its repairs had been completed, would now join B4 as soon as possible. To replace her, a veteran USN destroyer, *Upshur*, would join B5, as would *Campobello*, a brand-new Canadian-built anti-submarine trawler. Two more British destroyers had been found and were allocated to B4: *Witherington*, and an old four-stacker, *Mansfield*. These vessels had limited fuel capacity and were usually employed within a five- to six-hundred-mile range of St. John's. On this occasion, they were under orders to use up their fuel, then return to St. John's.

Just before sailing, "Happy" Day, whose ship, *Highlander*, was still undergoing repairs, decided not to transfer to another ship. He would put his faith in the repair facilities at St. John's. He would sail late but expected to catch up with the convoy before it had gone far. In the meantime, Lieutenant-Commander Gordon John Luther, RN, would command the group. Luther, formerly a Staff anti-submarine officer with the Home Fleet, was an advocate of the "seek and kill" school of anti-submarine warfare, whereas Day favoured a tight defence at all times. Although apparently a little uneasy about the arrangement, Day agreed to Luther leading the escort group until *Highlander* was able to rejoin the convoy.

Dönitz was increasingly uneasy about his lack of air support. It was, he noted, a situation in which the British commander, Horton, could "look at my cards without my being able to look at his."[4] The changing character of the war in the Atlantic made effective air power essential, but Göring wouldn't loosen his grip on "his" aircraft, no matter how pressing the reason.

On March 9, Dönitz received a report from B-Dienst, providing a wealth of information on the position of another eastbound convoy, HX228. "From past experience," noted Dönitz, "we had to assume that the enemy had located the *Neuland* group, which had been sailing westwards for some days, and that the convoy would take evasive action to keep out of its reach. I therefore at once transferred the group 120 miles further north. There I made a mistake. The next day the convoy sailed past the southern end of the patrol line. Had I not moved the boats, the convoy would have run straight into their midst. This shows how chess moves of this kind can often fail and how thinking ahead can sometimes be dangerous. It is, of course, possible that my British opponent guessed what my next move would be and therefore allowed the convoy to proceed on its old course. He, too, was thinking ahead. On the other hand, it is equally possible that under the prevailing bad weather conditions, the enemy had this time failed to discover the U-boat dispositions."[5]

Soon, however, U-boats were nosing around the convoy. One of HX228's escort vessels, the destroyer *Harvester*, rammed and sank U444. It was a Pyrrhic victory; *Harvester* took so much damage that she became easy meat for another U-boat, U432. A Free French corvette, *Aconit*, then proceeded to attack this U-boat most effectively with depth charges, sinking her. The spirit of the jungle pervaded the Atlantic war.

Another skirmish took place at this time. A convoy had been spotted heading for Newfoundland. The *Raubgraf* group of U-boats immediately set off to intercept it. What might have been a massacre was averted by dreadful weather – gales, blizzards, and mountainous seas – plus the prompt work of the convoy's escorts. One merchant ship was lost. No U-boats were sunk, but several were damaged by depth charges.

The U.S. Coast Guard put on its usual display of ships and blimps as Convoy SC122 began to move out. It was an impressive sight: eleven columns of ships occupying an area of sea some five miles wide with a perimeter in excess of thirteen miles. As soon as the convoy was clear of land, the ships and blimps disappeared with the lengthening shadows, their show of strength over. No doubt many of the sailors watching would gladly have given up the farewell display if only the ships and blimps involved could have made an appearance where they were most needed – in the Air Gap.

The night passed without incident.

The convoy plodded eastward in dreary morning weather. Soon it would turn northeast, heading for Newfoundland. A twin-engined B-25 Mitchell bomber flew out from shore and looked the convoy over. It turned and headed home.

One merchantman was lost to the convoy. The elderly Greek ship, *Georgios P.*, built in 1903, was having difficulty maintaining the convoy's speed of slightly under seven knots. She withdrew and turned back for New York. Escort commanders had little choice but to permit such ships to go on their way.

A fierce storm hit the convoy as darkness fell on the second day. Strong winds battered the ships, scattering them over many miles of ocean. Later, as the winds subsided, the escorts began the tedious and time-consuming job of rearranging the vessels in their proper order.

Eleven were missing. One of them was the British freighter *Clarissa Radcliffe*. The Canadian corvette *The Pas* spotted her and gave her directions to rejoin the convoy. She never did.

On March 8, Convoy HX229 departed New York with forty ships; the following day, the "extra" convoy, HX229A, departed with twenty-seven. Suddenly, after weeks of congestion and noise and taut tempers, the harbour was empty, a maritime ghost town.

Three major convoys struck out into the ocean, turning north-east for Newfoundland, their next stop. The merchant ships did not zigzag; Admiral Horton, the new boss at Western Approaches, considered it a waste of time and fuel for convoys making less than twelve knots.

The message from BdU went out on the evening of March 12: "Commence operations against HX229." All boats still engaged in the last few skirmishes with convoys SC121 and HX228 were to break off immediately. Those boats with sufficient fuel and torpe-does were to turn back and form two new patrol lines; before long, fresh boats from Germany would arrive to reinforce them. Dönitz intended to deliver a crushing blow by completely destroying the massive convoy. The thirteen boats of the *Raubgraf* ("Robber Baron") pack were already in position, astride the convoy route northeast of Newfoundland. In fact, Washington estimated the pack to be considerably larger than it was; they diverted SC122 far to the north to avoid it. The two other packs, *Stürmer* ("Daredevil") and *Dränger* ("Harrier"), would soon be assembled further east and would be lying in wait. (Dönitz had a predilection for flamboyant names for his wolfpacks, considering them good for morale.)

Convoys SC122 and HX229 were immediately diverted to the east. They had successfully avoided the *Raubgraf* wolfpack, but a line of U-boats some six hundred miles long was forming dead ahead. Contrary to widespread belief, the U-boats of a pack did not communicate with one another; indeed, once a patrol line had been established, individual boats, about twenty miles apart, were under orders to maintain strict radio silence until a convoy was sighted. With few exceptions, communications travelled via the BdU. In the ocean, all U-boats were equal – and Dönitz controlled them all from his headquarters. A special transmitter at Nauen, near Berlin, was used exclusively for U-boat signals. A second ultra-low-frequency station near Magdeburg in central Germany was able to transmit signals to submerged U-boats, reaching them without difficulty to a depth of some fifteen metres.

The submarines were still forming their lines. Boats arrived from Germany and France, taking their positions as directed by BdU. Other U-boats had gone to refuel from one of the "milk cows," the big Type XB (a converted minelayer) and Type XIV tanker U-boats sent out to top up the tanks of the combat subs. Refuelling at sea had extended the range of the U-boats, but it was an extremely tricky and hazardous procedure requiring calm seas and great skill and tenacity from the crews.

The eleven U-boats of the *Stürmer* pack were now proceeding at top speed to intercept Convoy HX229. Dönitz had some new weapons at his disposal, and he was keenly interested in their performance under operational conditions. One was the so-called FAT torpedo. The name had nothing to do with the weapon's shape, but was rather a description of its technical makeup: it was short for *Federapparat* (spring apparatus), a missile that could be preset to veer to the right or left after launching. It would continue to circle until it hit a target or ran out of fuel.

When word of the new weapon had first reached the British, they immediately set to work to develop a counter-weapon, believing FAT (also referred to as the "shallow searching torpedo") to be based on acoustic technology. The work wasn't wasted, for when the Germans did develop an acoustic torpedo, the British were ready with counter-measures. Both sides introduced new weapons throughout the Battle of the Atlantic. Among the most ingenious was MAD, the magnetic anomaly detector. It was a development of the magnetometer, developed in Britain before the war to plot distortions in Earth's magnetic field in order to locate underground mineral deposits. Gulf Research was working to increase the magnetometer's capability when the U.S. government took over the job for possible use in the hunting of U-boats. The new airborne version was based on the fact that the passage of a submarine through water causes changes in Earth's magnetic field. By the end of 1941 the Americans had succeeded in detecting submerged submarines at a range of four hundred feet. To achieve the best results, however, the aircraft had to be kept in line with Earth's magnetic field to within one-tenth of a degree, a staggeringly difficult proposition. On top of all that, the MAD equipment had to be shielded from the aircraft's own magnetic field. For this reason, the equipment was usually mounted in the tail or wing tip; a stylus recorded field strengths on a moving roll of paper. MAD entered service with the USN in July 1943. It proved to be of little value for widespread searches over great tracts of ocean; it was, however, a useful weapon in confined areas. One of its great advantages was its passivity. Submarines had no means of knowing that they had been detected, since, unlike sonar and radar, MAD did not have to transmit signals to do its job. One further limitation, however, was that an aircraft had to be directly over a submarine to fix its position accurately. The disadvantages of dropping depth charges or bombs from there were obvious; they would land far beyond the target. So the scientists at the California Institute of Technology got to work on the development of a "retro-bomb" that would have a reverse velocity equal to the forward velocity of the aircraft. As the bomb was launched, a small solid-fuel rocket propelled it backwards to reach a maximum velocity of 100 mph. The duration of the rocket's burn cancelled out the aircraft's forward momentum. On burnout, the bomb fell vertically onto the target. PBY Catalinas were chosen to carry the retro-bombs, such aircraft becoming popularly known as Madcats. The retro-bombs were launched in salvoes of eight from rails fitted under the wing. Typically, three salvoes were fired at half-second intervals, spreading the bombs over approximately 180 feet; ideally, then, the salvoes would strike along the entire length of the U-boat. A Madcat carried twenty-four bombs, enough for one concentrated attack. Usually, the Madcats operated in pairs.

Another shortcoming in the system was the inability of the aircraft crew to determine whether it really was a U-boat that they had detected. A wreck on the seabed would generate just the same echoes on the screen as did a fully functional submarine. All of which led to the development of another successful anti-submarine device: the sonobuoy. Essentially, it was a small floating radio transmitter, with a hydrophone suspended on a length of line. Whatever sounds the hydrophone picked up were passed on to the transmitter on the surface, thence to the aircraft. Production versions were cylinders slightly less than four feet long and four inches in diameter. Equipped with a parachute to slow its descent, the sonobuoy started transmitting shortly after hitting the water. The hydrophone separated from the main body, falling to the limit of the twenty-four-foot connecting cable. The device's batteries ran for approximately four hours, about the same time required for the sea to dissolve a soluble bung in the base, sending it all to the bottom of the sea, and, it was hoped, secure from the enemy's inquisitive eyes.

Yet another ingenious weapon, designed for use against sub-merged U-boats, was the air-launched homing torpedo, known officially by its cover-name, the Mark 24 mine, and unofficially as either "Wandering Annie" or "Fido." It was fitted with an acoustic device that could detect the "popping" of partial vacuums in the water – known as cavitations – by a submarine's propeller. To prevent the weapon homing on its own cavitation, the hydrophone was shielded and the propellers designed to cause as little cavitation as possible. On entering the water, Fido dived to a preset depth, then began to spiral upward, enabling the homing head to sweep a 360-degree arc in its search for underwater sound. The device worked most efficiently when its prey was moving at speed – a common enough condition in the current conflict, because of the U-boat commanders' natural desire to put as much distance as pos-sible between their boats and the attackers. Therein lay the strength and the weakness of the system: a U-boat commander could almost certainly escape from his attackers if he fought every instinct and slowed his boat down to minimum speed. Since the usefulness of the homing torpedo would be reduced to nil if the enemy knew about the weapon, it was originally thought that production should cease after one year, or early 1944. In fact, the device was manufactured for the rest of the war.

The first example went to England aboard the liner *Empress of Scotland* in the care of Group Captain Gresswell, the airman who had made the first Leigh light attack. After the journey, Gresswell recalled, "I had been home for a couple of days, when I received a buff-coloured envelope with 'OHMS' across the top, by ordinary post. Inside was a letter from His Majesty's Customs; they wanted to know why I had imported into the United Kingdom 'packing cases containing what is believed to be some form of aerial homing torpedo for use against submarines.' Why had I failed to declare them?"[6]

The flight deck of HMS *Implacable* is packed with Fireflies of 1771 Squadron, Barracudas of 828 Squadron, and Seafires of 880 Squadron, for a strike on the Norwegian refuge of the battleship *Tirpitz*. (Imperial War Museum A-26648)

The splendid German battle-ship *Tirpitz* secure at her moorings at Kaafjord, Norway, July 1944. Four month later, she was sunk by RAF Lancasters, wrecked by 12,000-pound Tallboy bombs. (Imperial War Museum C-4535)

A tongue-in-cheek diving diploma issued to Werner Hirschmann on completion of his training. Hirschmann became Engineering Officer on U190, and was captured in Canadian waters, May 1945. The translation reads: "Master Diving Diploma – We Masters of the Guild of Trim Tamers and Chief Engineer Torturers herewith make known that the most worshipful Lieutenant (Eng.) Hirschmann today before the undersigned took a submarine of medium size undamaged below the surface without danger to the galley and the training officer's nap and moved same in moderate oscillations up and down so that now he has been found worthy and is admitted into the brotherhood of the glorious diving boat people." (Werner Hirschmann collection)

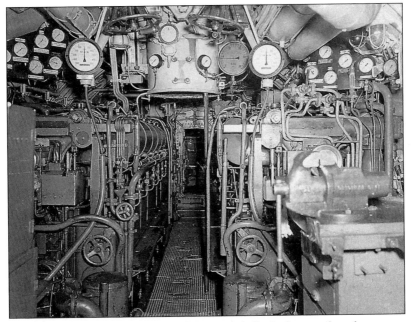

With machinery taking up most of the severely limited space aboard a WW II U-boat, living quarters had to be squeezed in wherever possible. (Werner Hirschmann collection)

On fine, sunny days at sea, every member of a U-boat's crew would do his best to get as much fresh air as possible – although good conditions made it more vital than ever to maintain a non-stop watch for aircraft. (Werner Hirschmann collection)

Depth charge attacks from the air destroyed many U-boats. Here, a D/C hits a U-boat's hull (upper circle) as a second lands beside the boat. A crewman is just discernible in the conning tower manning an anti-aircraft gun. (Imperial War Museum NY-3303)

Underwater repairs and maintenance on a U-boat could be arduous, particularly in winter. Here, a crewman surfaces after working on U190's hull. (Werner Hirschmann collection)

A Type IX U-boat is refuelled from a "milch cow" U-boat, officially a Type XIV. The abilty to refuel expanded the U-boats' range, but by mid-1943 Ultra decypts had revealed the supply boats' locations; all were soon sunk. (Imperial War Museum HU-54352)

Late in the war, the Germans attempted to speed up U-boat production by utilizing sub-contractors, with final assembly of the boats in large shipyards. Intense bombing by the USAAF and RAF rendered the scheme almost totally impracticable. (Imperial War Museum HU-75001)

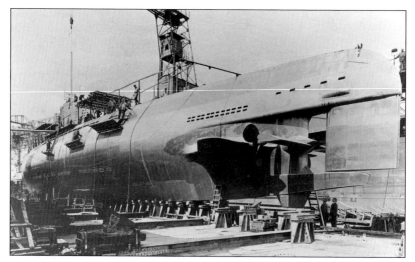

U3001, a type XXI U-boat, in dry-dock. The advanced U-boats with their high underwater speed proved to be a disappointment in action, due to innumerable technical problems. (Imperial War Museum HU-75000)

Under the watchful eyes of British sailors, German crewmen dismantle equipment on U826. Such scenes were repeated dozens of times after the surrender, May 1945. (Imperial War Museum A-28531)

U190, a long-range Type IX submarine in Newfoundland waters, May 1945, shortly after its surrender to the Canadian Navy. (Werner Hirschmann collection)

At Weymouth, Dorset, officers of U249 surrender their vessel to Polish naval personnel, May 1945. Many U-boat crew feared reprisals and were intensely relieved to be treated humanely in captivity. (Imperial War Museum HU-74996)

U776 approaches an unfamiliar landing: Westminster Bridge, London. The U-boat was one of 174 which surrendered in May 1945; more than two hundred others were scuttled by their crews. (Imperial War Museum HU-75002)

A far less complex weapon was the rocket projectile developed in Britain during 1942 primarily for attacks on tanks. Soon it was being used successfully on shipping strikes, and was found to be highly effective against U-boats, one hit usually being enough to pierce a submarine's hull. Terry Bulloch of 120 Squadron was delighted with the new weapons:

> They were under sponsons, little bits of metal bolted on just outside and below your window. There were four either side and they were fired electrically. You used to get into a twenty-degree dive in a Liberator, from 2,000 feet, with cruise power on . . . you would dive down, fire the first two at 600 feet, two at 400 feet, and a stick of four at about 200 feet. Then you would pull the thing out. You had to get the trim absolutely right, or else you'd damage the wing. At the bottom of your dive, the aeroplane's nose was up in the air, but you were still sinking. It was great fun, I loved it. The rockets were very accurate. You could see them go into the water. They had ballistic qualities, believe it or not, under water. One of mine went right through the pressure hull of the U514, and straight out the other side. To make sure of it, I turned back quickly and dropped eight depth charges in a straddle and followed that up with "Wandering Annie," an acoustic mine, and down he went to the ruddy bottom.[7]

Throw-ahead weapons were a useful addition to the Allied arsenal. The British Hedgehog consisted of twenty-four charges mounted on six rows of spigots, each tilted to compensate for the ship's rolling. Squid, the successor to Hedgehog, appeared late in 1943, a three-barrelled mortar firing projectiles each packed with two hundred pounds of Minol II, a powerful mixture of Amatol and aluminum.

You were pretty safe this far west. U-boats didn't like it; too many patrolling planes and ships. The experienced hands recounted endless tales of ships in convoy being blown to smithereens in the middle of the night, of tanker men struggling in the water while fuel-fed fires spread across the surface to consume them. The first-voyage hands took in every word while doing their best to look unconcerned. They convinced nobody.

Dönitz sent two packs of U-boats, one of eight boats, one of eighteen, to form a line across the path of SC122; a third pack of eleven boats took on HX229. B-Dienst had done a commendable job of plotting the positions of the convoys, although they were still apparently unaware of the existence of HX229A. This out-standingly valuable convoy was diverted out of danger. Confusion intensified when the *Stürmer* group established contact with both SC122 and HX229 more or less simultaneously. Bewildered, Dönitz's staff spent several hours trying to sort out the mess, and only then did it dawn on them that the U-boats were in contact with two separate convoys, not one.

The two escort groups differed in their makeup and in their strength. SC122 would have a formidable escort, with Commander Boyle leading in *Havelock* with eight other vessels, including the U.S. destroyer *Upshur* and the British trawler *Campobello*, forming a defensive screen around the merchant ships. *Campobello* had just been built at a Canadian yard and was now being taken to Britain by her Royal Navy crew. She had a popular position in the convoy, to the rear, and was therefore least likely to be attacked by U-boats, which usually got ahead of a convoy and waited for it to sail into their sights. *Upshur*, a veteran four-stacker destroyer, had served on the North Atlantic since the days before Pearl Harbor. Since then, *Upshur* had spent most of its time in the Caribbean.

HX229 would be slightly less well defended, having only *Volunteer*, plus two destroyers, *Witherington* and *Mansfield*, and a pair of corvette escorts. The temporary commander, Gordon Luther, was not well known to the other captains.

The U-boats hurrying to the rendezvous ran into frightful weather. A new Type IXC boat, U523, suffered buckled outer hull plates, caused by the immensely powerful seas. One of the U-boats, U333, had encountered a Wellington of 172 Squadron in the Bay of Biscay, that hotbed of Allied air attacks. In this case, the German crew was thankful that their vessel had been equipped with extra anti-aircraft guns. When the Wellington attacked, the U-boat crew fought back instead of diving to the comparative safety of the depths. U333 shot the Wellington down in flames, killing the crew.

The patrol line took form slowly, as individual boats arrived, directed by Dönitz's HQ. The U-boats occasionally dived, using their hydrophones to check for enemy ships. (In good conditions, hydrophones had a greater range than the human eye.) The weather remained awful. Convoy SC122 was still about half a day in front of HX229. Although none of the escorts was in need of fuel, several wanted to top up, a sensible precaution under the circumstances.

As night fell, the gale intensified. Two of the convoy's vessels became separated from the rest of the assembly, the Icelandic merchantman *Selfoss* and the trawler *Campobello*. *Selfoss* immediately turned and headed for Reykjavík. She arrived safely. *Campobello* sprang a leak. "We found that we were leaking badly somewhere under the coal in the bunkers," recalled Lieutenant G. B. Rogers, one of her crew. "The coal itself prevented us from pinpointing the actual leak though we tried trimming from the sides. . . . The inflow of water was greater than our pumping and bailing ability and after a time, the water reached the bottom of the boilers. As coal fires and hot boilers do not mix with cold sea in quantity, we finally had to draw fires and let the steam pressure down. This put paid to any more mechanical pumping and cut off all power throughout the ship."[8]

Eventually, the brand-new ship had to be abandoned. She was the first casualty of the battle. The corvette *Godetia* hurried to her aid, rescuing her crew. Not a man was lost.

About a hundred miles to the southwest, Convoy HX229 ploughed eastward through the angry sea. Lieutenant-Commander Luther still commanded the escorts. For a few hours on the 15th, the escort strength rose to six ships when *Pennywort*, which had been delayed at St. John's, rejoined the group. But the enhanced strength of the escort force was to be short-lived. The destroyer *Witherington* was obliged to heave to with deck plating damaged by the storm. The weather deteriorated during the night; monstrous seas came from the rear, overtaking the slow merchantmen, pummelling the ships' decks, smashing away lifeboats, hatches, and anything else not battened down. One particularly powerful wave hit *Canadian Star*, crashing through the saloon; two little girls who were sleeping there awoke to find themselves being washed out onto the deck. They were not hurt. By morning, the worst of the storm had blown itself out. Three ships had fallen out of the convoy's ranks. Two of these were visible a few miles to the rear; the third, the Liberty ship *Hugh Williamson*, was nowhere to be seen. (The convoy didn't hear any more from her; she proceeded in splendid isolation, threading her way through the U-boats unaided, arriving safely in England.)

Luther observed that the storm had been blowing the convoy along, directly toward England. He was due to make a turn to the northeast in a few hours. It now seemed a pointless move, doing nothing but adding time to the voyage. He ordered a signal to be sent to request a change in routing so that the convoy might have a direct run for home. But there were problems with *Volunteer*'s transmitters. Ordinary Telegraphist D. Greenhouse recounts what happened: "As a last resort, our Petty Officer Telegraphist Anderson decided to try the veteran transmitter which was installed when *Volunteer* was built in 1917! This was contained in a large wire cage which took up half the available space in the W/T office. The valves (tubes) in the 'thing' were like goldfish bowls. After much fiddling about, the monster showed signs of life and the PO Tel, amid crackling, blue flashes and sparks, began tapping out the call sign. The sparkers not actually manning the listening sets looked on in amazement. To our even greater astonishment, when the smoke and steam had subsided, he received a 'dah–de–dah' (K) 'carry on.' Carry on he did, in good, steady Morse code. All credit to the quality of workmanship and materials which must have gone into the manufacture and installation of that beautiful old transmitter."[9]

By the morning of the 16th, the convoys were approaching the CHOP (change of operational control) line, at which point the Admiralty would take over. The no-nonsense, intensely capable CO of B4, Commander "Happy" Day, was still in St. John's, waiting for repairs to be completed to his ship, *Highlander*. He expected to sail in a few hours, but he had more than five hundred miles to travel before he caught up with HX229. To the east, the six-hundred-mile line of *Stürmer* and *Dränger* U-boats had almost taken form, with the last U-boats due to arrive in a few hours.

During the night, a U-boat recently released from the *Raubgraf* group, U653, unintentionally sailed into the middle of HX229. The U-boat's bridge watch officer, Heinz Theen, was startled to see a light directly ahead. (Later, he decided it must have been a sailor lighting a cigarette.) By the time the skipper, Gerhard Feiler, had reached the bridge, ships could be seen all around the U-boat. "We did an alarm dive," Theen recalled. "As the ships of the convoy went over the top of us, we could hear quite clearly the noises of the different engines – the diesels with fast revs, the steamers with slow revs and the turbines of the escorts made a singing noise."[10]

U653 at once transmitted a sighting report. It was electrifying news. The convoy (the Germans still thought there was only one) was in sight. Now U653's job was to drop back to a safe distance and shadow HX229 until more U-boats arrived.

It was not a particularly difficult task, particularly here in the notorious Air Gap, out of range of most shore-based Allied aircraft. All they had to do was keep the merchant ships' masts in sight as they peeped over the horizon. But Gerhard Feiler, U653's commander, was concerned about the state of his vessel. The starboard diesel engine was giving trouble. He had only one torpedo left – and he believed it to be defective. Fuel was running low; in fact, U653 had been en route to a rendezvous with a tanker when she unexpectedly broke through the defences of HX229. BdU ordered the eight U-boats of the *Raubgraf* group to make for the convoy at top speed. They would be joined by two more U-boats that had just refuelled. In addition, Dönitz ordered eleven of the boats comprising the powerful *Stürmer–Dränger* line to join the assault on HX229; they were expected to make contact early the next morning. Confusing matters was a signal sent by the Americans to HX229A, ordering a diversion to the west of Newfoundland. B-Dienst believed the message referred to HX229.*

Thirty-eight U-boats were massing to attack the convoy, with another thirteen en route from France or Germany. It was probably the largest "wolfpack" ever assembled. The Admiralty advised the convoy of the U-boats' presence. Little more than an hour later, U758, under the command of Helmut Manseck, sighted the convoy and began to shadow it along with U653.

---

* In his postwar memoirs, Dönitz said he thought the signal to have been a fake, sent solely to confuse the U-boat HQ. It was an ominous possibility, for it meant that the Allies were aware that B-Dienst had broken their naval codes – and heaven only knew what fake information might have been fed to U-boat HQ.

I I

BATTLE IS JOINED

"On ye brave, who rush to glory or the grave!"
– Thomas Campbell

AT 0900, THE CONVOY altered course, as previously arranged. The change of course took U653 by surprise; even worse was the sudden appearance of one of HX229's escorts, the four-stacker destroyer *Mansfield*. Fortunately for the Germans, *Mansfield*'s radar was out of commission and lookouts couldn't spot the submarine in the poor conditions.

U653 dived, allowing the convoy to pass, then resumed its shadowing. Forty minutes later, U664, commanded by Adolf Graef, intercepted the convoy; three U-boats were now in contact. After about forty minutes, U615, commanded by Ralph Kapitsky, also made contact with the convoy, making four in all. Kapitsky was keen to make an underwater attack on one of the stragglers, until he discovered that his periscope was unserviceable. Another U-boat skipper, Heinz Walkerling of U91, also decided to make an underwater attack on the stragglers (he had not yet spotted the convoy itself). He dived, but apparently did not carry out his planned attack.

Shortly before noon, Lieutenant-Commander Luther, still in command of the sadly depleted escort force, despatched *Mansfield* to investigate a lengthy signal sent by U653 to BdU. *Volunteer's* Huff-Duff (HF/DF) operator had picked up the signal and had plotted it at 353 degrees. Frustratingly, no other escort was equipped with HF/DF, so it was impossible to get a "fix." Lieutenant-Commander L. C. Hill, in command of *Mansfield*, had orders to run out on the bearing of the U-boat's signal and search. Hill did so, but the U-boat eluded him. Meanwhile, Luther recommended to Commodore Mayall that the convoy turn ninety degrees to starboard. Mayall agreed. The manoeuvre failed to shake off the shadowers.

A fifth U-boat, U600, commanded by Bernhard Zurmuehlen, now joined the shadowers. The Admiralty ordered the destroyer *Vimy* to depart Iceland – more than nine hundred miles away – to reinforce Luther's escorts. Unfortunately, *Vimy* was undergoing repairs and would not sail for another thirty-six hours, by which time she had well over a thousand miles to travel.

At 1237, Luther asked Commodore Mayall to slow the convoy down to eight knots, so that the stragglers astern might rejoin. It took them four hours. Another new arrival, U84, commanded by Horst Uphoff, attempted an underwater attack, but found the sea too boisterous. Luther asked Mayall to bring the convoy back to its course of 028 degrees. Guessing that action was imminent, Luther decided to top up his tanks from one of the tankers in the convoy. In these difficult conditions, it proved infinitely easier to say than to do. After an hour spent trying to pick up the hose floating behind the tanker *Gulf Disc*, Luther abandoned the attempt, hoping that conditions might improve enough for him to try again later.

During the afternoon, BdU ordered U653 to break off, refuel, and head back to base for long-delayed repairs. U615 took over the job of "contact keeper." One by one, the individual U-boats intercepted the convoy and took their places in the pack. As twilight began to dim the scene, U603 (Bertelsmann) and U89 (Lohmann) joined forces with the U-boats already shadowing HX229. At 1800, the convoy reached the CHOP line. At 1905, the convoy changed course, now taking a direct route for England, abandoning any attempt to route the convoy around the *Stürmer–Dränger* line of U-boats.

At this stage of the war, most convoys had a designated rescue ship to pick up survivors from torpedoed ships. HX229 had none. Commodore Mayall ordered the rear ship in each column to act as a rescue vessel for the ships ahead of them. It was not a popular order; merchant skippers shuddered at the thought of coming to a halt with U-boats in the vicinity. It was asking – *pleading* – for trouble. You became an easy target. And yet, at the same time, you ached for the guys struggling in the water, some with dreadful burns, some injured, many having been smothered in fuel oil that coated their bodies with a foul and toxic layer and made them maddeningly difficult to rescue because they kept slipping from your grasp and falling back in the sea. But was it fair to ask a guy to risk his own life and ship to rescue them? Why didn't the Navy look after the job?

It was obvious to everyone that the Germans were just waiting for darkness before they attacked. A single VLR Liberator could have done wonders with the U-boats now that the convoy was making its way through the treacherous waters of the Air Gap. Still, not one VLR aircraft had been allocated to this part of the North Atlantic.

The daylight hours slipped away. The officers and men of the convoy and its escorts braced themselves. Night was falling. Clear weather; full moon; visibility for ten miles. Ideal conditions for a full-scale slaughter.

U603 had only four torpedoes left – hardly surprising, since the boat had been on patrol for seven weeks and had sunk two tankers. Three of the four "eels" were the new FAT model torpedoes. The skipper, Hans Bertelsmann, decided to fire all four in two salvoes

at ships on the starboard column of the convoy. U603's radio operator sent out the obligatory signal warning other U-boats that FAT
torpedoes were about to be launched. The first watch officer sat
inside the conning tower at the special sighting-glass connected to
the torpedo calculator used for torpedo attack. There was no
squinting into the periscope, as depicted in countless movies; no
slamming away of the hand grips, folding them into the periscope
mechanism. The first watch officer, Rudolf Baltz, called out final
adjustments. The computer digested them. At precisely eight
o'clock, Bertelsmann gave the order to fire.

U603 shifted as the torpedoes sped on their way, propelled by
compressed air and accompanied by an incongruously gentle
whoosh. The missiles picked up speed quickly until they attained a
velocity of twenty-eight knots, their gyroscopes keeping them on
course. But at the moment of firing, the convoy had been completing its final turn before nightfall. As a result, three of U603's
torpedoes missed. The fourth missile struck *Elin K*, a Norwegian
vessel, in her aft hold. The skipper, Robert Johannessen, barely had
time to get out of his cabin and up to the bridge before his ship
started to sink. There was nothing to be done for her. Johannessen
gave the order to abandon ship. In moments, the ship was standing
vertically in the water, and shivering convulsively as bulkheads collapsed deep within her, she disappeared with the last glimmers of
daylight. The crew escaped without serious injury, but a Dutch
ship, *Terkoelei*, hardly covered herself with glory when she sailed
past the lifeboats, making no effort to rescue the survivors.
Fortunately, a B4 corvette, *Pennywort*, picked the Norwegians up.

Lieutenant-Commander Luther ordered the standard response
to an attack in moonlight: a Half Raspberry. The colourfully named
manoeuvre consisted of all the escort vessels turning outward and
sweeping with radar and Asdic, but not using star shells. They made
no contact.

About ninety minutes later, U758, commanded by Helmut
Manseck, approached the convoy. He later recounted, "I had

shadowed the convoy all day, keeping at extreme range on the starboard side, just keeping the smoke and the tips of the masts in sight. I remember that the ships were doing well and not making much smoke. We had been about twelve miles out during the day and came in to four to five miles at dusk. . . . I could see six, eight, or ten ships and selected a solid, overlapping target of the third ships in the starboard columns. We fired our four torpedoes then turned sharply away to port. . . ."[1]

Manseck claimed to have sunk four ships. In fact, he hit two: the Dutch cargo ship *Zaanland*, and a recently built Liberty ship, *James Oglethorpe*.

Most of the crew of the Dutch ship were veteran sailors and escaped before their ship sank. *James Oglethorpe*'s crewmen were far less experienced. The captain, A. W. Long, presumably hoping to save his vessel, did not issue the order to abandon ship. In spite of this, many of his men attempted, unsuccessfully, to lower the lifeboats. One of the holds contained a cargo of cotton, which soon caught fire. The ship sagged to starboard. Captain Long and Second Officer Joseph Duke, with some thirty men, succeeded in putting the fire out, after which they attempted to return to St. John's, Newfoundland. But the ship never arrived. No clue to her fate was ever forthcoming.

On the port quarter of the convoy, a lookout on the corvette *Anemone* could barely believe his eyes. There, sitting calmly on the surface about three thousand yards away, was a U-boat. *Anemone*'s captain, Lieutenant-Commander P. G. A. King, promptly swung his ship in the U-boat's direction, heading for the enemy vessel at top speed. Incredibly, the U-boat's crew seemed not to have spotted the corvette. King ordered the forward gun crew to hold their fire. The enemy swept closer, growing larger with every passing moment. Another few seconds and it would be a point-blank target. But at three hundred yards, the U-boat dived, disappearing from view.

King was still confident of a kill. Conditions were perfect for a depth charge attack except for one inconvenient fact: the corvette was likely to sail right into the explosions. Wisely, King ordered only five charges to be dropped. He specified fifty-foot settings. As *Anemone* sped through the swirl left by the plunging U-boat, the charges exploded, damaging her radar and R/T equipment. The corvette's crew searched in vain for signs of the U-boat's destruction: oil, debris, bodies. The water settled. Asdic reported a new contact! King hurried in to attack again. The U-boat surfaced some fifteen hundred yards ahead. *Anemone* gave chase, gaining on the U-boat, which dived again. No matter; the Asdic operator had a solid contact. Determined to get this sub, King gave chase at top speed.

Two hundred yards from the attack position, an electrical fault ruined everything. Several of the vessel's firing bells rang prematurely. Obediently, the seamen manning the four side throwers launched their depth charges, accomplishing nothing but killing fish and wreaking more damage on the Asdic equipment located under the vessel. Frustrated but by no means ready to give up, King again stood off and gave the Asdic time to recover. Twenty minutes passed, an unreal interlude, during which men gazed into the sea, trying to read its secrets. Had they scored a hit? Was the U-boat at this moment lying on the seabed, its pressure hull fatally punctured, water pouring in? The crew shuddered when they thought of the deaths awaiting their counterparts on the U-boat. Rats in a trap, most of them. But they deserved it, didn't they? Slinking around, killing without warning.

The sea settled. Another Asdic contact! Three more attacks followed, two with standard depth charge patterns, and one using the recently developed Hedgehog, capable of firing a salvo of twenty-four small charges well ahead of the ship. Unfortunately, electrical problems continued to plague *Anemone*. Only four D/Cs fired. Frustrated, Lieutenant-Commander King turned back toward the convoy. He later recorded how his first attack appeared to have been a certain kill. Even with *Anemone*'s electrical problem reducing the number of D/Cs launched, the U-boat should have been hit, and sunk. It was, in fact, yet another example of how difficult it could be in the heat of battle to assess damage with any degree of accuracy. The U-boat in question, U89, suffered little damage, despite the vigorous efforts of King and his crew. U89 had been released from the *Raubgraf* group a few days before because of engine trouble and a shortage of fuel. The skipper, Dietrich Lohmann, had joined the convoy attack on his own initiative.*

Lieutenant-Commander Luther was worried about his escort group. It had been inadequate when the convoy left New York. Now it had been reduced to pathetic proportions. The protection of the entire convoy devolved on a single vessel: his ship, *Volunteer*. Luther received more bad news. A brand-new Liberty ship, *William Eustis*, was in trouble, listing heavily, her crew taking to the lifeboats. Again, the last merchantman in the column failed to stop and pick up survivors. Whatever his personal feelings about such conduct, Luther could not force the master of a merchant ship to act as a rescue ship. After making a wide Asdic sweep, he slowed and began the task of rescuing the crew himself. All of them escaped with their lives – hardly surprising, considering how well prepared they were; *Volunteer*'s crew noted with interest that many of them brought packed suitcases aboard the destroyer, and all wore rubber suits which they peeled off to reveal jackets and trousers and shoes.

The captain of *William Eustis* suddenly discovered that he had neglected to dump his code books and other confidential papers. Ashen-faced, he gazed out to sea, no doubt hoping that his ship had gone down. It hadn't. *William Eustis* would have to be sunk to ensure that her code books didn't fall in the hands of the Germans.

Luther fired four depth charges. They exploded directly beneath the ship, heaving her bodily out of the water. She crashed back into

---

* U89 had survived an attack in November 1942 by the highly successful RAF sub-killer Terry Bulloch, but was lost with all hands on the boat's next patrol a few weeks after its engagement with *Anemone*, sunk by ships and aircraft.

the sea, sinking soon afterwards and taking her cargo of seven thousand tons of sugar with her.

It was a critical time for the convoy. Three of the tiny force of escorts were some distance away, rescuing survivors; two more, *Anemone* and *Mansfield*, were still involved with U-boats: *Anemone* with U89, *Mansfield* with the shadowing U-boat. By now, six more U-boats were in contact with Convoy HX229. Aboard the thirty-three merchant ships, men stared anxiously into the dark waters. The hours passed, the sudden calm almost as unnerving as the frantic activity that preceded it. The convoy steamed on, the heavily laden vessels slogging their way through choppy water, leaving swirls of inky phosphorescence in their wake. The night seemed endless.

Few of the merchant sailors undressed at night; they took what sleep they could swaddled in warm clothes and lifejackets, ready to leap up and head for the deck at the first sign of trouble. Many preferred not to go below at all; in spite of the bone-chilling cold, they remained on deck to sleep fitfully in lifeboats or on deck cargo.

At 0218, U-boat U616 fired four torpedoes at the Town-class destroyer *Beverley*. All missed.

In the early hours of that eventful night, *Volunteer* returned to the convoy. *Mansfield* and *Beverley* followed shortly after. Tensions eased a little; the escorts were now almost back to strength, although it was a depleted strength. The more escorts, the better the chances of getting through in one piece. Eight U-boats were now in contact with the convoy. The minutes passed; dawn would come in ninety minutes. Another nerve-grinding night on the North Atlantic would be over. The U-boats, a nocturnal species in the main, would slink away over the horizon, safely out of reach of the escorts. But they would be watching, keeping their eager eyes on the smudges of smoke and the tips of masts on the horizon. They would shadow the convoy all through the daylight hours, waiting, always waiting, for the moment when they might mount another attack.

U600 had been shadowing the convoy for more than four hours. The boat surfaced ahead of the leading ships on the starboard flank of the convoy. Her skipper, Bernhard Zurmuehlen, fired a salvo of five torpedoes. He immediately reported to HQ that he had scored five direct hits. In fact, he hit three: an American tanker, *Irénée du Pont*, and two British ships, *Nariva* and *Southern Princess*. A USN ensign, Frank Pilling, was on his way to England aboard *Irénée du Pont*. He glimpsed torpedo tracks beneath the water, "two streaks of greasy light, parallel, moving fast, coming in at an angle. There was no time to shout a warning; in one instant there were the tracks, in another, a great shattering crash. Holding onto the rail, I was not thrown down, but seeing what appeared to be flying metal in the air, I rushed towards the opposite side of the ship. The second torpedo shook *Irénée* with amazing violence. She quivered and staggered so wildly for a moment that I lost my footing and lurched crazily before running forward to the port ladder."[2] The torpedoing did not bring out the best in the ship's company. Panic seemed to seize every member of the crew. Only two of the ship's lifeboats were launched; crew members dived into the sea without making any attempt to launch the others.

Nariva, carrying 5,600 tons of frozen meat, died with a monstrous explosion and a pillar of black smoke that sent tons of water and wreckage high into the air. Second Officer G. D. Williams recalled,

The ship was making water fast and the forward welldeck was soon awash. The order was given to abandon ship and the boats launched. We pulled away from the ship but then we saw the life-raft which was secured to the port mainmast shrouds released with a splash into the water and several men jump after it where they clung desperately and shouted for help. As my boat crew tried clumsily to backwater their oars we saw the raft drift slowly forward along the ship's side and, to our horror, we watched helplessly as a great inrush of water sucked the raft and its occupants into the cavernous hole blasted in the ship's side by the torpedo. . . . But then, thank God, the same rush of water that had drawn them into the hull of the ship, at the next roll, swept them out again, by which time we were so much closer and could grab the raft lines and drag the men to safety in our boat, one of whom turned out to be our dear, elderly chief engineer who, as if in gratitude for his rescue, became violently sick all over me.[3]

Captain Dodds kept the boats nearby, ready to reboard the ship after dawn if she hadn't sunk by then; for the moment, her cork insulation appeared to be keeping her afloat.

Southern Princess, the third ship struck by U600, was the largest in the convoy, a tanker laden with ten thousand tons of fuel oil, two railway engines, and several invasion barges. The torpedo had destroyed the bulkhead between the fuel cargo and the crew's accommodations. The explosion ignited gas in one of the cargo tanks, and a furious blaze resulted. It blistered paintwork on the next ship in line. Men watched in horror; every crew member on the ship would surely be consumed in that fire. In fact, the death toll was surprisingly light: only four men died.

The last ship in the column was the New Zealand Shipping Company refrigerator ship *Tekoa*, commanded by one of the heroes of the action, Albert Hocken. He had seen five ships torpedoed – without a single merchant ship stopping to pick up survivors. Now, in the surreal half-light provided by the crackling funeral pyre that was *Southern Princess*, he set about the task of saving her survivors, tossing lines, lowering cargo nets and rope ladders. The oil-soaked sailors flopped gasping on the New Zealand ship's deck; her sailors hosed them down before taking them below and providing hot showers and warm clothes. *Tekoa* picked up 146 men; *Anemone* rescued ninety-four men from *Nariva*; *Mansfield* rescued twenty from *Irénée du Pont*. Although *Southern Princess*'s captain had entertained hopes of salvaging her, they were not to be realized; she continued to blaze.

The destroyer *Beverley* picked up a radar contact at three thousand yards. It was U228, under the command of Erwin Christopherson, getting into position to attack a tanker. The radar blip vanished, to be replaced almost immediately by an Asdic contact. Seven depth charges went thudding into the sea, set to detonate at between fifty and 140 feet. The attack shook U228 and her crew, and the sub sprang a leak. Christopherson dived at once, descending to nearly two hundred metres before shutting down the motors. *Beverley* tried but could not regain Asdic contact.

Manfred Kinzel was on his first patrol as the commander of U338. A bright and energetic individual, he had enjoyed spectacular progress in his career, spending several years in the Luftwaffe before transferring to the navy. That he was highly regarded by his superiors – and that the need for more U-boat men was becoming critical – may be judged by the fact that this ex-airman had spent a mere three months aboard another submarine before taking a captain's course and assuming his own command.

During the relentless attacks on Convoy HX229, one of U338's lookouts had spotted several merchant ships dead ahead, no more than a mile away. Kinzel grinned. More by luck than judgement, he had come into contact with Convoy SC122; the two convoys were on a parallel course. SC122 appeared to have no escorts. Kinzel ordered an immediate attack: two torpedoes at the starboard column of ships, two at the port. The U-boat's crew heard only two explosions, but in fact four ships were hit. Two of Kinzel's missiles hit cargo ships, as intended: the British *Kingsbury* and the Dutch *Alderamin*. Another torpedo just missed *Kingsbury*, streaking on to hit the British tramp steamer *King Gruffydd*. The fourth torpedo struck the brand-new Canadian freighter *Fort Cedar Lake*. All four ships lost way, wallowing in the inky water as the ocean poured into their torn hulls. They had each been fatally hit; their masters ordered the crews to abandon ship. In the case of *King Gruffydd*, there was more than a little urgency; the ship carried five hundred tons of high explosive. In the event, however, she dived to the bottom without her cargo exploding. Five of her crew were trapped in the fo'c's'le, their screams clearly audible as the ship sank. Although burning fiercely, *Fort Cedar Lake* stayed afloat long enough for the crew to abandon their ship without a single casualty. The crew of the Dutch steamer *Alderamin* were not so fortunate. Two of the ship's lifeboats were badly damaged when Kinzel's torpedo struck home; a third boat capsized. The remaining lifeboat was lowered successfully, but with only the chief engineer and three men aboard. Regrettably, the officer's conduct left more than a little to be desired. On reaching the water safely, he released the falls and made all haste to get clear of the sinking ship, leaving the other survivors to fend for themselves on life rafts. The lifeboat had an outboard motor — several crewmen heard it start up — but the boat didn't return to pick them up. The corvette *Saxifrage* rescued thirty-seven men.*

If the log entry by *Oberleutnant* Herbert Zeissler is to taken literally, the crew of U338 seemed remarkably unimpressed by their victories: "We were pleased but not unduly excited. In some ways, we had expected success and we thought it quite natural that we should do this. We had done our training properly and we had complete confidence in our captain, Kinzel. . . . For breakfast we took out the best provisions we could find — *Knackwurst* and strawberries and cream."[4]

The first night of battle was over. The toll had been pitifully one-sided: twelve merchant ships sunk for only two U-boats slightly damaged. The day's first light — pale and etiolated — revealed a sadly depleted assembly of ships. The merchant seamen had spent a night of taut nerves, listening to explosions and cries for help. No one

---

*   By curious coincidence, the *Alderamin*'s master, Captain C. L. van Os, later became skipper of the freighter *Alpherat*, which was bombed and sunk near Malta the following December. Survivors were picked up by none other than the corvette *Saxifrage*.

had thought it necessary to tell them what was happening. Now, with the dawn, it was all too obvious. Men counted the ships, then recounted them. They experienced that strange conflict of emotions familiar to fighting men since the world's first wars: relief and guilt in more or less equal proportions. The loss of "the other guy," while regrettable, helped in some inexplicable way to improve one's own chances.

The only bright spot in a gloomy picture was that five additional escort vessels were at that moment hurrying toward the convoys.

The night's successes brought more U-boats sniffing about, laboriously identifying the ships, since there was still some confusion among the Germans as to which convoy was which. That morning, it was determined at last that SC122 was about 120 miles ahead of HX229 and on virtually the same course. In the early afternoon, two more U-boats made contact with SC122 and confirmed its position and the fact that it contained more merchant ships than HX229. Twenty-eight U-boats had now positioned themselves to attack the two convoys. And more U-boats were on their way from Germany to intercept a westbound convoy, ONS1. They were ordered to form a new group, *Seeteufel* (Sea Devil), to undertake the mission. The weather had improved. The sea was calmer, the winds lighter. Convoy SC122 now consisted of forty-four ships and six escorts: two destroyers, *Havelock* and *Upshur*, one frigate, *Swale*, and three corvettes, *Buttercup*, *Lavender*, and *Pimpernel*. Two more corvettes, *Godetia* and *Saxifrage*, would soon rejoin the convoy after completing rescue operations. To the sailors peering at the leaden swell, the ocean looked empty, but no one was fooled. They knew the U-boats were out there, somewhere, waiting for the moment to pounce. And they were right; two U-boats, U358 and U666, were travelling on the surface, making their laborious way around the convoy to place themselves in an advantageous position ahead of the Allied merchantmen in preparation for an attack later in the day.

Meanwhile, Convoy HX229A had enjoyed an almost trouble-free voyage, having been diverted far to the north. Its principal problem was ice. The large whaling ship *Svend Foyn* collided with an iceberg in the early morning of March 19.

Far to the south, U439 came across the burning ship *Fort Cedar Lake*. She was settling by the bows. As the Germans looked at the hulk, they heard an unfamiliar sound and looked up in surprise. Open-mouthed, they saw a large four-engined aircraft approaching from the east bearing the red-white-and-blue roundels of the RAF! The U-boat captain, Helmut von Tippelskirch, declared the aircraft to be a Sunderland flying boat and ordered an immediate crash dive.

In fact, von Tippelskirch had erred in his aircraft identification. The aircraft was one of the B-24 Liberators just delivered to 86 Squadron based at Aldergrove, Northern Ireland. These Liberators had been modified to VLR specifications and were capable of immensely long patrols; they were the aircraft that had been awaited for so many weary months. Heaven knows how many sailors' lives might have been saved if such aircraft had been in service a year before. Or even six months. An officer on the USN destroyer *Upshur*, Lieutenant Herbert Gravely, wrote, "I recall the joy when we first saw an aircraft with us. . . . We gave a real cheer when that first aircraft was spotted."[5]

At the controls of the Liberator was Flying Officer Cyril Burcher, an Australian. He had taken off from Aldergrove some eight hours earlier, intending to rendezvous with Convoy SC122. In the poor visibility, he had missed the convoy, and was in the process of retracing his steps when he spotted U439. The well-trained U-boat crew dived out of harm's way, foiling Burcher's attack. Twenty minutes later, Burcher's Liberator appeared over the convoy. Commodore Boyle requested a Cobra patrol at ten miles. This was a standard search ahead of and on either flank of a convoy aimed at spotting any U-boat getting into position for attack. Burcher and his crew didn't have to wait long for results; on the first sweep of the convoy's port flank, the crew spotted a U-boat. It was U338 with Manfred Kinzel in command. Burcher's last depth charges went down and appeared to do the U-boat serious damage. Oil spread over the surface. But it was almost certainly leaked deliberately by the U-boat, a familiar ploy.

By this time, Burcher's fuel was getting low. He had to head for home. He landed at Eglinton, near Londonderry, after well over eighteen hours in the air. Such was the value of the VLR Liberator.

For about two hours, the convoy was bereft of air cover, because fierce winds at Reykjavík, Iceland, prevented aircraft from taking off. About midday, the corvette *Godetia* suddenly turned to starboard. A torpedo track streaked across the convoy's port column of ships. It narrowly missed the American ship *Cartago* but hit the elderly freighter *Granville*, of Panamanian registry. The crew had been sitting down to a roast chicken lunch when the torpedo struck. One of the ships' two lifeboats was wrecked; the second capsized on launching. *Granville* started to break up. Twelve of her crew were lost, but the corvette *Lavender* succeeded in rescuing the other thirty-three.

Manfred Kinzel's U338 had been responsible for the sinking. *Upshur* and *Godetia* went in search of the sub. Both got Asdic contacts and launched twenty-seven depth charges, but U338 wasn't damaged.*

Dawn on the 17th found the ranks of Convoy HX229 sadly depleted. Only twenty-eight of the convoy's original forty merchant ships had survived. The escort group was diminished, too; only *Volunteer* and *Beverley* now protected the convoy, although *Mansfield*, *Pennywort*, and *Anemone*, busy with various tasks astern, were expected to rejoin the convoy during the morning.

The convoy reached thirty-five degrees west. At this point, the usual practice would have been for *Mansfield* to return to St. John's; on this occasion, however, the destroyer received a signal

---

* Kinzel and his crew ran out of luck a few months later, sunk by an acoustic torpedo carried by a Liberator of 120 Squadron. None survived.

from Halifax ordering her to remain with the convoy and refuel from one of the escort oilers. The corvette *Pennywort* had been busy with rescue operations. Completing these, she resumed her original course, not having been informed that the convoy's course had changed by twenty-five degrees. By the time the error was discovered and *Pennywort* had rejoined the convoy, some twelve hours had slipped away.

Ten U-boats trailed the convoy. More were on their way, summoned by signals from U603, the designated contact keeper. The U-boats kept their distance, confident of kills with the coming of night. In the meantime they waited, their crews resting and catching up on various maintenance duties. Lookouts kept a diligent watch. No Liberators appeared.

Convoy HX229 was still in the Air Gap, although SC122 had already reached the "other side" and could count on air support, given reasonable weather. In mid morning, Commodore Mayall decided to reorganize Convoy HX229 after its heavy losses. The first step was to reduce the number of columns from eleven to nine. A new column was organized on the starboard side of the convoy. Almost simultaneously, the Dutch ship *Terkoelei* took a torpedo and sank rapidly.*

Once again, the problem of rescue loomed large for Lieutenant-Commander Luther. The merchant ships in the convoy were understandably still reluctant to stop and pick up survivors. Too many U-boats about. It was a perilous business at night, almost suicidal in broad daylight. But the freezing, oil-soaked men couldn't be left to die. Someone had to drag the poor devils out of the water and tend to them.

Luther ordered *Mansfield* to carry out the rescue, with his own vessel, *Volunteer*, screening the operation.

---

* Ironically, she had been built by Blohm and Voss in Hamburg in 1923, as the *Essen*, and was probably sunk by U631, built by the same yard in 1942. Some doubt exists because U384 also attacked at the same time.

Forty-five minutes later, the destroyer *Beverley* spotted a U-boat about eight miles away, directly in the path of the convoy. At top speed, *Beverley* headed for its prey – whereupon the masthead lookout reported a second U-boat in the same area. Both U-boats dived when the destroyer approached, but the crew obtained a good Asdic contact. For the next two and a half hours, *Beverley* attacked one of them, U530, a Type IXC long-range boat under the command of former merchant officer Kurt Lange. At thirty-nine, Lange was one of the oldest U-boat skippers.

Beverley's attack caused near-panic aboard U530 when the lights went out and water started to splash into the hull via the torpedo tube hatches. Crewmen worked at top speed to repair the leak, but made little progress. Water still streamed into the hull.

Containers between the outer deck and the pressure hull were damaged and these too filled with water. With this growing weight of water in the boat itself and in the outer deck containers, the U-boat sank steadily. Lange decided to pump out the midships diesel tanks to get more buoyancy, but the pumps were also damaged and this could not be done. One man noticed that 'the younger men were very steady but the married ones looked scared' but another man says that 'we were all in terrible fear.' The U-boat went down to 240 metres and the crew, believing that 200 metres was their boat's limit, expected to be crushed at any moment. It was at this stage that the German sailors, with only the dim emergency lighting, with water swilling around their feet, with the hull of their boat creaking under pressure, heard quite clearly the passage of the destroyer directly overhead and believed they were about to meet their end.[6]

They had good reason to think so. The destroyer *Beverley* launched a massive Mark X depth charge packed with some two thousand pounds of high explosive. Sensibly, the destroyer made off at top speed, not wishing to be too close when the monster went off. As it happened, the crew had no reason for concern. The D/C's firing mechanism failed. The mine sank, an innocuous lump to be added to the other assorted junk on the seabed.

That evening, Lange surfaced, cautiously. To the intense relief of everyone aboard the battered U-boat, there was no sign of *Beverley* or any of the other escorts. The Germans looked, aghast, at the damage their U-boat had suffered: "The U-boat's upper deck was found to be crushed and the steel cladding of the conning tower was 'rolled up like a piece of paper.' The crew had much cause to be thankful for the workmanship of the *Deutsche Werft* at Hamburg which had built U530. This crippled U-boat took no further part in the convoy battle, and *Beverley's* activities had also caused at least two and possibly three other U-boats to take fright and lose contact with the convoy."7*

Lieutenant-Commander Luther had been disappointed when it appeared that air support would not be forthcoming in the critical hours leading up to nightfall. But then two slim-winged, fat-bellied RAF Liberators abruptly appeared, one from 86 Squadron, with Flying Officer Charles Hammond at the controls, the other from 120 Squadron, commanded by a veteran Coastal Command pilot, Flying Officer S. E. "Red" Esler.

Hammond had actually been seeking SC122. He had missed the convoy on his first approach, had flown off again following directions provided by *Volunteer*, then returned after four hours, still not having found SC122.

At 1705, Esler spotted two surfaced U-boats about ten miles away. He attacked out of the sun, dropping five depth charges. Delighted, the crew saw the U-boat lurch out of the water, then splash back again like a dead fish. But U221 wasn't dead, just severely shaken. The submarine got away. Not long afterward, Esler's crew

---

*   Lange survived the war, being posted to shore duty early in 1945.

spotted three more U-boats. Two of them dived to safety as soon as the Liberator appeared. The third stayed to fight, putting up a barrage of not very accurate machine-gun fire. Esler dropped his last depth charge. It landed alongside the U-boat but, surprisingly, failed to cause fatal damage.

The shadows lengthened. The men of the two convoys prepared themselves for their second night in the battle zone.

At 2006, the corvette *Pimpernel* of SC122's B5 escort group picked up a strong radar contact. U305 was on the surface six thousand yards away. It quickly dived, soon afterward torpedoing two vessels, a refrigerator ship, *Port Auckland*, and a cargo ship, *Zouave*. Loaded with seven thousand tons of iron filings, *Zouave* sank quickly, "because she was a rattling old tub," wrote the cook, S. Banda, who was relieved, he says, when she went down. "She literally fell to bits – there were rivets flying about like machine-gun bullets. There were no real regrets at her going down; none of us were aiming to rejoin after this voyage."[8]

Port Auckland took longer to sink. W. P. Shevlin, one of the ship's engineers, had a difficult time escaping: "I was lost in the absolute darkness. I thought it was 'finish.' I kept struggling but really did not know where I was. I was quite calm and did not panic. . . . I thought sadly of my wife and my family and thought how sad the news would be to them."[9]

Commander Boyle ordered a Half Raspberry search for the U-boat. It was unproductive. He directed the corvette *Godetia* to pick up survivors from *Zouave* and *Port Auckland*; the Belgian crew was experienced at this vital work, having already rescued the crew of *Campobello*. As the last man was pulled shivering from the water, the corvette's radar picked up a good contact, but lost it after a few minutes. The U-boat escaped.

Darkness crept over Convoy HX229, now some eighty miles to the rear of SC122. Three destroyers – *Volunteer*, *Beverley*, and *Mansfield* – formed an uncomfortably sparse escort, although the corvettes *Anemone* and *Pennywort* rejoined shortly after nightfall.

Luther now had his full complement of escort vessels – but not for long.

Apart from *Volunteer*'s HF/DF equipment picking up a U-boat signal – which was soon lost – and a medical emergency involving acute appendicitis suffered by a seaman, it was a quiet night.

CLIMAX OF THE BATTLE

"The battle . . . is not to the strong alone; it is to the vigilant, the active, the brave"
– Patrick Henry

THE MORNING OF March 18 saw heavy weather with fierce winds. Seamen welcomed the rough conditions. The worse the weather, the fewer the U-boats.

Short of fuel, *Mansfield* had to leave HX229. She made for Londonderry with a strong gale pushing her along. Her departure reduced the escort to four ships: *Volunteer, Beverley, Anemone,* and *Pennywort.* Visibility worsened. Five Liberators were scheduled to provide the convoy with continuous air cover through the day. They didn't materialize. The first aircraft searched for five hours for the convoy, then flew back to Aldergrove, Northern Ireland, and landed, having spent in excess of sixteen hours aloft and seeing nothing but ocean. Four more Liberators took off; not one found the convoy. Squadron Leader Desmond Isted did, however, encounter U610, commanded by Walter von Freyberg-Eisenberg-Allmendingen. As U610 dived to safety, a depth charge from Isted's Liberator – which, predictably, the Germans identified as a

Sunderland – exploded right over the U-boat. It damaged both periscopes, both compasses, and a compressor, as well as various instruments. Flying Officer R. Goodfellow of 120 Squadron arrived on the scene. He detected the U-boat by his aircraft's radar, but he was too late to attack.

At about this time, two vessels, one British, one German, entered the picture. *Highlander*, lead ship in B4 escort group, rejoined the convoy after lengthy repairs in St. John's. And U221, under the command of Hans Trojer, succeeded in working its way to the front of Convoy HX229. Trojer then dived to periscope depth, waiting until the convoy came to him. The paucity of escorts enabled U221 to slip into the body of the convoy without being spotted. Third Officer R. H. Keyworth of the refrigerator ship *Canadian Star* saw a torpedo hit the Liberty ship *Walter Q. Gresham*; moments later he saw a torpedo streaking toward his own ship. It struck home. "It felt as though the whole ship had blown up underneath me. There was a tremendous amount of cordite. I can still almost taste it."[1]

Two torpedoes had hit the ship. She began to settle by the stern. Two of the lifeboats were wrecked, but the other two had space for the crew and twenty-four passengers. Lieutenant-Commander Luther ordered an Artichoke, a search to the rear of the convoy, the usual response to a daylight torpedo attack. It produced no results, although the corvette *Pennywort* picked up a weak Asdic signal; she dropped six depth charges without apparent effect. Luther called off the search and ordered *Anemone* and *Pennywort* to rescue survivors. The stormy sea didn't help matters. It was particularly hard on the men hanging on to the rafts. "We soon had twenty-two men on a ten-man raft," recalled Second Officer Clarke-Hunt. "Most of them had to hang on the side somehow. We lost six of these fairly quickly; you would see them getting cold, a certain look came into their eyes and then they just gave up."[2]

The grim weather prolonged rescue efforts for more than two hours. It was no simple matter to drag wounded, oil-soaked men from the sea. Most were dead weights, slippery with oil, utterly exhausted, unable to assist in their own rescue.

Third Officer R. H. Keyworth of *Canadian Star* came close to expiring during the ordeal:

> It was useless to bail; the sea just swept through the boat from end to end. I could see the men, one by one, their eyes glazing . . . eventually losing their grip and being washed up and down the boat and eventually out of it altogether. Then I started to get a feeling of cosiness, ready to relax, just as though I had come in and sat by a warm fire and just couldn't keep awake. I had a perfectly clear vision of my mother outside my home in Wellington, New Zealand, and at the gate, at the bottom of the long garden path, was the postman with an envelope in his hand. I knew very well that this told her that I had been lost at sea. As I lapsed further into this semiconscious state, the postman started to move. I couldn't bear the thought of my mother being distressed and I managed to rouse myself from this drifting-away feeling. The postman stopped. I started going again and the postman started walking up the path again so, once more, I pulled myself together and he stopped. I should think this process was repeated seven or eight times. By the time he was three-quarters up the path, I saw a corvette. I think now that if I had gone right into the coma, I would have seen the postman reach my mother and that the vision I had been seeing enabled me to reach to the bottom of my endurance and it saved my life." [3]*

---

* Third Officer Keyworth was subsequently awarded the MBE. Two other *Canadian Star* officers were also decorated, and *Oberleutnant* Hans Trojer, U221's commander and a veteran who had been active in U-boat warfare since the early days of the war, received the coveted Ritterkreuz. He and his crew died in September, sunk by a Halifax of Coastal Command.

Commander E. C. L. ("Happy") Day resumed command of the convoy after a lengthy stay in St. John's for repairs to his ship, *Highlander*. He was confronted by a problem: the captain and crew of the American freighter *Mathew Luckenbach* had decided to leave the convoy, preferring to rely on their superior speed – some fifteen knots – to take them through to England. It was a democratic decision. Officers and men had gathered in the mess hall. The captain explained that the two convoys, HX229 and SC122, had lost nineteen ships so far. The escorts had achieved little. It now looked as if the U-boats would sink every ship. In his opinion, *Mathew Luckenbach* had a better chance of reaching port alone. The captain intended to depart the convoy under cover of darkness. He asked for a show of hands. The entire crew had been in agreement; every man signed a statement to that effect. Thus *Mathew Luckenbach* became what the Navy called a "romper" or "runner," a ship abandoning a convoy to sail alone. It is hard not to sympathize with the freighter captain. He felt with more than a little justification that the safety of his ship and its crew was being jeopardized by remaining with this slow-as-molasses convoy – which was optimistically categorized as fast. The U-boats were picking off the ships one by one. If things went on at this rate, it could well turn out to be the worst convoy disaster of the war. The captain was determined not to be part of it.

Convoy HX229 had almost caught up with SC122; indeed, to the Germans it appeared to be one huge convoy. Twenty-four U-boats were in contact, lurking far enough away to be invisible to the convoy's lookouts. The weather was settling down nicely as the day drew to a close. Bright moonlight would soon cast a pale mantle over the columns of ships, making it easier for the helmsmen to keep station, but also making it easier for U-boats to attack. As the last minutes of March 18 ticked away, a U-boat suffering mechanical problems came upon HX229. U406 was commanded by Horst Dieterichs, who would later report that his vessel was severely hampered by "carbon deposits and thick sludge in both crank cases; this choked up the filters whenever we ran at high speeds, thereby causing a dangerously low oil pressure. Sabotage would have been an easy explanation but poor quality fuel seemed to be more likely."[4] U406 was in no condition to attack the convoy, but its signals soon brought ten more U-boats. The corvette *Anemone* spotted U615 shortly after 0300. Curiously, it was situated up-moon and downwind of the convoy, in a poor attack position. *Anemone* hurried to intercept. The destroyer *Volunteer* also joined in, on Commander Day's orders. The corvette dropped ten charges set to explode at depths ranging from 150 to 385 feet. U615 survived unharmed, but two other U-boats, U134 and U440, entered the fray and suffered some damage. While five of the escort vessels were busy sub-hunting, another U-boat, U441, arrived and promptly launched torpedoes at five merchant ships. The captain, Klaus Hartmann, claimed one ship sunk, another on fire, and two more hit. In fact, not one of Hartmann's torpedoes had found its mark.

U608, under the command of Rolf Struckmeier, fired three torpedoes at the destroyer *Highlander*. All three missed. *Highlander* had been hunting U439, but the destroyer's Hedgehog had failed. The destroyer returned to the convoy.

The pace of the action slowed. With the first glimmer of dawn, there seemed to be no U-boats in the immediate vicinity. There were. The corvette *Anemone* suddenly spotted two of them astern of the convoy. Both dived simultaneously – "perhaps just as well," commented Lieutenant-Commander King, "because had both U-boats remained on the surface, and fought it out with their guns, it would have been two against one and *Anemone*, with her single gun, could only have engaged one U-boat at a time, leaving the other to shoot unmolested."[5]

A few hours earlier, the River-class frigate *Swale*, one of SC122's escorts, reported a radar contact at 0448. A moment later, a merchant ship erupted in flames. She was the elderly Greek merchantman *Carras*, the leading ship in SC122's starboard column. Captain

Mazavinos gave the order to abandon ship. *Zamalek*, a small steamer, picked up the crew of thirty-four; not a man was lost or injured.

The frigid early hours of March 19 brought calm seas and good visibility. Another night gone. Another night closer to England. Morale improved perceptibly. Maybe there was a chance of getting through this nightmare of a voyage after all. For the moment, no U-boats were in evidence lurking around the convoy; energetic action by the escorts had scared them off. Now the crews had a few hours to take care of maintenance and repairs and, perhaps, get a little sleep. Inevitably, the action would resume when darkness fell.

The U.S. Coast Guard cutter *Ingham*, commanded by A. M. Martinson, took four days to battle her way through heavy seas from Iceland to join up with SC122. She was a large and impressive vessel, well-equipped, with a good crew. The escort commander, Lieutenant-Commander R. C. Boyle, was delighted to welcome her, and was appreciative of her captain's willingness to place himself and his crew under Boyle's command – particularly as Martinson was the senior in rank. Accompanying *Ingham* on the rough trip from Iceland was the USS *Babbitt*, a venerable but still-efficient destroyer commanded by Lieutenant-Commander Samuel F. Quarles. Approaching the convoy, Quarles was dismayed by the number of U-boats in the area: "There were so many between us and the convoy that we felt as if we were about to take on the whole German submarine fleet."[6] *Babbitt*'s radar picked up a good contact some ten miles from the convoy. There followed a classic submarine-versus-destroyer battle. In the destroyer, the sonar operator listened intently to sounds from beneath the surface; in the sub, the hydrophone man listened just as intently, constantly adjusting his receiver, trying to sort out the jumble of aquatic sounds so that he might read off the bearings, building up a mental picture of the enemy vessel and its movements. *Babbitt*'s adversary was U190, a new Type IXC on its first patrol. No matter how well they had been trained, it is doubtful that the crew were in any way prepared for the ferocious stress and physical pain they were about to endure. The first salvo of depth charges sent U190 plunging to a fearsome depth of 240 metres – widely believed to be too deep for a U-boat to survive. Every man aboard went through the torments of the damned as the pressure increased; it felt as if red-hot needles were jabbing their ear drums; their lungs seemed to be working at half power; their insides shrivelled while the pressure in their sinuses built up moment by moment. Around them, the boat creaked and squealed in pain as it took the frightful loads and absorbed them, apportioned them. Lights dimmed and went out. Dials popped. Pipes bent as if in pain. Men cringed, wincing at every cracking explosion, feeling as if great steel-toed boots were kicking their guts. There was something intensely personal about being depth-charged; each explosion seemed to be aimed at you and you alone. Every few minutes another pipe fractured, and showers of water played on the men and spurted into the reeking interior of the U-boat, another misery to be endured until the engineering boys could attend to it. The boat became a claustrophobic torture chamber, retreating further and further from one danger, only to run an appalling risk of succumbing to another.

Babbitt's attack lasted five endless, agonizing hours. Then it ceased – replaced by blessed, unreal silence. The captain, Max Wintermeyer, ordered the boat surfaced – gradually, carefully, ten metres at a time. Men began to relax, heaving great sighs of relief. One or two managed smiles, brief, brittle things. Someone chuckled, as if to tell everyone that he had known all along that he would survive . . .

At 180 metres, the worst thing in the world happened: *Babbitt* resumed the attack. Wintermeyer dived, going back to those terrifying depths. Again the crew waited, gasping for air, listening to the complaints of the steel, trying to control their emotions and themselves. Some shivered as if suffering from extreme cold; some endured it with stoicism, staring at their feet, enduring the agonies of air pressure, wondering how much life they had left.

Several hours later, U190 cautiously surfaced, the crew convinced that they had been attacked by a group of escorts, not just one. Seriously damaged, the boat returned to base for repairs.

The morning of March 19 had brought better weather, brighter and calmer. It also brought air cover. The dreaded Air Gap had been traversed. As if to symbolize the progress, a B-17 Fortress appeared, circling, looking everything over before proceeding to patrol the waters around the convoy.

All alone, some forty miles ahead of the convoy, the American freighter *Mathew Luckenbach* steamed along, heading for England. The ship had abandoned Convoy HX229, but without knowing it had almost caught up with Convoy SC122. *Mathew Luckenbach* was directly in the path of U527, a Type IXC U-boat. The sub's captain, Herbert Uhlig, had seen aircraft in the vicinity, so prudently decided to make a submerged attack. But such an attack brought his speed down to a pathetic few knots. In fact, the elderly merchantman seemed for a while to be outpacing its attacker. It took hours to get into position. At last Uhlig gave the order to fire. Two torpedoes hit *Mathew Luckenbach* with a great booming bang. She began to list. Captain Atwood H. Borden gave the order to abandon ship. None of the crew had been hurt, and all managed to scramble aboard lifeboats or rafts. It was a lucky escape, and the crew was doubly lucky that Lieutenant John Waters of the U.S. Coast Guard cutter *Ingham* happened to be looking in their direction at the time. At a distance of several miles, he glimpsed a column of water rising out of the sea. *Ingham* went to investigate and soon picked up the survivors. *Mathew Luckenbach* was low in the water but still afloat. Captain Martinson of *Ingham* suggested that the crew return to their ship and attempt to sail her to port. The suggestion met with little enthusiasm.

Ten miles away, Captain Uhlig of U527 wanted to finish off the stubborn merchant ship, but the sight of two warships, and a Fortress patrolling above, deterred him. After watching the crippled ship for some hours, he decided finally to attack. To his astonishment, a torpedo from another U-boat hit the ship and she went down rapidly. U523 was responsible – though three other U-boats were also getting into position for attack when she went down.

At 0300, a 220 Squadron Boeing Fortress took off from Benbecula, a storm-battered strip in Scotland's Outer Hebrides. Within moments of lifting off, the big aircraft was over water, the waves glinting dully in the moonlight. The Fortress was the first of the day to head out to meet Convoy SC122. Ahead lay a long flight of nearly six hundred miles of unchanging vista. Water, countless acres of it, pewter-coloured, frigid, merciless. And endless sky.

Then at last, the convoy! Like a herd of cattle in the ocean, the ships plodded along, their progress barely discernible. The Fortress conducted a patrol of the convoy but found no sign of U-boats. It was a different story for the Fortress of 206 Squadron with Pilot Officer Leslie G. Clark at the controls. Rendezvousing with Convoy HX229 at 0905, Clark was asked to patrol at a range of about thirty miles. He soon encountered a snow squall. Clark flew into it, calculating that any U-boat skipper would expect an aircraft to steer well clear of such conditions. He was right. A surfaced U-boat loomed out of the murk. Clark and his crew acted with commendable promptness, dropping four depth charges before U384 had time to dive. They had delivered a mortal blow. The U-boat disappeared beneath the surface, leaving huge patches of oil on the surface. The captain, *Oberleutnant* von Rosenberg Gruszczynski, and his entire crew lost their lives. Half an hour later, another Fortress appeared near SC122, also from 220 Squadron. Almost immediately, the crew, under the command of Flying Officer Bill Knowles, spotted a U-boat astern of the convoy. It was U666 on its first patrol; the Fortress attacked and damaged the boat, but it managed to limp back to St. Nazaire, arriving on April 10.*

---

* It was sunk with all hands the following February.

Five big Sunderland flying boats also came out to escort Convoy SC122, taking off from Lough Erne, Northern Ireland. The Sunderlands' job was to fly parallel track sweeps, covering as much area as possible, to make their presence known to the largest number of U-boats. It was tedious work for the aircrews, but an effective method of keeping the U-boats at bay. This patrol turned out to be uncommonly productive. Two Sunderlands caught U-boats on the surface. A 228 Squadron Sunderland spotted U608 well astern of SC122 and depth-charged it without inflicting any damage. Clare Bradley and his crew of a Canadian squadron, 423, also sighted a U-boat astern of the convoy, apparently preparing to attack a merchant ship that had fallen astern of the convoy because of boiler trouble. Stragglers were the favourite prey of ambitious U-boat skippers like Manfred Kinzel of U338, who had already sunk five merchant ships from SC122. Kinzel confidently expected to add this vessel, a CAM-ship, *Empire Morn*, to his tally of victories. The Sunderland's arrival spoilt his plans. Kinzel hastily ordered an immediate dive. The big Sunderland roared overhead, dropping two depth charges; it should have been six, but four hung up. The remaining two charges proved highly effective, however, smashing a hole in U338's pressure hull and putting the sub out of the battle. Such was the inestimable value of strong, well-coordinated air cover. For the hard-pressed men of the convoys, the presence of Liberators, Sunderlands, and other Allied aircraft was a splendid boost to morale and proof that the voyage was at long last nearing its end. England was only a few hundred miles over . . . *there*. As long as the visibility held, the air force would make the last leg of the journey infinitely easier.

By now, many of the boats clustering around the convoys were damaged and low on fuel, their crews stretched almost to the limits of endurance. "The merchant ship, escort, and aircraft carrier crews may have felt that their enemies were invisible, safe, and always full of confidence, but a U-boat man, who may not have seen his home base or another friendly U-boat for several weeks, felt immensely lonely and isolated. After the four days of this convoy battle, he was physically and mentally exhausted, never free from the fear that he was about to be pounced upon by ship or aircraft and depth-charged into eternity."[7] Condemned to fight in their reeking iron coffins, either soaking in sweat or shivering, the U-boat crews continued to spend day after endless day in a state of grinding tension, their imaginations painting horrific pictures of what *might* happen at any moment of any day. Even night brought no security. The British had made vast improvements to their radar; now they could spot a surfaced U-boat at twenty miles or more in pitch darkness. A moment's droning might be followed by the searing glare of a Leigh light. And the deadly thud of depth-charge explosions. Little wonder that *Blechtoller* (tin can madness) had become a familiar problem in U-boat crews. Depth meant safety, but no one knew how deep a U-boat could go. Those who had tested a U-boat to its limit took the hard-won information to the bottom.

As the weather continued to improve, so did visibility, making it easier for patrolling aircraft to keep the convoys in sight. Although good visibility was of equal benefit to the predatory U-boats, the convoys were by now better prepared, with eight escorts each. The British destroyer *Vimy* had finally arrived after its journey from Iceland, and the American destroyer *Babbitt* rejoined the convoy after its lengthy battle with U190.

Patrolling in the vicinity of SC122 was a Liberator of 120 Squadron commanded by the capable Red Esler, who had encountered U221 and U608 two days before. Esler had been sent to cover the convoy late in the afternoon; the visibility remained good after dark, so he stayed. It was as well that he did. The Liberator crew spotted U590 in the act of diving. Esler dropped two depth charges; they were near-misses, but the convoy heard no more from the U-boat. Shortly afterward, Esler approached the convoy from astern. He noted the presence of what he thought was one of the escort vessels. His navigator, Flight Sergeant T. J. Kempton, was in the Liberator's nose and had a better view. He reported that the vessel wasn't an escort but a U-boat! Esler attacked immediately — only to find that the depth charges wouldn't release. Frustrated, he continued to patrol for more than two hours before returning to his base at Aldergrove. He and his crew had flown for thirty-six of the past seventy hours and had attacked five U-boats.

The rest of the night passed quietly for the ships of SC122. The Germans relaxed their efforts. The convoy had drawn too close to the British Isles and the fleets of Coastal Command aircraft. Dönitz ordered his U-boats to break off at daylight and search the convoys' paths. There was always the possibility of coming across stragglers and other targets of opportunity.

Dawn on March 20 saw aircraft of RAF Coastal Command arriving in strength to shepherd the ships home: Fortresses, Liberators, and Sunderlands dotted the sky. They found no "trade" in the immediate vicinity of the convoys, but several aircraft spotted U-boats further west. A Sunderland of 201 Squadron commanded by Flight Lieutenant Dudley Hewitt dropped six depth charges on a U-boat in the act of submerging. The charges blew it back to the surface, where it emerged at an angle of about forty-five degrees and remained there for a moment before splashing back. Hewitt circled, banking steeply, his gunners blazing away at the U-boat's conning tower. The airmen watched as sailors scrambled out, trying to reach their deck gun. The Sunderland gunners kept up a steady fire and the big flying boat continued to circle. Hewitt dropped his last depth charges. They straddled the submarine, sending up massive blossomings of spray. Hewitt and his crew were confident that they had disposed of the U-boat, and indeed received credit. But subsequent investigation showed that two U-boats were involved: U527, which had sunk *Mathew Luckenbach* the day before, and U598. By curious coincidence, both U-boats had engaged Hewitt's Sunderland and both survived.

Another Sunderland, this from the Canadian 423 Squadron based at Castle Archdale, Northern Ireland, encountered U631 and straddled her with five depth charges. The delighted Sunderland

crew were confident that they had sunk or, at least, severely damaged the U-boat. In fact, the Sunderland's depth charges merely
gave the Germans an uncomfortable few minutes' shaking up. They
got more shaking up a short time later when they encountered a
Sunderland of 201 Squadron commanded by Flying Officer W. C.
Robertson. The U-boat didn't dive when the Sunderland appeared,
but instead fought it out while a problem with the conning tower
hatch was cleared. Countless rounds of ammunition passed between
the Sunderland and U631, but no damage was done and no casualties were sustained by either side.

It was the last encounter in the battle for Convoys SC122 and
HX229, rated by the Germans as the greatest convoy battle of the
war. It came at a time of shattering losses for the Allies. Captain
S. W. Roskill, the British naval historian, states that "in the first ten
days [of March 1943], in all waters, we lost forty-one ships; in the
second ten days, fifty-six. More than half a million tons of shipping
was sunk in those twenty days; and what made the losses so much
more serious than the bare figures can indicate, was that nearly
two-thirds of the ships sunk during the month were sunk in
convoy."[8] The propagandists in Berlin called it a major German
victory. It was. And it had cost only one U-boat, U384, a Type VIIC,
with its crew of forty-seven. To achieve this victory, Allied naval
and air forces had used a phenomenal total of 378 depth charges:
229 by HX229's surface escorts, 69 by SC122's escorts, and 80 by
Coastal Command aircraft.*

~

The devastating losses suffered by SC122 and HX229 shook Allied
confidence in the convoy system. Were convoys at the end of their

---

* Shortly after the battle, however, U665, on its way back to base, was sunk with
all hands in the Bay of Biscay by a Whitley V. Another returning U-boat, U338,
which had sunk five ships in the battle, fought it out with a Halifax of 502 Squadron.
The U-boat's gunners shot down the plane and all but one of its crew were killed.

usefulness? Was it time to think up new methods of protecting the merchant ships, now more vital than ever as plans for the invasion of Europe spawned ever more lists of arms and supplies? There were those who said that the invasion could never take place while the U-boat wolfpacks still roamed the seas.

More bad news emerged from a top-level conference in Washington. Ernest King, the single-minded American admiral, announced his intention of withdrawing U.S. escort ships from the principal northern routes across the Atlantic. From now on, he said, the USN would concern itself with the southerly routes only. Canadian and British officers were dismayed; just as Dönitz's U-boat force seemed to be becoming even more powerful, King was pulling out of the main areas of danger in the Atlantic. It was, said some, typical of the man's bloody-mindedness. The admiral's personality was a source of endless comment among his colleagues. Sir John Slessor observed, "He is often alleged to have been very anti-British, but I think it more true to say that he was rather excessively pro-American."[9] Brigadier Dykes, the British Secretary to the Combined Chiefs of Staff in Washington, was less diplomatic, describing King as a man of great strength of character with a very small brain. Slessor pointed out that King's "weakness as a colleague in an Allied organization for the high direction of war was that it never seemed to occur to him that he could possibly be wrong, or that it was conceivable that his own judgement, and the efficiency of the United States Navy, were not in every way superior to anyone else's."[10] According to Slessor, King had a morbid fear of an independent air force; he made few friends in the RAF when he declared that the poor equipment, inadequate strength, and insufficient training of Coastal Command were entirely due to the fact that it was part of the RAF and not the RN. Another of his *bêtes noires* was the Allied Anti-submarine Survey Board, set up to bring about an efficient coordination between American, British, and Canadian operations in the Atlantic. After successfully blocking every recommendation made by the board, King succeeded in having it dissolved. He also managed to squash an eminently sensible suggestion put forward to create a Combined Procedure Board to work out a single, combined system of operational, intelligence, and signals procedures that would be used by all Allied anti-submarine units in the Atlantic. The effect of the system would have been that a British, American, or Canadian unit could move rapidly from, say, British command to American command without having to retrain crews in procedures. But King, apparently seeing some sinister conspiracy at work here, would have none of it. He seemed constitutionally incapable of accepting the idea of any of his ships serving, even temporarily, under British officers.

Since late in 1941, the United States Navy had exercised strategic control over the Western Atlantic. Now the USN confined its authority to the area from New York south. The Royal Canadian Navy took over responsibility for trade convoys and their escorts in an area running eastward from New York and southward from Greenland along the meridian of forty-seven degrees west. Canadian Rear-Admiral L. W. Murray assumed command as commander-in-chief, at Halifax. It was agreed that anti-submarine air operations were now to come under the operational direction of the naval commander responsible for protecting shipping in any given area, the air officer commanding exercising general operational control. Canada was to be responsible for air cover of HX, SC, and ON convoys to the limit of aircraft range from Labrador, Newfoundland, and the Canadian maritime provinces. It was a highly satisfactory development for the Canadians, who had been the subject of so much criticism earlier in the Atlantic conflict. Now they took responsibility for a significant part of the traffic. Canadian escorts underwent intensive training to ready them for their new responsibilities. During the summer months, Commander P. B. Martineau toured the Canadian units engaged in anti-submarine endeavours. He reported, "The general situation has improved out of all recognition since my visit in October–November 1942. . . . The cooperation between the RCN and the RCAF is excellent."[11]

It was, in fact, the beginning of better times in the Atlantic.

13

WINGS OVER THE OCEAN

"While sky and sea and land
And earth's foundations stand
And heaven endures"
– A. E. Housman

IN MAY, WITH THE addition of the VLR Liberators of 10 Squadron, based in Newfoundland, the notorious Air Gap finally ceased to exist. The pessimism of only a few weeks earlier vanished. Now the U-boat wolfpacks no longer persisted against air-escorted convoys, and the rate of sinkings rapidly dropped to proportions that approached the negligible. John Slessor, the commander-in-chief of Coastal Command since February 1943, said that the U-boat campaign against the North Atlantic convoys was defeated by midsummer, with less than fifty VLR aircraft, in conjunction with the surface escorts and a couple of light carriers. He couldn't resist adding: "I'm afraid there is no disguising the fact that King's obsession with the Pacific and the Battle of Washington cost us dear in the Battle of the Atlantic."[1]

The Allies had for years grappled with the problems of covering the vast reaches of the Atlantic with a strictly limited number of aircraft. Inevitably, their attention was drawn to a comparatively small area of water, about three hundred miles long by 120 miles wide: the Bay of Biscay. Five out of every six U-boats operating in the Atlantic passed through the bay on their way to or from the Atlantic, more than a hundred a month on average. Clearly, this was the place to slaughter U-boats. But the enemy was wily. And inventive. U-boats were soon observed to be carrying crude-looking wooden aerials for the Metox radar detector, often called *das Biscaykreuz* (the Biscay Cross), which gave the U-boats warning of the presence of radar operating in the vicinity. Many Allied aircrews found to their cost that U-boats were no longer the sitting (or diving) ducks that they had been in the past, their anti-aircraft armament having been greatly enhanced. Some maritime air force units began to make their own modifications; an Australian squadron, No. 10, added four forward-firing Browning machine guns to the two turret-mounted Brownings in the noses of their Sunderlands. Thus equipped, one of their aircraft attacked U426. The U-boat's gun crew opened fire, but the battery of machine guns in the Sunderland's nose quickly silenced them. The flying-boat crew saw half a dozen bodies lying in the conning tower. A cluster of depth charges sent U426 to the bottom, stern first. The captain, Christian Reich, and his entire crew were lost. By May 1943, more than 50 per cent of the U-boats sighted in the Bay of Biscay were attacked; seven were sunk.

A Sunderland of the Canadian 422 Squadron had a brisk battle with U625, off the coast of Northern Ireland. The aircraft was about five hundred miles out in the Atlantic, on its way to escort a convoy, when it came across the U-boat, its crew bathing and sunning themselves. "We couldn't believe our eyes," recalls the crew's navigator, Frank Cauley. "We went in and dropped our depth charges."[2]

The U-boat replied, using its powerful armament: two 20-millimetre cannon and a number of machine guns. They scored hits on the Sunderland. Fragments of shrapnel snapped through the thin metal walls, buzzing like infuriated wasps, but fortunately hitting none of the crew. The mainly Canadian crew were on their first op, with an RAF pilot and navigator checking them out. One of the Germans' shells hit the Sunderland below the waterline, punching a jagged, ugly hole that threatened to flip the big flying boat over onto its back the moment it touched down. There were dozens more small shrapnel holes in the hull, which seemed in imminent danger of ripping, like a sheet of stamps.

The crew found it relatively easy to plug the large hole in the hull, using patching materials carried in the aircraft. The small holes presented a different challenge – until the flight engineer, Sergeant E. E. Higgins, had a bright idea. The aircraft was well supplied with chewing gum; so Higgins suggested that each crew member chew five sticks and form them into a wad. He pressed them into the holes while the pilot, Warrant Officer W. F. Morton, took the Sunderland up to chilly levels where the wads froze solid. Thus plugged up, the Sunderland returned to base. Landing was a nerve-wracking business, with every crew member all too aware of what might happen if the gum plugs were knocked out by the stresses of landing. They held.*

Some months later, another Canadian aircraft, a Canso of 162 Squadron, also encountered a U-boat offering spirited defence. At the time, the unit was based at Wick in northern Scotland. Ten days earlier, the same aircraft, with Flying Officer R. E. MacBride at the controls, had sunk U477. Today the skipper was the squadron CO, Wing Commander Bill Chapman. He had an experienced crew, that of Flying Officer Jim McRae, the co-pilot on this trip. Like so many aircrew on maritime patrol work, McRae's crew had completed some fifty operational sorties over the Atlantic and had yet to see a submarine.

The Canso took off and headed for the search area, two hundred miles north of the Shetland Islands. The sea was calm, which helped McRae to spot the feathery wake of a periscope as it sliced through

---

* Someone told the Wrigley Company about the incident. Soon each crew member received a gift pack of gum.

the water. The crew quickly prepared for action; the navigator, Flying Officer Dave Waterbury, plotted the position, while McCrae saw to the settings on the bomb control panel. Then he picked up the hand-held K20 camera, hoping to record the attack on film.

Chapman approached, aiming a few degrees off the target's port bow. He dropped four depth charges from fifty feet. They landed in a perfect straddle. Chapman held his course while he continued to press down on the button operating the rear-facing camera. At the same time, Dave Waterbury had gone aft to one of the observation blisters to use the second K20 camera. Chapman climbed to a thousand feet and circled. He saw the U-boat emerge from the water and start a slow circle to starboard. Soon it came to a stop, beginning to go down by the bows. Chapman made another run over the boat to get more pictures. At this point, a member of the crew left his intercom button in the "on" position, effectively putting the system out of action.

Elated, the crew sat back for another run over the sinking U-boat. Only it wasn't sinking. The conning tower had reappeared. Chapman glimpsed the puffs of anti-aircraft fire. The U-boat was fighting back! And effectively! The Canso shuddered. Black smoke streamed from the port engine. The propeller couldn't be feathered; it kept windmilling, adding enormously to the drag.

Chapman headed back to the Shetlands. But the Canso couldn't maintain height even with the remaining engine at full power. There was nothing for it, a landing had to be attempted. The flight engineer, Leatherdale, lowered the wing floats. A moment later, the Canso bounced off the top of a wave. A mile further on, it touched again. Power off, haul back on the controls. A safe landing.

But it was not without its problems. Water sloshed into the hull through a hole punched by flak. The plane was sinking. The crew launched two five-man dinghies from the blisters. Well equipped, the dinghies carried two cases of survival gear, an emergency radio, two cameras, and a Very pistol. With the calm sea, the prospects looked bright.

Then the port dinghy burst; moments later, the starboard dinghy began to deflate. It had been holed earlier, but no one had noticed. In spite of the crew's efforts, the craft wouldn't retain enough air to support more than two men. All the emergency gear went over the side.

A Sunderland appeared, signalling that help was on the way. Then a Warwick came along. It dropped a lifeboat, which landed about 150 yards away. The crew tried to manoeuvre the dinghy in its direction, but with every man hanging on, it proved impossible. Dave Waterbury, the navigator, then stripped to his shorts, donned his Mae West, and set off to swim to the lifeboat. He reached it but found it damaged, its deck awash. Then began the laborious and exhausting business of paddling the sinking lifeboat to the dinghy. He succeeded but was utterly drained by the time the lifeboat and dinghy came together.

Transferring to the lifeboat was beyond the strength of several of the crew. Leatherdale, the RAF engineer, had already slipped away, unable to cling to the dinghy any longer. Two of the three wireless operator/air gunners were in desperate condition; twenty-year-old Gerald Staples, from Fredericton, New Brunswick, and Frank Reed, twenty-one, from Blytheswood, Ontario, died soon after a second Warwick appeared, directing a rescue launch. The survivors' ordeal was over. They had been in the water more than eight hours.*

The same squadron, 162, won a Victoria Cross only a few days later. Again the Allied aircraft in question, another Canso, took severe punishment from the heavy armament of a U-boat. The aircraft had taken off from Wick, Scotland, at 0930. After nearly ten hours in the air, the skipper, David Hornell, turned for home and spotted a U-boat northwest of the Shetlands. Hornell headed for the sub, U1225, and encountered fierce flak. Shots hit the starboard wing, which caught fire; the starboard engine streamed oil. The

---

* Chapman earned a DSO, McRae, Waterbury, and Bergevin (the third WOP/AG) received the DFC, Sergeant R. F. Cromarty, the second flight engineer, won the DFM.

Canso became almost impossible to control. Hornell and his co-pilot, Bernard C. Denomy, fought with it during every moment of their approach, determined to complete the attack despite their damage.

Hornell managed to drop four 250-pound depth charges in an excellent straddle. They exploded, forcing the nose of the U-boat up out of the sea. The members of the Canso crew hardly noticed; they were too busy trying to keep their aircraft aloft. The situation was becoming critical. After bombing, the pilots had managed to get the big amphibian up to about two hundred feet. Now the speed was falling off dangerously, with the aircraft shuddering, sounding as if it was about to disintegrate. The starboard engine, still burning, broke away from its mountings and tumbled into the sea. Not an instant to lose. Hornell and Denomy struggled to get the Canso down on to the water. It bounced twice, then settled, immediately beginning to sink while still emitting great billows of smoke. The crew scrambled out and launched the two dinghies, one of which burst. Eight men had to share a four-man dinghy, four in, four out, in the sea, hanging on for dear life. Five hours later, quite by chance, a Catalina of 333 (Norwegian) Squadron spotted them. The pilot, Lieutenant C. F. Krafft, circled the dinghy for hours while sending radio messages requesting help. The weather deteriorated; the sea became rougher. After some fourteen hours in the sea, the dinghy overturned. Despite their exhaustion, the crew managed to right it. Denomy got aboard and dragged the others in after him.

At last a Warwick of 281 Squadron appeared, its skipper a Canadian, Flying Officer J. A. J. Murray. He dropped the lifeboat – but it fell downwind of the dinghy and drifted away in the brisk wind, a crushing disappointment to the chilled airmen. Soon afterward, Donald Stewart Scott, of Pakenham, Ontario, one of two flight engineers in the crew, died. The other engineer, Fernand St. Laurent, of Pointe-au-Père, Quebec, died soon after. The skipper, David Ernest Hornell, of Mimico, Ontario, could no longer see;

he was becoming weaker by the minute, slipping in and out of consciousness.

Finally, after some twenty-one hours, help arrived in the form of an RAF high-speed launch. But it was too late for David Hornell. He died while the launch sped for shore. He won the Victoria Cross for his conduct, Denomy the DSO.*

In response to the increasing pressure from the skies, the Germans started moving their U-boats through the Bay of Biscay in what came to be known as "group transits," U-boats clustered in close formation – ironically, a form of convoy for the force dedicated to the convoys' destruction. The tactical advantages were obvious: less chance of the U-boats being spotted by Allied aircraft, and less chance of being caught off-guard, because more eyes were engaged in lookout duty. In theory, the group transit idea also enabled the U-boats to provide mutual anti-aircraft fire. In practice, when spotted, the formations usually broke up and began zigzagging, eventually crash-diving. Although the group tactics reduced the number of U-boat kills in June to two, in July excellent results were achieved by the Allies, with eleven subs destroyed.

In mid June, a naval hunter-group under the command of a feisty U-boat killer, Captain F. J. Walker, RN, began operations from Plymouth with HM ships *Starling*, *Wren*, *Woodpecker*, *Kite*, and *Wild Goose*. He was eventually responsible for twenty-one kills. He trained his group to move to prearranged positions in the event of an attack.† The snag, as usual, was the shortage of suitable vessels. The efficacy of the idea was well demonstrated at the end of July when an entire group of three outward-bound U-boats was sunk by a team of air force and naval vessels, U461 being despatched by a Sunderland of 461 Squadron RAAF, U462 by a Halifax of 502

---

* Ed Matheson, the navigator, and Graham Campbell, a WOP/AG, won the DFC. The other two WOP/AGs in the crew, Sergeant I. J. Bodnoff, and Sergeant S. R. Cole, won the DFM.
† "Johnny" Walker died prematurely, suffering a stroke in 1944.

Squadron RAF, and U504 by *Wren, Woodpecker, Kite,* and *Wild Goose.* The concept clearly had exciting possibilities.

By August, the inevitable happened: the Germans began running submerged during the day, usually hugging the Spanish coast. The Spaniards, under the fascist dictator Francisco Franco, made no secret of their friendship with the Axis powers, although they did not participate actively in the war. When Coastal Command aircraft hunted U-boats close to shore at night, their radar screens became a chaotic jumble of "coast returns." Adding to the confusion in most cases was the presence of innumerable fishing boats. The "blip" made by a tunny boat was virtually identical to that made by a U-boat. Many a fishing crew was startled out of their wits when struck by the blinding brilliance of a Leigh light. Such incidents not only wasted valuable time, but sent out warnings to any U-boats in the vicinity that anti-submarine aircraft were active nearby.

Unfortunately, the Admiralty found it necessary to withdraw Walker's hunter-group team at the end of August, a questionable decision since the Atlantic convoys had not been seriously threatened for many weeks. But the British wanted not only to maintain but to increase the pressure on the U-boats in the Bay of Biscay, and asked the Americans for six squadrons of aircraft to lend weight to the offensive. Admiral King replied that the U.S. Navy had no anti-submarine aircraft to spare. He did, however, agree to send some PBYs and Venturas to Iceland, which, he said, would enable the British to withdraw comparable forces from there and transfer them to the Bay. A week later, the U.S. Chiefs of Staff confirmed that a surplus of VLR aircraft now existed in Newfoundland and that two USAAF VLR Liberator squadrons could be sent to England for two months. The USN was of course in control of all American anti-submarine operations, no matter whether flown by the USN or the USAAF. It was one of the anomalies of inter-service cooperation – or lack of it.

～

The spring of 1943 marked the climacteric of the Battle of the Atlantic. The curious thing is how few on the Allied side realized it. The year had begun with fears of renewed U-boat strength. Routing convoys around the wolfpacks had become increasingly difficult; there were simply too many of them. Losses of merchant ships had outpaced the entire shipbuilding efforts of the United Nations. Gloomy days indeed – yet by April 1943 the darkest days had already passed. The distinctive, slim-winged, chubby-bodied shape of the VLR Liberators became the symbol of the new era. Then another blow for the Germans: astonished Kriegsmarine men spotted single-engine biplanes *in the middle of the Atlantic!* Antiquated-looking contraptions, they buzzed along in the vilest weather, wings seeming to flap as they coped with the gusts and gales. They were Swordfish, now being flown from escort carriers, the latest in the parade of new developments that transformed the Atlantic battle. They had proved astonishingly efficient as a naval torpedo bomber – and in any number of other roles. Whatever needed doing, or carrying, a Swordfish could usually be relied upon to look after it. Soon Swordfish could be seen with large radar blisters between their landing-gear legs, and with rows of rocket projectiles beneath their wings. When the load became too onerous even for a Swordfish, JATO (jet-assisted takeoff) could be achieved with the aid of more rockets fastened to those flimsy-looking wings.

The escort aircraft carriers were modestly proportioned vessels, many converted tankers and merchantmen with their superstructure cut off and replaced by landing decks. The earliest were basic indeed, with no hangars, no facilities for servicing below deck. Their aircraft, principally Swordfish or Avengers, Wildcats (originally known as Martlets in British service), Sea-Hurricanes, or Fulmars, spent their time on deck, alternately lashed by storms and cooked under the sun, often buried in snow and ice. Remarkably, serviceability was maintained at an impressive level. Even more impressive were the relatively few landing and takeoff accidents. It was a tribute to the excellence of the training of the aircrews and the skill of the batsmen (or officially, Deck Landing Control Officers), the gallant souls who positioned themselves on tiny islands and wielded what looked like oversized Ping-Pong bats to assist the pilots in bringing their aircraft back on to the carrier. Landings could usually be counted on to be the most demanding part of any flight, particularly when the deck was heaving fifteen or twenty feet, sometimes more, every minute or two – a seaborne seesaw of Brobdingnagian proportions. Two pairs of practised eyes were required for a successful return to solid deck: those of the pilot and the batsman. The pilot would approach the deck nose held high to slow his aircraft down, in a gentle curve so that he had a good view of the carrier throughout his approach.

The batsman braced himself against the wind, a slight figure topped by a yellow skull cap. By raising the bats above his head, he informed the approaching pilot that he was too low. Lowering the bats meant, Aircraft too high! Get rid of some height. Quickly! Left bat down told the pilot to raise the port wing. Right bat down told him to raise the starboard wing. Other messages were a little more complicated. One arm waved in a circle told the pilot to abandon that landing attempt and go around again for another try. A slicing motion meant, Cut the engine!

Occasionally things went wrong. A vicious wind suddenly darted across the deck; a light snow shower turned into a blinding squall. Misjudgements occurred no matter how experienced the pilot. Sometimes thing went wrong for no apparent reason. A perfectly acceptable approach became a grotesque crunching of metal and a ripping of fabric. Usually the incidents were of minor consequence. A shaking-up; a dent in one's professional pride. But occasionally it became horrific. Fire engulfed aircraft; men were burned to death before the asbestos-garbed crew could get to them. Little wonder that the deck invariably had its audience of off-duty crewmen when the ship was receiving aircraft – the "goofers." An approaching pilot saw two rows of pale faces, one on either side of the ship, putting him in mind of a crowd at a golf tournament lining the fairway. The spectators knew the various aircraft and what could be expected of them. Swordfish would sometimes wind up on their bellies, their undercarriage legs splayed like those of a dancer doing the splits. The Seafire, a pretty aircraft, but flimsy, had landing gear that wasn't designed for the rough and tumble of carrier work. The result was so many collapses for every so many landings; it was like some mechanical natural law. The Sea-Hurricane, though outdated, was well enough behaved. The Wildcat, the toughest of the naval fighters, had a playful tendency to ground-loop unless handled with a firm and practised hand. Sometimes an aircraft overran the arrester wires stretched across the flight deck. Beyond the arrester wires was a barrier designed to stop aircraft that happened to miss the wires. The barrier could bring an aircraft to a halt in a few feet, its propeller whacking the wires with a discordant twang, blades folding back as if made of rubber.

Occasionally, even more serious accidents befell the unfortunate crews of the escort carrier aircraft. Bill Hutcherson was radio officer on *Crystal Park*, sailing westward shortly after D-Day. He watched a Swordfish from an escort carrier diligently searching the ocean in the vicinity of the convoy. Night fell, and the Swordfish crew couldn't find their carrier: "Flying over us several times, he tried, desperately, to discern the carrier down in the total darkness and, finally, seemed to make up his mind, as he began a slow descent, marked by flame from his exhaust. Unfortunately, he picked the wrong ship and crashed into the bridge of a large tanker. Almost immediately, a flare of fire shot into the air as the fuel tanks of the plane erupted."[3]

The escort carrier was the final piece of the jigsaw puzzle, the element that changed the odds once and for all. With aircraft patrolling above, it was almost impossible for a U-boat to slip into the ranks of a convoy and sink ships at will. And they couldn't hide; the aircraft had radar to sniff them out.

The German cipher-breakers had made great progress in pro-viding up to date information on convoy movements, but improved Allied air power virtually cancelled this advantage. For example, the Germans lost six U-boats in attacks on Convoy SC130 without sinking a single ship. One of the U-boats carried Peter Dönitz, son of the U-boat leader and watch officer on U954, to his death.* The tables had turned irrevocably in the Atlantic. The despondency of only a few weeks before gave way to optimism in the Allied camp. All the efforts and innovation, the daring and the sacrifice, had at last paid off.

Escort carriers were not without their problems. Some of the earliest were converted merchant ships, not unlike the MAC-ships, built in American yards. They were known as CVEs. Although the acronym officially stood for Convoy Vessels – Escort, the word soon got around that it meant "Combustible, Vulnerable, and Expendable." They became popularly known as Woolworth carri-ers. The British complained about the quality of the ships. With some justification, however – and, no doubt, a good measure of asperity – the Americans pointed to their own navy's experience with them, declaring themselves well satisfied. In reply, the British pointed out that the USN employed them largely in the benign conditions of the Caribbean, whereas the RN operated them in the consistently frightful North Atlantic. The speedily fabricated ships simply couldn't cope with the terrible weather, declared the British; not only were they plagued by defects, they were downright unsafe. That these fears were valid was demonstrated all too well in March 1943, when *Dasher* blew up in the Firth of Clyde as it was return-ing with engine failure and buckled plates having completed one convoy run. On the fatal day, the carrier had completed flying and had struck down all but one of her aircraft. Two Swordfish were being refuelled. Witnesses said the detonation was more a "pouff" than a bang, typical of a gasoline vapour explosion. But if the

---

*   Another Dönitz son, Klaus, lost his life on a motor torpedo boat in May 1944.

sound was insignificant, the results weren't. The explosion vented through the after bulkhead of the engine room low down, up through a large hatch just forward of the elevator mechanism, up through the ship's side to starboard via the Fleet Air Arm mess-deck, and presumably through the bottom in several places. All light and power failed at once; the emergency generators cut in, but died after twenty seconds. The explosion blew the elevator into the air, severely damaging the after end of the flight deck. A violent fire erupted in the hangar. Moments later, the engine room began to burn, and the ship flooded rapidly from the forward engine room bulkhead to her stern. She listed to starboard at about ten degrees and then settled quickly by the stern, sinking in eight minutes. Only the captain and 148 of the crew of 526 were saved.

Inevitably, the disaster resulted in much finger-pointing. The British complained that the ship had been built with a one-inch-diameter hole between the gasoline stowage and the main shaft tunnel, plus many more openings below. It seemed likely that a worker smoking in the shaft tunnel had tossed the butt down from the Fleet Air Arm mess-deck and had ignited the vapour. The fact that *Dasher* started life as a passenger ship also contributed to the tragedy; the cabin doors were not fitted with escape hatches, and many men died when the doors jammed.

After the tragedy, the RN made extensive modifications on the CVEs, which had to be carried out after delivery, since American production-line practices did not permit changes once a design had been "frozen." This added to the delay in getting the precious escort carriers to the convoys.

Escort carriers had a curious history in the tradition-bound RN. The Admiralty considered them to be naval vessels first and floating airfields second. Their Lordships had always looked upon naval aviation as a sort of ugly stepchild; its existence could not be denied, but all those buzzing aircraft and oily mechanics did seem to lower the tone of naval operations. When the escort carriers arrived, the RN had few senior officers with experience of carrier operations.

But did that really matter? A ship was a ship, wasn't it, even a carrier? All that was needed was a senior officer with sufficient experience to command her. This thinking resulted in some odd and a few thoroughly dangerous situations. Two escort carriers, *Nairana* and *Campania*, were in the mid-Atlantic protecting a slow convoy. It had been agreed that one carrier should fly routine patrols, while the other stood by. The conditions were hideous: gale-force winds, tempestuous seas with huge and immensely powerful waves, and almost no visibility. *Campania* advised her sister carrier that the weather was too dangerous for flying. No one with the slightest knowledge of flying could argue with that decision. *Campania*'s aircraft were struck down. Aboard *Nairana*, the duty Swordfish crew of Lieutenant George Sadler, 835 Squadron, anticipated receiving a similar order. But Captain R. M. T. Taylor, RN, had other ideas. Bubbling with Nelsonian enthusiasm, he declared it a fine night to catch a U-boat on the surface. Perhaps he could already imagine the history books describing how his aircraft flew when no one else's could, resulting in a brilliant victory over the predatory U-boats. Far less enthusiastic were Sadler and his crew and the met officer, Mike Arrowsmith, who informed Taylor that the weather was impossible for flying. The ship was in an occluded front, he explained. Barometric pressure was falling, the speed and direction of the wind were constantly changing, and things would undoubtedly get worse before they got any better. Making impossible conditions virtually suicidal was the fact that radio silence was in force; no homing assistance could be expected from the carrier. Taylor was not to be deterred. Details, mere details, he seemed to think – he, who would not be required to set foot in an aircraft that ghastly night. Sadler was ordered to go.

The crew clambered aboard while the ferocious wind rattled their aircraft, doing its best to shake the biplane to pieces. The flight deck stirred and groaned, battered by what felt like a full-fledged hurricane. Sadler started his engine and ran it up. He eased the throttle forward. The big biplane rolled, the tail rising almost immediately. With that wind rushing over its ample flying surfaces, the Swordfish leapt into the air after a run of only a few yards. It vanished from the anxious gaze of the deck crew, consumed in one gulp by the black maw. Straight and level flying was impossible, and the visibility so poor that bearings could not be taken. Nevertheless, the crew did their best to complete their designated patrol, their Swordfish bouncing and pitching, punished by the howling wind. After half an hour of chaotic and totally unproductive flight, came a radio message from the carrier: Return at once! It was far easier said than done. By now, Sadler and his crew were a long way astern of the convoy; they had to fly into the teeth of a 50-mph gale to rejoin it – no simple matter in a Swordfish with a cruising speed of about 85 mph. Despite the foul conditions, Stan Thomas succeeded in navigating the aircraft back to the carrier, using ASV radar for the last lap. But the big ship remained obstinately invisible in the swirling murk. Sadler descended until his altimeter indicated two hundred feet. Still he could see nothing. Eyes aching from the strain of trying to pierce the darkness, he pushed on. Nothing to be seen, nothing . . . until, like a dim photographic image suddenly coming into focus, the carrier materialized. The island sped by *above* the Swordfish. Sadler hastily reset his altimeter as he swung his aircraft to one side to avoid the carrier. Now the indicated barometric pressure should be at least reasonably close to the truth. It was something. But not much. Sadler attempted a dummy approach. Another cautious turn in the black bag that enveloped them, with not even a glimpse of the carrier to make sense of it all. Keeping the Swordfish the right way up became a major effort. The carrier's deck lights appeared. And disappeared. The angry sea tossed the vessel about like a cork in a whirlpool. The landing deck reared thirty feet or more. Sadler glimpsed the batsman, half crouched like a runner about to start a race. The rain blurred his vision. Raindrops struck his goggles like lead shot. The deck loomed . . . then, a waveoff. Full power! Sadler eased the Swordfish into a turn. He glimpsed crewmen on the deck gazing at him, open-mouthed. They vanished to the rear. It was the first of eleven landing attempts. All failed. Sadler received further instructions: Circle the carrier until dawn, then land.

Morning brought a sickly grey light. Conditions were still awful, but at least Sadler could see the flight deck. It was just as well; he had little fuel left. He decided to touch down about halfway along the deck, where there was relatively little movement. With the faithful batsman guiding him, he approached once more. The deck pivoted before him, the gigantic seesaw in action again. Closer, closer . . . then, the wonderful cross-arms signal: Cut engine! With a thump and a rattle, the stalwart Swordfish touched down and, caught by the third arrester wire, came to a safe stop. The ordeal was over. Half-giddy with relief and stiff with cold, the crew clambered out, assisted by the entire flight-deck handling party.

Sadler was involved in another incident a few days later. Two Sea-Hurricanes from *Nairana* were patrolling ahead of the convoy. They spotted a brace of U-boats. The Hurricanes lacked the firepower to sink them, so they called the carrier and asked for reinforcements. George Sadler and Johnny Hunt were flown off. George asked to be armed with Oscar, the new acoustic torpedo which could be dropped at some distance from the target; it homed on the sound vibrations of the U-boat's propellers. But for his own reasons, Captain Taylor insisted that the attack be made with rocket projectiles and depth charges. He appeared not to realize that the U-boats would be able to pick up the approaching planes on their Metox radar. Which they did – and then lost no time in diving out of danger. The attack was foiled before it began. The aircraft dropped depth charges, more in hope than expectation. Neither U-boat was damaged.

Soon after that, Captain Taylor left *Nairana*, a classic square peg, an individual thrust into a highly responsible job for which he had no inclination and remarkably little training. His replacement was Captain Villers Nicholas Surtees, DSO, RN. Lieutenant-Commander

Barry Barringer, commanding officer of 835 Naval Air Squadron, wrote eloquently of the man:

> Surtees had many of the qualities that are needed to rise to high command in the Navy. He was a man of decision, although his decisions were not always right. He was a man of considerable courage and powers of endurance – during our convoys to Russia he hardly left the bridge. And he was a man determined to do his duty as a naval officer no matter what the cost; the Navy was the be-all and end-all of his life; he had few other interests and no other love. In the days of Nelson he would undoubtedly have made a first-rate commander of a ship of the line, ever anxious to follow his Admiral's instructions to "lay alongside and engage the enemy more closely." However, we were not in the days of Nelson, and as captain of an aircraft carrier in the Second World War, Surtees had two serious weaknesses. First, he found it difficult to communicate, especially with those from a different background. This may have been because he was a reserved man, a bit of a loner and a bit of a misogynist. He wasn't good with people. His second weakness was that he knew little about flying. So why, you may very reasonably ask, was he given command of an aircraft carrier? You might have thought that anyone would have been able to grasp the fact that an aircraft carrier – which operates aircraft – ought to be commanded by a person with at least *some* knowledge of flying. Yet the Admiralty now saw fit to hand over one of its best escort carriers to an ex-cruiser officer who had been brought out of retirement by the war and had never in his life served in an aircraft carrier let alone flown an aeroplane.[4]

Surtee's appointment was unlikely to generate much enthusiasm among the aircrews. The captain knew so little about aeroplanes that he frequently ordered the crews to do the impossible – without apparently realizing the dangers involved. On one occasion the captain ordered an anti-submarine patrol to be flown in weather so vile that no U-boat commander in his right mind would have come anywhere near the surface. Winds howled at sixty knots with gusts to one hundred knots, plus heavy snow squalls and icing. In spite of these thoroughly dangerous conditions, a Swordfish succeeded in taking off, an accomplishment in itself. The difficulty was, in that monstrous blow, the Swordfish could make little headway; in fact, it was barely keeping pace with the convoy.

Then, making a dangerous situation lethal, the engine stopped. The crew sent a Mayday call. They jettisoned their depth charges and flares. Unfortunately, the latter could only be jettisoned live. As they descended, they lit up. The wind quickly carried them over the convoy, an unfortunate development, but hardly critical in the circumstances. At an altitude of some three hundred feet, the Swordfish's engine spluttered back to life, and the pilot, Bob Selley, managed to get the aircraft down safely on *Nairana*'s deck. Instead of congratulating the airmen for their skill and courage, Surtees berated them for endangering the convoy with his flares. He simply didn't comprehend what appalling difficulties the aircrew had faced.

Having such men commanding aircraft carriers was criminal. How could intelligent decisions be made? How could the best interests of the ship's company be served? In a similar vein, D. M. "Pappy" McLeod was serving on the British carrier *Victorious* with a fighter squadron: "The Captain asked Commander (Air) if there was any reason why the Corsairs dropped below the flight deck and disappeared over the bow on take-off. Commander (Air) said, 'No reason, sir,' and the Captain said, 'Well, tell them to stop it!'... Our CO, Freddie Charlton, replied, 'You stupid old fart, give us an extra ten feet of deck and we won't sink on take-off.'"[5]

∾

In May 1943, no less than thirty-eight U-boats were sunk in action and another five lost in accidents. Dönitz sent a revealing message to his commanders: "The struggle for our victory, becoming ever more hard and bitter, leads me to reveal to you in all clarity the seriousness of our situation at the moment and of our future. . . . The German nation has long felt that our arm is the sharpest and most decisive and that the outcome of the war depends on the success or failure of the Battle of the Atlantic."[6]

In late May, Dönitz withdrew his U-boats from the North Atlantic to the relative safety of the "Black Pit," south of the Azores. It was a terrible time for him. Although he tried hard to mask his distress, he had been deeply shaken by the loss of his son. Now it seemed that his U-boat force was being destroyed about him – and he could do nothing to save it. The Allies had, with stunning speed, turned defeat into victory. The aircraft, the radar technology, the vast array of weapons, the ever-stronger escort groups, they all added up to impossible odds for the U-boats. With the priceless assistance of Ultra, for instance, the Allies were able to locate and destroy Dönitz's ten "milk cows." In June and July, Dönitz lost fifty-four boats – significantly, forty-four of them to aircraft. Six went down on one notable day, July 30. Dönitz promptly ordered even heavier anti-aircraft weapons for his subs; some now carried as many as eight rapid-firing guns.

But Dönitz's only real hope lay in the new generation of U-boats emerging from the factories. They had many of the qualities he considered essential to victory. Before any of the new boats came into being, however, the veteran Type VII was given a fresh lease on life with a simple but highly effective device. Ironically, the basic idea had been around, waiting to be developed, since the mid-1920s. Its Dutch inventor, J. J. Wichers, called it a *snuiver*, or "sniffer." He placed two pipes in the submarine: one sucked in air; the other expelled exhaust from the diesel engines. The device added immeasurably to the U-boat's capabilities. For the first time in its history, it was possible to run on diesels underwater at periscope depth. Moreover, batteries could be charged below the surface. These were highly significant advances, and the wonder is that the *snuiver* had excited little or no interest in either the RN or the German navy in the years leading up to the Second World War. In May 1940, the Germans had occupied the principal Royal Netherlands Navy base at Den Helder and found two submarines fitted with the *snuiver*, soon to be renamed the *Schnorchel*; two others had gone to England. Still, no one seemed to care.

The *Schnorchel* had some disadvantages, the Germans discovered. It was noisy – a serious shortcoming for U-boats, which relied on hydrophones to warn them of the presence of enemy ships. For this reason, if diesels were run underwater, they had to be turned off at least three times each hour.

The device could also be used to bring fresh air into a U-boat beneath the surface. But this was a tricky procedure, requiring a high degree of skill and experience. It involved closing the main valve with the diesels running, then reducing the air pressure in the U-boat and sucking in fresh air. But clumsy handling could lead to disaster; at least two U-boats are believed to have been lost in such attempts. Werner Hirschmann, engineering officer of U190, recalls an incident late in the war involving the *Schnorchel*. Almost the entire crew lost consciousness because of an excess of carbon monoxide in the boat. "While snorkelling earlier on, I had been unable to maintain the exact depth keeping the snorkel head just above the surface. We did have a kit with chemical in a vial, but the chart indicating the meaning of the colour changes had been left behind in Lorient!"[7] At great risk, the boat had to surface in broad daylight to air out the interior and save the crew from death.

As soon as the *Schnorchel* became known to Allied sailors, they saw it in every wave, every splash. Heaven knows how much ammunition was wasted on false sightings of *Schnorchel*-equipped U-boats.

Within a few months, the Germans made other technological innovations. Newly developed, low-emission *Wanze* (bug) detectors began to be fitted to Dönitz's boats. Then came *Naxos*, the first detector to pick up Allied centimetric radar emissions; soon the *Fliege* (fly) detector arrived, still later, the *Mücke* (gnat).

During the month of August 1943, the first German acoustic torpedoes appeared. Designed principally for use against warships, the acoustic torpedo became part of the arsenal of Dönitz's U-boats – they had a choice: acoustic for use against escorts and other warships, plus the G7e and the FAT torpedoes for merchant ships. Just as Allied aircraft used Window (called Chaff by the Americans) to confuse enemy radar operators with false echoes, the Germans in the Battle of the Atlantic introduced *Aphrodite*, a gas-filled balloon festooned with metal foil. The basic idea was similar to that of Window: to create false echoes and bewilder the enemy. This rather basic device was soon replaced by *Thetis*. The Germans even tried to confound radar by applying a rubberized coating to U-boats; it was not notably successful.

The Allies continued to introduce new anti-submarine warfare devices. In addition to Fido, the acoustic torpedo, and Squid, a mortar that fired three full-sized depth charges simultaneously (the Hedgehog fired only small D/Cs), they developed Foxer, a noise-maker designed to distract the German acoustic torpedo.

Of all these developments, the *Schnorchel* was undoubtedly the most significant. It went a long way to restoring the invisibility of the submarine. It didn't turn the tables, but its use resulted in the Allies having to employ huge fleets of ASW vessels right up to the end of the war.

Had the conflict lasted much longer, the Allies would have had to contend with the revolutionary "electro-boats," which could travel at over seventeen knots beneath the surface. These U-boats, known as Types XXI and XXIII, incorporated vastly increased battery capacity. By the end of 1944, the Germans had produced ninety Type XXI boats and thirty-one of the smaller Type XXIII. Production of these advanced boats was well organized, utilizing many plants fabricating components that were later brought together for final assembly. Kaiser in America had pioneered such techniques with the construction of Liberty ships. The Germans were never able to utilize it fully. The reason: Allied bombing made transportation difficult, at times almost impossible. Nevertheless, some impressive production figures were recorded. Dönitz noted that submarines of the size of the Type XXI U-boats could be completed in from "260,000 to 300,000 man-hours, whereas under the old method a boat of similar size required 460,000 man-hours."[8] But he faced another problem: How could the crews for these complex and speedy U-boats be trained? The Baltic, that traditional training ground for Dönitz's crews, was virtually closed by intensive mining and constant patrols by Allied aircraft. Dönitz also points out in his memoirs that "the shipbuilding program had been drawn up at a time when enemy air attacks on German industry were still comparatively few. Its implementation, however, had to be achieved under the hail of bombs which, from the autumn of 1943, came pouring down upon the German armament industry in ever-increasing volume. Destruction of factories and dislocation of communications caused an endless series of transfers of work from one industrial centre to another."[9] So much for the "experts" who claim that strategic bombing had little effect on German industrial output.

~

The massive battleship *Tirpitz* still furrowed brows at the Admiralty. With her fully laden weight of 52,600 tons, she was even larger than *Bismarck*. And her great speed and tremendous firepower represented a grave threat to the vital Atlantic lifelines. *Tirpitz* carried eight 15-inch guns, twelve 5.9-inch guns, and an array of lighter guns of 37-millimetre and 20-millimetre calibre. But it was her steel cladding that placed her in a class by herself; her armour plate was twelve inches thick on the sides and at least eight inches thick on deck, far heavier and stronger than the armour carried by any

British battleship, even those of the new *King George V* class. How seriously the Admiralty regarded her may be gauged by an order to the effect that only a Home Fleet which included at least two *King George V*-class ships plus an aircraft carrier could be considered adequate to face her.

Launched in April 1939, *Tirpitz* had been completed in February 1941 and began sea trials in March. While the trials were proceeding, the British sank *Bismarck*, ending the German dream of having the two super-ships roaming the Atlantic, wreaking havoc. Thereafter, Hitler became paranoid about the possibility of losing *Tirpitz*. Still convinced that the Allies would attempt an invasion in Norway, he ordered *Tirpitz* to Trondheim, escorted by a screen of destroyers, a floating fortress to protect his northern empire. Churchill became almost as fixated on *Tirpitz* as was Hitler, declaring the ship to be the most important target in the world. On the night of January 28, 1942, a force of Halifaxes and Stirlings had bombed her, without scoring a single hit. Soon after, *Tirpitz* left Trondheim with her destroyer escort. The British submarine *Seawolf* spotted her. The news flashed to Admiral Tovey, commander-in-chief Home Fleet, who was at sea with a potent force including the battleships *King George V* and *Duke of York*, the battle cruiser *Renown* and the aircraft carrier *Victorious*, plus a heavy cruiser and a dozen destroyers. Bad weather closed in. Not until the morning of March 9 did conditions improve sufficiently to mount an air strike. Twelve Albacore torpedo-bombers – a not very successful development of the Swordfish – took off from *Victorious*. They found their target, but failed to hit it. *Tirpitz* put into Narvik, returning to Trondheim a few days later.

The British, convinced that *Tirpitz* would soon be roaming the Atlantic, destroying convoys at will, seized upon a daring idea. Reasoning that the great ship would require unusually large docking facilities, they believed that the Germans intended to make use of the huge dock built at St. Nazaire in the 1930s for the *Normandie*. The British mounted a commando raid to wreck the dock. They calculated that with the St. Nazaire dock out of action, should *Tirpitz* ever require repairs, she would have to put in to a German port – and the RN would undoubtedly get her before she arrived.

The raid on St. Nazaire succeeded. But *Tirpitz* never needed the big dock; she was snugly harboured in Trondheim, Norway. The Admiralty agonized over her. She had to be watched constantly, tying up large sea and air forces. More RAF bombing raids took place – with not a single bomb hitting the battleship. One reason was the installation of new and highly efficient smoke-making equipment by the Germans.

Tirpitz was a menace, a dark shadow on Allied war plans. Her impact on the RN may be gauged by the dismal story of Convoy PQI7, bound for Soviet Russia. It left Iceland on June 27, 1942, with a strong escort of destroyers and other vessels. On the evening of July 4, Ultra intelligence revealed that *Tirpitz* was heading out to sea, in company with the cruisers *Admiral Scheer* and *Hipper* and the pocket battleship *Lützow*. The news sent shock waves through the Admiralty. The ailing First Sea Lord, Admiral Sir Dudley Pound, immediately ordered the convoy's escort vessels to withdraw to the west, the merchantmen to scatter and proceed individually. It was an extraordinary order, a virtual sentence of death for the convoy. Why didn't Pound simply order the ships to turn about?

Convoy PQI7 suffered catastrophic losses; only eleven of the original thirty-seven merchantmen arrived in the Soviet Union; nearly four thousand trucks and other vehicles were lost, plus 430 tanks and 2,500 aircraft. More than 150 seamen lost their lives. The disaster forced Churchill to suspend the convoys, at least temporarily, much to Stalin's displeasure. PQI8 did not sail for nine weeks.

In October, the British attempted again to sink *Tirpitz*. Conventional methods had failed; now was the turn for the unconventional. A Norwegian Resistance leader, Leif Larson, sailed a fishing boat from the Shetlands carrying six British frogmen and their unusual vessels: steerable torpedoes called Chariots. Bad weather sank the lot. Once again, *Tirpitz* had prevailed.

Now the RN attempted to deal with the German battleship with the aid of midget submarines, known as X-craft. The four-man crews fastened limpet mines to the ship's hull using powerful magnets. Their Amatol charges lifted *Tirpitz* some six feet out of the water, wrecking lighting, jamming doors, twisting her steel frame, and damaging her engines. Two of the naval officers involved, Lieutenants Cameron and Place, were awarded the Victoria Cross.

Tirpitz now needed a full refit in a German dockyard. But the Germans shied away from the appalling risks of the journey to the Fatherland. Instead, they repaired the battered vessel as best they could in Norway, then stationed her in Altenfjord. She remained there until the spring of 1944, undergoing repairs. "But," complained Dönitz in his memoirs, "the greatly increased air superiority which the enemy had in the meanwhile acquired precluded any possibility of her being employed during the long daylight of the northern summer against enemy convoys. At this time of the year, the enemy could always obtain timely and accurate information of any move made by *Tirpitz* through air reconnaissance; and apart from that, he was now in a position to afford continuous protection to his convoys at all times by means of aircraft carriers . . . The value of having the *Tirpitz* in northern Norway lay, as before, in the fact that by her presence there she tied down the enemy heavy ships to the north European zone and prevented their being sent to some other theatre of war."[10]

Could she be destroyed from the air? Although air attacks had failed in the past, the technology of bombing had advanced significantly. Altenfjord lay beyond the range of the RAF's bombers; but could she be attacked by aircraft from a carrier?

In the spring of 1944, the fleet carriers *Victorious* and *Furious* joined forces with the escort carriers *Emperor*, *Searcher*, *Pursuer*, and *Fencer* at Scapa Flow. They formed two groups, each comprising twenty-one Barracuda bombers and forty fighters, Corsairs,

Hellcats, and Wildcats. On April 3, they struck, the fighters strafing the shore-based gunners and the flak and radar control centres. Fourteen bombs hit *Tirpitz*. On their way out of the target area, the Fleet Air Arm airmen saw numerous fires on the big ship. More than a hundred sailors had been killed. It had been a successful strike – except that it did little really serious damage. The fires were soon put out. The 1,600-pound bombs had been dropped too low by the Barracudas. They didn't penetrate the ship's heavy armour.

The naval aviators tried again on April 28. This time the weather failed them. It did again on May 15 and on May 28. More attacks in July and August were frustrated by weather and by the smoke-making facilities around the fjord. To the airmen's chagrin, they discovered that a 1,600-pound bomb had in fact hit the ship just forward of the bridge. It penetrated eight decks – then failed to explode.

It was clear that larger bombs were needed to eliminate *Tirpitz*. Enter the Dam Busters, the RAF's famous 617 Squadron, which had earned undying glory with its spectacular attack on the Möhne and Eder dams in May 1943. At that time the squadron had as its CO the personable – and seemingly indestructible – Guy Gibson. Leonard Cheshire had taken over after Gibson; now he had in turn been replaced by a quiet and introspective Welshman, Willie Tait, who had won two DSOs and a DFC in previous tours. His boss, Air Vice-Marshal the Honourable Ralph Cochrane, had sought and obtained "Bomber" Harris's agreement to a plan to sink *Tirpitz* using the recently developed six-ton "Tallboy" bombs. Although Altenfjord was just outside the range of Lancasters flying directly from the United Kingdom, it would be possible with a refuelling stop in Russia, specifically Yagodnik, near Archangel.

On September 11, twenty Lancasters from 617 Squadron and eighteen more from 9 Squadron commanded by Wing Commander James Michael Bazin, plus a film unit aircraft, took off and headed for the Soviet Union. Twelve of the Lancasters carried "Johnnie

Walker" or "JW" mines, designed to attack ships on their under-sides where the steel was thin; in the case of *Tirpitz*, only three-quarters of an inch. When the mine reached a depth of sixty feet during its descent,

a hydrostatic valve released a flow of hydrogen from a high pressure container in the rear of the weapon and passed it, via a pressure-reducing valve, to eject the water out of the buoy-ancy chamber in the nose. The weapon became lighter than the surrounding water, its descent ceased and it started to rise, nose-first. The fins on the side of the weapon were so arranged that when the JW ascended or descended through water, it traveled at an angle of about thirty degrees to the ver-tical, thus giving a horizontal displacement of about thirty feet during each such move. When the nose of the weapon was uppermost, the nose fuse was made live so that if the weapon struck anything hard during its ascent (e.g., the bottom of a ship) the warhead would detonate. The "JW" warhead con-tained 100 pounds of Torpex/aluminum formed into a shaped charge, with a concave area at the front lined with soft metal. The explosive was detonated from the rear, so that the force of the explosion was focused on the metal liner. The latter would dissolve into a slug of molten metal that was hurled forward from the warhead at a very high velocity. This slug had enormous penetrative power and, once inside the bowels of the ship, it could cause severe local damage. That effect would be compounded by the ingress of water . . . the inclu-sion of powdered aluminum in the explosive charge meant that when it detonated, large amounts of gas were generated. The huge bubble thus formed was capable of lifting the ship suddenly at the point of detonation. Then, an instant later, the bubble collapsed, causing that part of the ship to drop several feet . . . and could break its back.[11]

The Tallboy had been introduced into service a few months before. A twenty-one-foot-long monster of a bomb, it had been designed by Barnes Wallis, the inventor responsible for the drum-like bomb that wrecked the Ruhr dams. The attack on *Tirpitz* was code-named "Paravane."

The RAF crews spent several days amid the dubious attractions of Yagodnik, the officers on a houseboat, the NCOs in underground billets. It rained for seventy-two hours without pause. Everything got wet – food, bedding, floors; the airfield became a quagmire. Frustration soured every moment at Yagodnik. Would the damned rain never stop? Was everyone condemned to spend the rest of their lives here in this hellish place?

The weather cleared. Early on September 15, the Lancasters took off. They flew low in an attempt to slip under the Germans' radar, then poured on power to climb to their bombing height. As they approached the fjord, the crews saw the smoke screen beginning to take form across the target. Tait's bomb aimer, Flight Lieutenant W. A. Daniels, probably got the clearest view of the battleship, but a smoke screen was already obscuring most of her when he released his Tallboy.

Disappointed, the crews headed back to Yagodnik. One of the squadron's bomb aimers said he thought he saw a hit on *Tirpitz*. The comment sounded more like wishful thinking than a definitive report. The Lancasters flew home; one, Flying Officer Levy's, didn't arrive. It seems likely that the Rhodesian and his crew had the bad luck to fly into a hill, but no confirmation has ever been forthcoming. Levy and his crew were the only Allied casualties.

On the 20th, a PRU (photo-reconnaissance unit) Mosquito brought back a photograph. It cheered everyone up, for it showed that a Tallboy had indeed hit *Tirpitz*, leaving a gigantic hole in her foredeck. But she was still afloat.

The Germans patched her up and sailed to an anchorage off Haak Island, near Tromso, a remote spot on Norway's northern coast. Now she was about a hundred miles closer to Britain.

Cochrane decided on another raid – but this one would fly from Lossiemouth in northern Scotland, direct to the target, and back again. No time-wasting – and politically sensitive – stops in the Soviet Union this time. Extra fuel tanks were squeezed into the Lancasters, and the Merlin 28 engines were replaced by the more powerful Merlin 24s. In the cause of lower weight, much of the armour plate came out, as did the nose and dorsal turrets. For three days and nights, the ground crews sweated over the modifications and the changing of engines.

On October 29, Tait led thirty-seven Lancasters to Tromso, only to find fog drifting into the fjord. The target quickly disappeared from view. The Lancasters bombed on estimated positions, dropping thirty-two Tallboys. Not one found its mark.

On November 12, airmen readied themselves for yet another operation against *Tirpitz*. In the chilly predawn darkness at Lossiemouth, northern Scotland, thirty Lancasters of 9 and 617 squadrons, plus a 463 Squadron aircraft carrying a film crew, started engines. The din rumbled across the field, washing over the ground crews standing huddled against the chill to watch "their" aircraft set off. One by one, the heavily laden bombers dragged themselves off the ground after longer than usual runs, engines bellowing at full power. They headed out over the North Sea, invisible in the blackness below. Their landfall: Tromso. The first hints of daylight began to paint the city's faint outline as the bombers crossed the coast, beginning their climb. Crew members scowled as they tried to penetrate the gloom, searching for the fighters said to have been posted to the area to deal with any attacks that the British might be tempted to mount on *Tirpitz*. The sun rose. Bathed in icy sunshine, the Lancasters climbed to fourteen thousand feet. The mountain peaks slipped below. Then, suddenly, as if the world had ceased to be, the hills dropped away. And there, "like a spider in her web of torpedo nets"[12] lay *Tirpitz*. Although the Germans failed to activate their smoke screen, a veritable storm of flak rose to greet the bombers. Black puffs dotted the sky, wisps of smoke sped past the aircraft, fading, disintegrating as they went. The bomb aimers counted the seconds. A lifetime to wait, a lifetime of quivering needles in tiny dials, followed by the instant of release and a bound of joy from the aircraft as the great bombs fell away, objects of graceful line, like enormous fish with slightly offset fins that sent them spinning faster and faster as they fell, preparing them for the task of smashing their way through inches of solid steel plate.

The banging of the guns echoed within the craggy walls of the fjord. The bombs screamed as they picked up speed.

A Tallboy hit *Tirpitz* on her foredeck. She staggered. Another bomb hit her abaft her funnel. She vanished from sight, obscured by smoke and debris. A magazine blew up; a stalagmite of flame and spinning debris rose with a kind of stately deliberation before collapsing. A third Tallboy hit the ship but failed to explode.

Mortally wounded, *Tirpitz* had a hole some two hundred feet wide blasted in her side. She listed, a little at first, then more severely.

After bombing, the 9 and 617 Squadron Lancasters flew away, diving to pick up speed. One Lancaster remained over the ship, the crew filming the death of *Tirpitz*. The great ship turned over, as if too weary to remain upright any longer. Inside, more than a thousand seamen were trapped, never to be rescued.

Tirpitz was no more. The job had taken three minutes.

~

Late in the war, Dönitz tested his new *Elektro-U-Boote* – "electroboats" – in action. In February 1945, U2322, under the command of Fridtjof Heckel, sank a small British merchant ship, *Engholm*, off Eastern Scotland. When warships gave chase, U2322 evaded them with ease, making use of its phenomenal underwater speed. In March 1945, Dönitz pulled together a number of Type VII boats equipped with *Schnorchel*s. They constituted the last wolfpack. Sent to attack the American east coast, two were sunk, the rest surrendered. A Type IX U-boat, U190, arrived off Halifax, Nova Scotia, on March 30, 1945, then waited two weeks, until April 16, when she launched an acoustic torpedo at the minesweeper HMCS *Esquimalt* on patrol near Halifax harbour. The ship went down at once, the last Canadian warship lost in the Second World War. Only thirty-nine of her crew of sixty-five survived.

Late in April 1945, a Type XXI U-boat, U2511, put to sea. In command was a veteran U-boat skipper, Adalbert Schnee, whom Dönitz considered "exceptionally brilliant." U2511 was the last word in underwater weaponry. Almost twice the size of a Type VIIC, it boasted spacious living quarters for the crew plus a deep-freeze for the storage of food. No more rotting vegetables and decaying sausage for the new generation of U-boat men. U2511's six bow torpedo tubes could be reloaded at the press of a button, the process taking little more than ten minutes, compared with as long as twenty minutes per tube in the older boats.

U2511's voyage was to be of short duration. Schnee wrote, "First contact with the enemy was in the North Sea with a hunter-killer group. It was obvious that with its high under-water speed, the boat could not come to harm at the hands of these killer-groups. With a minor course alteration of 30 degrees, proceeding submerged, I evaded the group with the greatest ease. On receipt of order to cease fire on May 4, I turned back for Bergen; a few hours later I made contact with a British cruiser and several destroyers. I delivered a dummy under-water attack and in complete safety came within 500 yards of the cruiser. As I found out later during a conversation when I was being interrogated, by the British in Bergen, my action had passed completely unnoticed. From my own experience, the boat was first-class in attack and in defence; it was something completely new to any submariner."[13]

At last Dönitz had the submarine he wanted, the weapon that was truly an underwater craft. But it was too late. The war was lost; German armies were in full retreat, the machinery of state disintegrating around them. On April 30, Hitler killed himself. He had

already named his successor: Karl Dönitz.* The next day, Dönitz
sent a message to the German armed forces announcing the capit-
ulation: "I expect discipline and obedience. Chaos and ruin can be
prevented only by the swift and unreserved execution of my
orders. Anyone at this juncture who fails in his duty and condemns
German women and children to slavery and death is a traitor and
a coward. The oath of allegiance which you took to the Führer
now binds each and every one of you to me, whom he himself
appointed as his successor."[14]

The war in Europe ended a few days later. Dönitz was arrested
by the victorious Allies. The former U-boat chief informed his
captors that he had nothing to apologize for. At the Nuremberg
trials, the prosecution claimed that Dönitz should be punished by
death for his "*Laconia*" order forbidding U-boats from rescuing survivors of sunken ships. When the American Fleet Admiral Chester
W. Nimitz admitted that the USN had pursued a similar policy in the
Pacific, the sentence was commuted. Dönitz served ten years in
Spandau. He died in 1980, apparently still unconvinced that the
British had succeeded in breaking the Enigma code in 1941.

As for the U-boats themselves, on May 7, 1945, Dönitz ordered
them to surface and surrender. The Battle of the Atlantic had
ended, one of the longest in history. The battlefield had no corpses,
no groaning wounded, no abandoned weapons. Everything had
been swallowed by the ocean. Much of it lies there still, a memo-
rial to thousands of brave sailors and airmen. Soon the last evidence
of the battle will vanish. But it will not be forgotten. It was without
question one of the crucial battles of the Second World War, for on
it depended all the other battles. In the end the Allies won, but it
cost some 2,500 merchant ships, totalling 14 million tons, 30,000
merchant seamen and 70,000 naval personnel killed, wounded,

---

*   In his memoirs, Dönitz claimed to have been taken "completely by surprise" by
this action, adding that the Führer had never given him the slightest indication that
he considered Dönitz a possible successor.

and captured, 5,000 airmen, and about 2,500 aircraft. Of the 1,162 U-boats built by the Third Reich, the Allies sank about seven hundred; 200 were scuttled; 156 surrendered at the end of the war. Had the war lasted longer, the extraordinary *Elektro-U-Boote* would have entered the fray in significant numbers and would undoubtedly have cost the Allies dearly.

About forty thousand German sailors went to war in U-boats; three out of four of them died in action. More than half a century has elapsed since the last U-boat disappeared into the depths. The bitterness of wartime has cooled; most of the survivors of the battle now see their former enemies as fellow participants in a mad game, a game in which the only reward was survival. Below the sea or on the turbulent surface, everyone shared similar dangers and discomforts. Everyone felt the cold grip of terror squeezing their guts. Everyone grappled with panic.

Dönitz's men fought hard and well, suffering horrendous casualties as the war entered its last few years. Dönitz had every reason to be proud of them – just as the Allies had every reason to be proud of their sailors and airmen.

APPENDIX

THE COST: LOSSES IN THE NORTH ATLANTIC, 1939-1945

1939

ALLIED MERCHANT SHIPS SUNK

	Tonnage	No. of Ships
September	104,829	19
October	110,619	18
November	17,895	6
December	15,852	4
Total	249,195	47

U-BOATS SUNK

U39	September 14 (0)*
U42	October 13 (0)
U40	October 13 (0)
U45	October 14 (2)

---

*Number of ships sunk during U-boat's last patrol

U35   November 29 (0)
U36   December 4 (0)

Total sunk: 6

1940

ALLIED MERCHANT SHIPS SUNK

	Tonnage	No. of Ships
January	35,970	35
February	74,759	17
March	11,215	2
April	24,570	4
May	48,087	9
June	296,529	53
July	141,474	28
August	190,048	39
September	254,553	52
October	286,644	56
November	201,341	38
December	239,304	42
Total	1,804,494	375

U–BOATS SUNK

U55   January 30 (2)
U41   February 5 (1)
U33   February 12 (0)
U54   February 13 (0)
U53   February 24 (5)
U31   March 11 (0)
U44   March 13 (0)
U50   April 10 (0)
U64   April 13 (0)

U49   April 15 (o)
U102   June 30 (1)
U26   July 1 (1)
U122   July 7 (1)
U25   August 3 (o)
U51   August 20 (1)
U32   October 30 (1)
U31   November 2 (.5)
U104   November 21 (1)

Total sunk: 18

1941

ALLIED MERCHANT SHIPS SUNK

	Tonnage	No. of Ships
January	214,382	42
February	317,378	69
March	364,689	63
April	260,451	45
May	324,550	58
June	318,740	68
July	97,813	23
August	83,661	25
September	184,546	51
October	154,593	32
November	50,215	10
December	50,682	10
Total	2,421,700	496

U–BOATS SUNK

U70   March 7 (1)
U99   March 17 (6.5)

U100   March 17 (0)

U47   March 18 (4.5)

U551   March 23 (0)

U76   April 5 (2)

U65   April 28 (1)

U110   May 9 (3)

U556   June 27 (0)

U651   June 29 (2)

U401   August 3 (0)

U452   August 25 (1)

U570   August 27 (0)

U501   September 10 (1)

U207   September 11 (3)

U206   November 29 (0)

U208   December 11 (0)

U451   December 21 (0)

U567   December 21 (1)

Total sunk: 19

1942

ALLIED MERCHANT SHIPS SUNK

	Tonnage	No. of Ships
January	276,795	48
February	429,891	73
March	534,064	95
April	391,044	66
May	576,350	120
June	623,545	124
July	486,965	98
August	508,426	96
September	473,585	95
October	399,715	62

November   508,707   83
December   262,135   46

Total   5,471,222   1,006

U–BOATS SUNK

U93   January 15 (0)
U581   February 2 (1)
U252   April 14 (0)
U90   July 24 (0)
U588   July 31 (0)
U335   August 3 (0)
U210   August 6 (0)
U379   August 8 (2)
U578   August 10 (0)
U464   August 20 (0)
U253   (believed sunk) September (0)
U756   September 1 (0)
U705   September 3 (1)
U261   September 15 (0)
U116   (believed sunk) October (0)
U597   October 12 (0)
U661   October 15 (1)
U619   October 15 (2)
U353   October 16 (0)
U216   October 20 (1)
U412   October 22 (0)
U599   October 24 (0)
U627   October 27 (0)
U520   October 30 (0)
U658   October 30 (0)
U184   (believed sunk) November (0)
U132   November 13 (2)
U411   November 13 (0)
U98   November 15 (0)

U173   November 16 (1)
U611   December 8 (0)
U254   December 8 (0)
U626   December 15 (0)
U357   December 26 (0)
U356   December 27 (3)

Total sunk: 35

1943

ALLIED MERCHANT SHIPS SUNK

	Tonnage	No. of Ships
January	172,691	27
February	288,625	46
March	476,349	82
April	235,478	39
May	163,507	34
June	18,379	4
July	123,327	18
August	10,186	2
September	43,775	8
October	56,422	12
November	23,077	6
December	47,785	7
Total	1,659,601	285

U–BOATS SUNK

U337   (believed sunk) January (0)
U519   (believed sunk) January (0)
U553   (believed sunk) January (0)
U529   (believed sunk) February (0)
U265   February 3 (0)

U187   February 4 (o)
U609   February 7 (o)
U624   February 7 (1)
U442   February 12 (2)
U620   February 13 (1)
U225   February 15 (o)
U69   February 17 (o)
U201   February 17 (o)
U268   February 19 (1)
U225   February 15 (o)
U606   February 22 (2)
U522   February 23 (3)
U87   March 4 (o)
U633   March 10 (o)
U432   March 11 (1)
U444   March 11 (o)
U130   March 12 (4)
U163   March 13 (o)
U384   March 19 (1)
U665   March 22 (1)
U524   March 22 (1)
U469   March 25 (o)
U169   March 27 (o)
U381   (believed sunk) May (o)
U456   (believed sunk) May (.5)
U663   (believed sunk) May (o)
U124   April 2 (2)
U635   April 5 (1)
U632   April 6 (1)
U167   April 6 (1)
U526   April 14 (o)
U175   April 17 (o)
U191   April 23 (1)
U189   April 23 (o)
U710   April 24 (o)
U203   April 25 (o)
U332   April 29 (o)

U227	April 30 (0)
U465	May 2 (0)
U659	May 4 (0)
U109	May 4 (0)
U125	May 5 (0)
U638	May 5 (1)
U192	May 6 (0)
U531	May 6 (0)
U630	May 6 (1)
U438	May 6 (0)
U447	May 7 (0)
U209	May 7 (0)
U528	May 11 (0)
U186	May 12 (0)
U89	May 12 (1)
U753	May 13 (0)
U640	May 14 (0)
U266	May 15 (3)
U463	May 16 (0)
U657	May 17 (0)
U646	May 17 (0)
U954	May 19 (0)
U273	May 19 (0)
U258	May 20 (1)
U569	May 22 (0)
U752	May 23 (0)
U467	May 25 (0)
U436	May 26 (0)
U304	May 28 (0)
U440	May 31 (0)
U563	May 31 (0)
U418	June 1 (0)
U594	June 4 (0)
U308	June 4 (0)
U217	June 5 (0)
U202	June 11 (0)
U417	June 11 (0)

U118   June 12 (o)
U334   June 14 (o)
U564   June 14 (o)
U338   June 20 (o)
U449   June 24 (o)
U194   June 24 (o)
U647   (believed sunk) July (o)
U535   July 5 (o)
U951   July 7 (o)
U232   July 8 (o)
U435   July 9 (o)
U487   July 13 (o)
U160   July 14 (o)
U135   July 15 (o)
U558   July 20 (o)
U459   July 24 (o)
U404   July 28 (o)
U614   July 29 (o)
U461   July 30 (o)
U462   July 30 (o)
U504   July 30 (o)
U383   (believed sunk) August (o)
U454   August 1 (o)
U706   August 2 (o)
U106   August 2 (o)
U489   August 4 (o)
U525   August 11 (o)
U338   (believed sunk) September (o)
U341   September 19 (o)
U229   September 22 (o)
U221   September 27 (o)
U420   (believed sunk) October (o)
U460   October 4 (o)
U422   October 4 (o)
U336   October 5 (o)
U643   October 8 (o)
U610   October 8 (o)

U419   October 8 (0)
U402   October 13 (0)
U389   October 14 (0)
U279   October 15 (0)
U470   October 16 (0)
U844   October 16 (0)
U964   October 16 (0)
U540   October 17 (0)
U841   October 17 (0)
U631   October 17 (0)
U378   October 20 (1)
U274   October 23 (0)
U566   October 24 (0)
U282   October 29 (0)
U584   October 31 (0)
U306   October 31 (0)
U732   October 31 (0)
U648   (believed sunk) November (0)
U405   November 1 (0)
U340   November 2 (0)
U707   November 9 (0)
U966   November 10 (0)
U508   November 12 (0)
U226   November 16 (0)
U842   November 16 (0)
U280   November 16 (0)
U211   November 19 (0)
U538   November 21 (0)
U600   November 25 (0)
U542   November 26 (0)
U86   November 29 (0)
U391   December 13 (0)
U972   December 15 (0)
U645   December 24 (0)

Total sunk: 150

1944

ALLIED MERCHANT SHIPS SUNK

	Tonnage	No. of Ships
January	36,065	5
February	12,577	2
March	36,867	7
April	34,224	5
May	0	0
June	4,294	2
July	15,480	2
August	5,685	1
September	16,535	3
October	0	0
November	7,828	3
December	5,458	1
Total	175,013	31

U–BOATS SUNK

U263	(believed sunk) January (0)
U364	(believed sunk) January (0)
U377	(believed sunk) January (0)
U426	January 8 (0)
U757	January 8 (0)
U231	January 13 (0)
U544	January 16 (0)
U305	January 17 (1)
U641	January 19 (0)
U571	January 28 (0)
U271	January 28 (0)
U592	January 31 (0)
U666	(believed sunk) February (0)
U762	February 8 (0)

U734   February 9 (o)
U238   February 9 (o)
U545   February 11 (.5)
U283   February 11 (o)
U424   February 11 (o)
U406   February 18 (o)
U386   February 19 (o)
U264   February 19 (o)
U257   February 24 (o)
U761   February 24 (o)
U91   February 25 (o)
U358   March 1 (1)
U709   March 1 (o)
U603   March 1 (o)
U744   March 6 (1)
U625   March 10 (o)
U575   March 13 (1)
U653   March 15 (o)
U392   March 16 (o)
U976   March 25 (o)
U961   March 29 (o)
U193   (believed sunk) April (o)
U302   April 6 (2)
U962   April 8 (o)
U448   April 14 (o)
U986   April 17 (o)
U342   April 17 (o)
U311   April 22 (1)
U488   April 26 (o)
U240   (believed sunk) May (o)
U846   May 4 (o)
U473   May 6 (o)
U765   May 6 (o)
U731   May 15 (o)
U241   May 18 (o)
U675   May 24 (o)

U476   May 25 (o)
U990   May 25 (o)
U292   May 27 (o)
U740   (believed sunk) June (o)
U1191   (believed sunk) June (o)
U477   June 3 (o)
U955   June 7 (o)
U441   June 8 (o)
U373   June 8 (o)
U970   June 8 (o)
U741   June 10 (o)
U980   June 11 (o)
U715   June 13 (o)
U423   June 17 (o)
U767   June 18 (1)
U1225   June 24 (o)
U971   June 24 (o)
U269   June 25 (o)
U629   June 25 (o)
U317   June 26 (o)
U719   June 26 (o)
U478   June 30 (o)
U988   June 30 (believed to be 3)
U678   July 6 (o)
U243   July 8 (o)
U415   July 14 (o)
U319   July 15 (o)
U672   July 18 (o)
U212   July 21 (o)
U214   July 26 (o)
U333   July 31 (o)
U743   (believed sunk) August (o)
U925   (believed sunk) August (o)
U667   (believed sunk) August (4)
U671   August 4 (o)
U736   August 6 (o)

U608   August 10 (0)

U385   August 11 (0)

U981   August 12 (0)

U270   August 13 (0)

U741   August 15 (0)

U618   August 15 (0)

U621   August 18 (0)

U107   August 18 (0)

U984   August 20 (0)

U413   August 20 (1)

U445   August 24 (0)

U855   (believed sunk) September (0)

U247   September 1 (0)

U484   September 9 (0)

U1006   October 16 (0)

U297   (believed sunk) November (0)

U1200   November 11 (0)

U322   November 25 (0)

U482   (believed sunk) December (1)

U1020   (believed sunk) December (0)

U650   (believed sunk) December (0)

U400   December 17 (0)

U1209   December 18 (0)

U877   December 27 (0)

U772   December 30 (4)

Total sunk: 111

1945

ALLIED MERCHANT SHIPS SUNK

	Tonnage	No. of Ships
January	29,168	5
February	32,453	5
March	23,684	3

April	32,071	5
May	5,353	1
Total	122,729	19

U–BOATS SUNK

U1172	(believed sunk) January (2)
U327	(believed sunk) January (0)
U248	January 16 (0)
U1199	January 21 (1)
U1051	January 26 (0)
U1279	February 3 (0)
U683	(believed sunk) February (0)
U989	February 14 (0)
U309	February 16 (0)
U1278	February 17 (0)
U1273	February 17 (0)
U1276	February 20 (0)
U300	February 22 (1)
U480	February 24 (1)
U1014	February 24 (0)
U927	February 24 (0)
U1018	February 27 (2)
U1208	February 27 (1)
U296	(believed sunk) March (0)
U1302	March 7 (4)
U275	March 10 (1)
U681	March 11 (0)
U260	March 12 (0)
U714	March 14 (2)
U1021	March 14 (0)
U1003	March 23 (0)
U399	March 26 (2)
U722	March 27 (1)
U905	March 27 (0)
U1106	March 29 (0)

U1169   March 29 (o)
U965   March 30 (o)
U246   (believed sunk) April (1)
U396   (believed sunk) April (o)
U325   (believed sunk) April (o)
U1055   (believed sunk) April (o)
U321   April 2 (o)
U242   April 5 (o)
U1195   April 6 (2)
U774   April 8 (o)
U1001   April 8 (o)
U1065   April 9 (o)
U878   April 10 (o)
U486   April 12 (o)
U1024   April 13 (o)
U1206   April 14 (o)
U285   April 15 (o)
U1063   April 15 (o)
U1274   April 16 (1)
U636   April 21 (o)
U326   April 25 (o)
U1017   April 29 (o)
U1107   April 30 (2)
U320   May 8 (o)

In addition, the following U-boats were lost en route from Germany to Norway at war's end: U236, U393, U534, U579, U733, U746, U1007, U1008, U1210, U2338, U2359, U2365, U2503, U2521, U2523, U2524, U3032.

Total sunk or lost: 71

(Sources: For merchant shipping statistics, S. W. Roskill, The War at Sea, 1939-1945, London, HMSO, 1954-61; for U-boat statistics, Clay Blair, Hitler's U-Boat War, Vols 1 and 2, New York, Random House, 1996.)

NOTES

PROLOGUE

1. Interview with Werner Hirschmann.
2. William L. Shirer, *The Rise and Fall of the Third Reich* (New York: Simon and Schuster, 1960), p. 165.
3. Ibid. p. 637.

CHAPTER ONE: THRUST AND PARRY

1. Charles Lamb, *War in a Stringbag* (London: Arrow Books, 1978), p. 29.
2. Ibid., p. 37.
3. John Keegan, *The Price of Admiralty* (New York: Viking, 1989), p. 100.
4. Ibid., p. 100.
5. Time-Life Books Inc., *The U-Boats* (Chicago: Time-Life, 1979), p. 22.
6. David Shermer, *World War I* (London: Octopus Books, 1973), p. 167.
7. Clay Blair, *Hitler's U-Boat War*, Vol. 1 (New York: Random House, 1996), p. 36.
8. Karl Dönitz, *Memoirs: Ten Years and Twenty Days* (New York: Da Capo Press, 1997), p. 13.
9. Ibid., p. 20.
10. Ibid., p. 21.
11. Ibid., p. 132.
12. W.A.B. Douglas, *The Creation of a National Air Force: The Official History of the Royal Canadian Air Force,* Vol. 2 (Toronto: University of Toronto Press, 1986), p. 375.

13. Dönitz, *Memoirs*, p. 68.

14. William L. Shirer, *The Rise and Fall of the Third Reich* (New York: Simon and Schuster, 1960), p. 643.

15. Len Deighton, *Blood, Tears and Folly: An Objective Look at World War II* (London: Pimlico, 1995), p. 33.

16. Dönitz, *Memoirs*, p. 61.

17. Robert Payne, *The Life and Death of Adolf Hitler* (New York: Praeger Publishers, 1973), p. 374.

18. Martin Gilbert, *Churchill: A Life* (New York: Henry Holt, 1991), p. 634.

CHAPTER TWO: THE HAPPY TIME

1. John Keegan, *The Price of Admiralty* (New York: Viking, 1989), p. 227.

2. Karl Dönitz, *Memoirs: Ten Years and Twenty Days* (New York: Da Capo Press, 1997), p. 112.

3. Martin Gilbert, *Churchill: A Life* (New York: Henry Holt, 1991), p. 671.

4. Frank Curry, *War at Sea: A Canadian Seaman on the North Atlantic* (Toronto: Lugus Productions, 1990), p. 30.

5. Mac Johnston, *Corvettes Canada* (Toronto: McGraw-Hill Ryerson, 1994), p. 15.

6. H.A. Taylor, *Test Pilot at War* (London: Ian Allan, 1970), p. 138.

CHAPTER THREE: HOSTILE WINGS

1. Cajus Bekker, *The Luftwaffe War Diaries* (London: Macdonald, 1967), p. 257.

2. Gordon Turner, *Empress of Britain* (Erin, Ontario: The Boston Mills Press, 1992), pp. 189, 190.

3. Clay Blair, *Hitler's U-Boat War*, Vol. 1 (New York, Random House, 1996), p. 203.

4. W.A.B. Douglas, *The Creation of a National Air Force: The Official History of the Royal Canadian Air Force*, Vol. 2 (Toronto: University of Toronto Press, 1986), pp. 469-70.

5. Ibid., pp. 469-70.

6. Ibid., p. 472.

7. Martin Gilbert, *Churchill: A Life* (New York: Henry Holt, 1991), p. 669.

8. Mack Lynch, ed., *Salty Dips*, Vol. 3 (Ottawa: Ottawa Branch, Naval Officers' Associations of Canada, 1988), p. 29.
9. Ibid., p. 32.
10. Ibid., Vol. 2 (1985), p. 120.
11. Ibid., Vol. 3, p. 120.
12. John Slessor, *The Central Blue* (London: Cassell, 1956), pp. 482-3.
13. Ibid.
14. Gilbert, *Churchill*, p. 686.
15. Ibid., p. 686.

CHAPTER FOUR: SEARCH AND KILL

1. Martin Gilbert, *Churchill: A Life* (New York: Henry Holt, 1991), p. 691.
2. Mack Lynch, ed., *Salty Dips*, Vol. 1 (Ottawa: Ottawa Branch, Naval Officers' Associations of Canada, 1983), pp. 65-6.
3. Len Deighton, *Blood, Tears and Folly: An Objective Look at World War II* (London: Pimlico, 1995), p. 88.
4. Ibid., p. 87.
5. Sayer, Les, and Vernon Ball, *TAG on a Stringbag* (Borth, Dyfed: Aspen Publications, 1994), p. 305.
6. Ibid., p.307.
7. Ibid., p. 308.
8. Laddie Lucas, ed., *Out of the Blue* (London: Grafton Books, 1987), p. 170.
9. Ibid., p. 171.
10. Ralph Barker, *The Ship-Busters* (London: Chatto & Windus, 1957), p. 96.
11. Ludovic Kennedy, *Pursuit: The Sinking of the Bismarck* (London: Collins, 1974), p. 190.
12. Ibid., p. 217.

CHAPTER FIVE: NEW APPROACHES

1. Kenneth Poolman, *The Catafighters* (London: William Kimber, 1970), pp. 34-5.
2. Anthony Cave Brown, *Bodyguard of Lies* (New York: Harper & Row, 1975), p. 15.

3. Ibid., p. 16.
4. Ibid., p. 252.

CHAPTER SIX: AMERICA MOVES CLOSER TO WAR

1. H.A. Taylor, *Test Pilot at War* (London: Ian Allan, 1970), p. 79.
2. W.A.B. Douglas, *The Creation of a National Air Force: The Official History of the Royal Canadian Air Force*, Vol. 2 (Toronto: University of Toronto Press, 1986), p. 474.
3. Alfred Price, *Aircraft versus Submarine* (London: William Kimber, 1973), pp. 60–61.
4. Ibid., p. 64.
5. Ibid., p. 65.

CHAPTER SEVEN: OPERATION DRUMBEAT

1. Karl Dönitz, *Memoirs: Ten Years and Twenty Days* (New York: Da Capo Press, 1997), p. 159.
2. Martin Gilbert, *Churchill: A Life* (New York: Henry Holt, 1991), p. 712.
3. Dönitz, *Memoirs*, p. 197.
4. Clay Blair, *Hitler's U-Boat War*, Vol. 1 (New York: Random House, 1996), p. 453.
5. Michael Gannon, *Operation Drumbeat* (New York: Harper & Row, 1990), p. 169.
6. Ibid., p. 183.
7. Ibid., p. 183.
8. John Keegan, *The Price of Admiralty* (New York: Viking, 1989), p. 229.
9. Gannon, *Drumbeat*, p. 235.
10. Interview with Percy Kelly.
11. Dönitz, *Memoirs*, p. 202.
12. Ibid., p. 203.
13. Blair, *U-Boat War*, Vol. 1, p. 486.
14. Adolf Galland, *The First and the Last* (London: Methuen, 1955), p. 158.
15. W.A.B. Douglas, *The Creation of a National Air Force: The Official History of the Royal Canadian Air Force*, Vol. 2 (Toronto: University of Toronto Press, 1986), p. 488.

16. Blair, *U-Boat War*, Vol. 1, p. 541.

17. Ibid., p. 546.

18. Arthur Harris, *Bomber Offensive* (London: Macmillan, 1947), p. 137.

19. Marc Milner, *North Atlantic Run* (Toronto: Penguin Books, 1990), p. 155.

20. Frank Curry, *War at Sea: A Canadian Seaman on the North Atlantic* (Toronto: Lugus Productions, 1990), p. 120.

CHAPTER EIGHT: WINNING AND LOSING

1. W.A.B. Douglas, *The Creation of a National Air Force: The Official History of the Royal Canadian Air Force*, Vol. 2 (Toronto: University of Toronto Press, 1986), p. 516.

2. Karl Dönitz, *Memoirs: Ten Years and Twenty Days* (New York: Da Capo Press, 1997), p. 263.

3. Max Arthur, *There Shall Be Wings* (London: Hodder & Stoughton, 1993), p. 257.

4. W.A.B. Douglas, *The Creation of a National Air Force: The Official History of the Royal Canadian Air Force*, Vol. 2 (Toronto: University of Toronto Press, 1988), p. 523.

5. Ibid., p. 524.

CHAPTER NINE: TURNING POINT

1. W.A.B. Douglas, *The Creation of a National Air Force: The Official History of the Royal Canadian Air Force*, Vol. 2 (Toronto: University of Toronto Press, 1986), p. 525.

2. Ibid., p. 530.

3. Ibid., p. 536.

4. Ibid., p. 544.

5. *Toronto Star*, April 10, 1943.

6. Douglas, *Creation of a National Air Force*, p. 544.

7. Ibid., p. 544.

8. Ibid., p. 545.

9. Ibid., p. 546.

10. Ibid., pp. 549-50.

11. Karl Dönitz, *Memoirs: Ten Years and Twenty Days* (New York: Da Capo Press, 1997), p. 324.

12. Ibid., p. 327.

CHAPTER TEN: THE BIGGEST BATTLE

1. Martin Middlebrook, *Convoy* (London: Penguin Books, 1978), p. 101.
2. Ibid., p. 98.
3. Karl Dönitz, *Memoirs: Ten Years and Twenty Days* (New York: Da Capo Press, 1997), p. 317.
4. Ibid., p. 325.
5. Ibid., pp. 326-27.
6. Alfred Price, *Aircraft versus Submarine* (London: William Kimber, 1973), p. 131.
7. Max Arthur, *There Shall Be Wings* (London: Hodder & Stoughton, 1993), p. 259.
8. Middlebrook, *Convoy*, p. 148.
9. Ibid., p. 151.
10. Ibid., p. 153.

CHAPTER ELEVEN: BATTLE IS JOINED

1. Martin Middlebrook, *Convoy* (London: Penguin Books, 1978), p. 174.
2. Ibid., p. 188.
3. Ibid., p. 189.
4. Ibid., p. 199.
5. Ibid., p. 213.
6. Ibid., p. 228.
7. Ibid., p. 229.
8. Ibid., p. 235.
9. Ibid., p. 236.

CHAPTER TWELVE: CLIMAX OF THE BATTLE

1. Martin Middlebrook, *Convoy* (London: Penguin Books, 1978), p. 248.
2. Ibid., p. 250.
3. Ibid., p. 252.

4. Ibid., p. 258.
5. Ibid., p. 261.
6. Ibid., p. 264.
7. Ibid., p. 273.
8. Quoted in Karl Dönitz, *Memoirs: Ten Years and Twenty Days* (New York: Da Capo Press, 1997), p. 329.
9. Sir John Slessor, *The Central Blue* (London: Cassell, 1956), p. 491.
10. Ibid., p. 491.
11. W.A.B. Douglas, *The Creation of a National Air Force: The Official History of the Royal Canadian Air Force*, Vol 2 (Toronto: University of Toronto Press, 1986), p. 553.

CHAPTER THIRTEEN: WINGS OVER THE OCEAN

1. John Slessor, *The Central Blue* (London: Cassell, 1956), p. 499.
2. Interview with Frank Cauley.
3. From an unpublished manuscript by Bill Hutcherson.
4. E.E. Barringer, *Alone on a Wide, Wide Sea*, (London: Leo Cooper, 1995), p. 110.
5. Mack Lynch, ed., *Salty Dips*, Vol. 3 (Ottawa: Ottawa Branch, Naval Officers' Associations of Canada, 1988), p. 181.
6. Dan Van der Vat, *Stealth at Sea: The History of the Submarine* (London: Orion Books, 1994), p. 342.
7. Interview with Werner Hirschmann.
8. Karl Dönitz, *Memoirs: Ten Years and Twenty Days* (New York: Da Capo Press, 1997), pp. 356-7.
9. Ibid., pp. 356-7.
10. Ibid., p. 385.
11. Alfred Price, *Sky Battles/Sky Warriors* (London: Arms and Armour Press, 1993/94), p. 100-101.
12. Paul Brickhill, *The Dam Busters* (London: Evans Brothers, 1951), p. 241.
13. Dönitz, *Memoirs*, p. 429.
14. Ibid., p. 451.

BIBLIOGRAPHY

Arthur, Max. *There Shall Be Wings*. London: Hodder & Stoughton, 1993.

Barringer, E. E. *Alone on a Wide, Wide Sea*. London: Leo Cooper, 1995.

Blair, Clay. *Hitler's U-Boat War*. New York: Random House, 1996.

Brickhill, Paul. *The Dam Busters*. London: Evans Brothers, 1951.

Brown, Anthony Cave. *Bodyguard of Lies*. New York: Harper & Row, 1975.

Curry, Frank. *War at Sea: A Canadian Seaman on the North Atlantic*. Toronto: Lugus Productions Ltd., 1990.

Dallies-Labourdette, Jean-Phillipe. *U-Boote: 1935–1945*. Paris: Histoire & Collections, 1996.

Dear, I. C. B., ed., *The Oxford Companion to World War II*. Oxford: Oxford University Press, 1995.

Deighton, Len. *Blood, Tears and Folly: An Objective Look at World War II*. London: Pimlico, 1995.

Dönitz, Karl. *Memoirs: Ten Years and Twenty Days*. New York: Da Capo Press, 1997.

Douglas, W. A. B. *The Creation of a National Air Force: The Official History of the Royal Canadian Air Force Volume II*. Toronto: University of Toronto Press, 1986.

Franks, Norman. *Search, Find and Kill*. London: Grub Street, 1995.

Friedman, Norman. *British Carrier Aviation*. Annapolis: The Naval Institute Press, 1988.

Gannon, Michael. *Operation Drumbeat*. New York: Harper & Row, 1990.

Gilbert, Martin. *Churchill: A Life*. New York: Henry Holt & Co., 1991.

Gretton, Sir Peter. *Crisis Convoy*. London: Peter Davies, 1974.

Hadley, Michael L. *U-Boats Against Canada.* Kingston, Ont.: McGill-Queen's University Press, 1985.

Harbron, John D. *The Longest Battle: The RCN in the Atlantic 1939–1945.* St. Catharines, Ont.: Vanwell Publishing Limited, 1993.

Hoare, John. *Tumult in the Clouds.* London: Michael Joseph, 1976.

Johnston, Mac. *Corvettes Canada.* Toronto: McGraw-Hill Ryerson, 1994.

Kaplan, Philip, and Jack Currie. *Wolfpack: U-Boats at War, 1939–1945.* London: Aurum Press, 1997.

Keegan, John. *The Price of Admiralty.* New York: Viking, 1989.

Kennedy, Ludovic. *Pursuit: The Sinking of the Bismarck.* London: Collins, 1974.

———. *The Death of the Tirpitz.* Boston: Little, Brown & Company, 1979.

Lamb, Charles. *War in a Stringbag.* London: Arrow Books, 1978.

Lamb, James B. *On the Triangle Run.* Toronto: Macmillan of Canada, 1986.

Middlebrook, Martin. *Convoy.* London: Penguin Books, 1978.

Monsarrat, Nicholas. *Three Corvettes.* London: Cassell & Co. Ltd.,1945.

———. *The Cruel Sea.* London: Cassell & Co. Ltd., 1951.

Naval Officers' Association of Canada. *Salty Dips,* vols. 1, 2, and 3.

Parker, Mike. *Running the Gauntlet.* Halifax: Nimbus, 1994.

Payne, Robert. *The Life and Death of Adolf Hitler.* New York: Praeger Publishers, 1973.

Poolman, Kenneth. *The Catafighters.* London: William Kimber, 1970.

Popham, Hugh. *Sea Flight.* London: Futura Publications, 1974.

Price, Alfred. *Aircraft versus Submarine.* London: William Kimber, 1973.

———. *Sky Battles/Sky Warriors.* London: Arms & Armour Press, 1993/94.

Sarty, Roger. *Canada and the Battle of the Atlantic.* St. Catharines, Ont.: Vanwell Publishing Limited, 1998.

Sayer, Les, and Vernon Ball. *TAG on a Stringbag.* Borth, Dyfed, U.K.: Aspen Publications, 1994.

Schull, Joseph. *The Far Distant Ships.* Ottawa: King's Printer, 1950.

Shermer, David. *World War 1.* London: Octopus Books, 1973.

Shirer, William L. *The Rise and Fall of the Third Reich.* New York: Simon and Schuster, 1960.

Slessor, John. *The Central Blue.* London: Cassell & Co., 1956.

Taylor, H. A. *Test Pilot at War.* London: Ian Allan, 1970.

Turner, Gordon. *Empress of Britain*. Erin, Ont.: The Boston Mills Press, 1992.

Van der Vat, Dan. *Stealth at Sea: The History of the Submarine*. London: Orion Books, 1994.

Waters, John M. *Bloody Winter*. Annapolis: United States Naval Institute, 1984.

ACKNOWLEDGEMENTS

The author is grateful to the following veterans of the Battle of the Atlantic who contributed to this book. Like most veterans – naval, air force, or army – they were impressively patient when explaining technicalities, and self-deprecating about their own accomplishments. Becoming acquainted with them was a major pleasure of researching this book.

William G. Baldwin, Manotick, Ontario; Philip K. Bamford, St. John, New Brunswick; Elwood H. Brander, Burlington, Ontario; Allen R. Burgham, Kingston, Ontario.

Donald Cash, Lunenburg, Nova Scotia; Frank Cauley, Gloucester, Ontario; Bill Chapman, Nepean, Ontario; Fred Colborne, Edmonton, Alberta; Alan H. Cole, Ste-Agathe, Quebec; David M. Croskery, Braeside, Ontario; E. John Cruchley, Sarnia, Ontario.

Dr. R.H.N. Davidson, Toronto, Ontario; John P. Dobson, Port William, Nova Scotia; Bill Doherty, Burlington, Ontario.

Bob Fear, Oakville, Ontario; John G. Fenton, Cold Brook, Nova Scotia.

Werner Hirschmann, Toronto, Ontario; Bob Huntington, Cambridge, Ontario; Bill Hutcherson, Richmond, British Columbia.

William C. Lawrence, Trail, British Columbia.

Dr. Bruce Macpherson, Etobicoke, Ontario; James M. McRae, Yarmouth, Nova Scotia; J. Doran Moore, Burlington, Ontario; Donald C.F. Moors, Halifax, Nova Scotia.

Joseph M. O'Grady, Hamilton, Ontario; George W.C. Offley, Ottawa, Ontario.

Charles Presley, Ajax, Ontario; Robert J. Pinner, Burlington, Ontario.

Harry H. Rasmussen, Hamilton, Ontario; Richard H. Reed, Yarmouth, Nova Scotia.

Les Sayer, Colchester, England; James Stewart, St. Andrews, New Brunswick; Edward John Stiles, Lucknow, Ontario; Aubrey Sutherland, Chester Basin, Nova Scotia.

George R. Weir, Regina, Saskatchewan; Ken West, London, Ontario; Hewlett White, Scarborough, Ontario.

Harry C. Taylor, Rexdale, Ontario.

David J.C. Waterbury, Chester Basin, Nova Scotia; David H. Withey, Liverpool, England.

In addition, the author would like to express his appreciation of the staff of the Burlington Central Library, who located many out-of-print books. Roger Sarty of the Canadian War Museum, Ottawa, and the staff of the Imperial War Museum, London, England, were also unfailingly helpful; their knowledge and professionalism were greatly appreciated.

Finally, thanks to Lynn Schellenberg and to the staff at McClelland & Stewart, in particular, Doug Gibson, publisher, and Alex Schultz, editor.

INDEX

(Note: The names of ships appear in inverted commas)